LANDSCAPE SITE GRADING PRINCIPLES

GRADING WITH DESIGN IN MIND

Bruce G. Sharky

WILEY

Cover image: Wiley
Cover design: Measurement, topography and courtyard Images: © Bruce Sharky; Center landscape Image: © Design Workshop

For general information about our other products and services, please contact our Customer Care Department within the United States at (800) 762-2974, outside the United States at (317) 572-3993 or fax (317) 572-4002.

Wiley publishes in a variety of print and electronic formats and by print-on-demand. Some material included with standard print versions of this book may not be included in e-books or in print-on-demand. If this book refers to media such as a CD or DVD that is not included in the version you purchased, you may download this material at http://booksupport.wiley.com. For more information about Wiley products, visit www.wiley.com.

Library of Congress Cataloging-in-Publication Data:

Sharky, Bruce.
  Landscape site grading principles: grading with design in mind / Bruce Sharky.
    pages cm
  Includes bibliographical references and index.
  ISBN 978-1-118-66872-6 (cloth : acid-free paper); 978-1-118-93139-4 (ebk); 978-1-118-93140-0 (ebk)
  1. Landscape construction. 2. Building sites. 3. Grading (Earthwork) 4. Landscape architecture. I. Title.
  TH380.S53 2014
  624.1'52—dc23
                              201400839

Printed in the United States of America

10 9 8 7 6 5 4 3 2 1

Gracías Nolita

CONTENTS

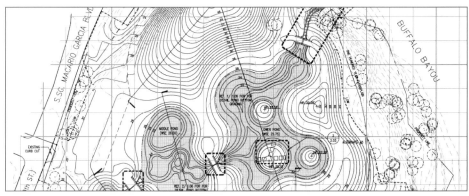

COURTESY OF THE SWA GROUP

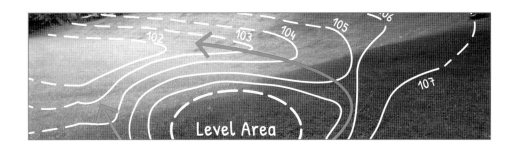

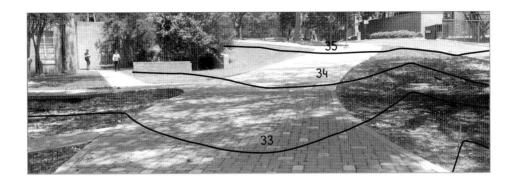

13 Detailed Grading with Slopes, Contours, and Spot Elevations

RHHA

PREFACE

LANDSCAPE SITE GRADING PRINCIPLES embodies a new approach for teaching site grading for designers who think and learn visually. Knowledge and skill in site grading are essential areas of service for landscape architects and allied design professionals. Demonstration of competency in site grading is a significant component in the test for obtaining professional licensure to practice landscape architecture. Site grading plans must not only solve practical requirements and meet various governmental standards but also create landforms that contribute to the aesthetic ambition of the overall landscape site and architectural design concepts. *Landscape Site Grading Principles* will provide students with the necessary background, knowledge, and problem-solving skill set to develop landscape-grading plans that meet standards of care related to meeting public health, safety, and welfare design standards.

The predominant site grading textbooks used in site grading courses take an engineering approach. *Landscape Site Grading Principles* teaches grading principles through visual means to better meet the needs of the visual learner. It provides a hands-on approach to allow students to better understand grading principles. This is accomplished by integrating text with illustrative diagrams and actual examples photographed in the everyday landscape.

Finding a more effective approach to teaching site grading has been a goal of mine. I have found that students seem to better grasp grading concepts when I utilize a more hands-on approach. For example, I have taken blackboard chalk out with me on campus walks with students to draw hypothetical contours and spot elevations on the ground, walls, and other surfaces. I find doing this helps students visualize what they have struggled to visualize reading existing textbooks. I have also used PowerPoint presentations, but this method, while visual, does not necessarily help students visualize how to apply my description of the images on the screen to manipulating the site contours and making the required spot elevation calculations for their assignments. While most students view grading and other technology-related courses as something other than design, in fact grading is just as much a design subject, and just as visual, as any other aspect of landscape design. Although landscape grading does involve a certain amount of computation, many students do not readily "see" what they are creating from calculating spot elevations and reconfigured contours. With the publication of *Landscape Site Grading Principles*, faculty will be able to help students more readily visualize grading concepts and solutions and become successful at solving site grading problems while creating aesthetic solutions.

Site grading education continuously evolves, and curricula change, reflecting the changing nature of the design professions and the nature of professional practice. Site grading is typically taught as a stand-alone course in a landscape architecture and architecture curriculum technical stream. Although this approach will most likely continue, there is a growing consideration of greater integration of site grading and technology with the design studio stream. *Landscape Site Grading Principles* is written to address the ambition for more effective integration of design and site grading by placing emphasis on the design implications of site grading.

Landscape Site Grading Principles recognizes that students enter landscape architecture and related professions with an academic preparation and set of life experiences influenced greatly by computers and other technology. Walking around a high school or college campus, one will quickly notice that most of the students' heads are tilted downward as they walk across campus or sit amongst their friends, with thumbs flying, either texting their friends or doing Google searches. College students come into academic life well versed in and adept at a range of computer skills, and they expect the computer to be their primary means of doing their course assignments, including those in landscape architecture studio and technology courses. While these students are highly computer literate, they may not have a sound grasp of the physicality of the world. This is particularly true of concepts of scale and of the substance and dimensions of the material world they pass through every day. This statement may not apply for everyone, but it is important for technical courses—such as site grading—to give students more hands-on experience of the materials and elements they will be designing. *Landscape Site Grading Principles* will provide as close a hands-on experience as possible of the physical elements that a course in grading must address for the students. Actual examples photographed in the everyday landscape are liberally integrated with the text, to help students better see, and hopefully grasp, landscape-grading concepts.

Landscape Site Grading Principles will prepare students to become competent in landscape grading while understanding the design implications of the subject. This goal will be accomplished in several ways. First, the book presents principles of site grading and the knowledge necessary for gaining competency. Second, it presents the material using a variety of visual and graphic aids in support of the written explanations. Third, step-by-step examples will walk the student through the process for solving several types of grading problems. Chapters will also contain professional examples of grading plans, to help students better understand how principles are applied in different circumstances.

Much of the content in the first half-dozen chapters is material that was previously taught in specific preparatory courses that were considered prerequisites to courses in site grading but have gradually been eliminated from the curricula. This background material has been included in the early chapters to provide students of landscape site grading with the necessary preparation and context for the professional conventions and knowledge needed to understand landscape site grading as an important piece of the project design continuum.

Although writing is often a solitary endeavor, even the writer who goes solo has many people to acknowledge, credit, and thank for their unique contributions. Foremost, I must thank my teachers: the students who have taken my landscape site grading courses and from whom

I learned much, through their eyes, about site grading and design. Undoubtedly, significant credit must be given to Sarah Zelenak, an MLA student assigned to me as a graduate research assistant. Sarah has had the heart and skill to translate my rough diagrams, sketches, and markups of many photographs into a format suitable for publication. She provided the professional graphic polish that I think makes this textbook unique with its reliance on imagery to convey concepts presented in the text.

Margaret Cummins of John Wiley & Sons saw the potential of this book from reading my original book proposal and guided me with her good counsel through the review process. She was assisted by Michael New, also of Wiley, in the day-to-day questions I had once the writing of the book was under way. Thanks also to Professor Bradley Cantrell, Director of the Robert Reich School of Landscape Architecture, for his support by assigning a graduate research assistant to assist me in the graphic preparations. Professor Van Cox, Brad's predecessor, assigned my graduate assistant Jia Li, who translated early hand-drawn diagrams and graphic ideas I was experimenting with during the early stages of research. Both Sarah and Jia are extraordinary talents. I would recommend both as they develop their professional careers.

Appreciation for their contributions is due to a number of landscape architecture firms who responded to my request for outstanding examples of designs where site grading played a central role in their projects. I appreciate all the firms and their contributions, particularly in their selection of exemplary design projects that I hope will serve as an inspiration to students of site grading. In particular I would like to thank:

Doug Reed and Alex Strader of Reed-Hilderbrand

Sarhar Coston-Hardy of the Olin Studio

Tegan Holly of RHHA

Izabela Riano of Michael Van Valkenburgh

M. Reed Dillingham of Dillingham Associates

Dale Horchner and Kurt Culbertson of Design Workshop

Rhett Rentrop of SWA Group

Tary Arteburn of Studio Outside

Robert Loftis of Morrow Reardon Wilkinson Miller

Jennifer Harbourt of Reich Associates

Professor Sadik Artunc allowed me to select several of his original site grading exercises to adapt in this book. Marshall Roy, IT analyst of the LSU College of Art + Design, helped debug troublesome computer files and resolve software issues. Kevin Duffy helped in the photography studio to set up map photographs. Vincent Cellucci, coordinator of my college's Communication Across the Curriculum studio, was one of two people who inspired me to take on the project. The other was Professor Michael Pitts of the LSU School of Architecture, who—unbeknownst to him—inspired my own effort by his writing project on sustainable design in architecture. Unavoidably, there are probably some omissions. I offer my apologies, but most importantly my appreciation. Though you may have been omitted in print, I thank you.

Photographs, diagrams, and images are the author's unless otherwise noted. Reference is given where photographs, plans, and other images are from third-party sources.

Finally, I thank my wife, Nola, whose support made this work possible. While I did try to keep up with various duties around the house, our usual summer travels together were supplanted by my writing alone, with my head down at my computer and iPad. This project would not have happened without her encouragement and patience.

SOME BACKGROUND ON THE SUBJECT OF SITE GRADING

SITE GRADING INFORMS DESIGN

Inspired landscape designs contain at least one vital ingredient: an inspired grading design. Many designers consider landscape grading as the generative basis for many of their successful landscape site designs. The ambition of this text is to present an approach to grading that will prepare students not only to grasp and master concepts of landscape site grading but to develop site-grading and drainage design solutions that are both practical and aesthetically pleasing. Students reading this text will appreciate that the underlying approach considers grading as an integral component of site design. Design should be in their thoughts as they walk from their design studio class and into the classroom where their grading course is held. Just as they spend their design studio class time and their evenings striving to develop exciting and inspiring landscape design solutions, they should experience this same enthusiasm in the hours they spend developing grading assignments.

Cultures throughout history have modified the native landscape to accommodate their activities and to facilitate their survival. The Native Americans who settled in what is now Bandelier National Monument in New Mexico found a river valley suitable for habitation and managing their crops (Figure 1.1-A). Modifications of the existing landscape were required to enable them to adapt to the landscape they found. In some cases the modifications were substantial, and in other cases little change was required. In contrast, the designers of Teardrop Park, a high-rise residential development in Lower Manhattan, New York City, were challenged with making substantial modifications of the existing ground to realize the award-winning site design (Figure 1.1-B). In both cases the resulting landform seems natural—that is, it does not appear that very much modification of the existing ground occurred, while in fact a great deal of site grading was required.

Figure 1.1-A Bandelier National Monument, New Mexico   **Figure 1.1-B** Teardrop Park, New York City

Figures 1.2-A and 1.2-B provide an example of a utilitarian application of site grading to accommodate human activities. What appears as a flat lawn area is in fact a sophisticated site-grading design with subtle slopes to disperse rainwater. The site also required an equally sophisticated soil preparation and underground drainage system to support a healthy lawn capable of withstanding a large crowd.

Site grading is an integral aspect of specialized landscape designs. Elaborate and aesthetically pleasing landforms are developed in designs for specialized uses such as golf course greens, skateboard parks (Figure 1.3-A), and outdoor event spaces (Figure 1.3-B). Site grading is as much an art form as a disciplined application of specific practical and functional considerations.

Figure 1.2-A Bryant Park, New York City, in the early morning

Figure 1.2-B Bryant Park, New York City, later in the afternoon

Figure 1.3-A Alamosa Skate Park in Albuquerque, NM

Figure 1.3-B Stern Grove Amphitheater, San Francisco, CA

LET'S BEGIN

Some time ago, someone gave me a round metal badge (see Figure 1.4) with the message "Time for Design." I have long forgotten who gave me the badge and the organization behind the badge. For the last several years I have worn the badge at the first few class meetings of the introductory site-grading course I teach. I have found that students generally do not think of grading as having much to do with design, at least at the beginning of the course. Their impression is that design studio is about design, and the site-grading course is about math. When they come to the grading class they turn off the design side of their brains. It seems they set aside what they have learned in design studio when working on grading exercises and projects. I go out of my way, during the early meetings of the landscape site-grading course, to stress the importance of design and to explain, verbally and with visual examples, how site grading is fundamental to achieving creative as well as functionally appropriate, responsive landscape designs. The process of grading and the exploration of reshaping the land can inform design.

THE IMPORTANCE OF GRADING IN DESIGN

Students readily understand the need for, and importance of, design studio courses in the curriculum. And of course they spend most of their waking hours—including late into the night—on their design projects. When a design project is due, students will be working on their designs in my grading class. I have worked to figure out how to reprogram design students to understand and believe in the importance of landscape site grading during their academic preparation, because they will surely come to realize grading's important role after graduation, during their early professional careers.

I have given all this a lot of thought, asking why grading often takes a back seat to design and some other courses. I have come up with a number of possible explanations. A majority of design students are visual learners, but grading texts do not approach the subject of landscape site grading in visual terms. The nonvisual approach used in existing textbooks employs

Figure 1.4 Grading involves design and can be the generative basis of an outstanding site design

left-brain content in presenting the material, and walks students through grading as basically problem solving, learning to apply mathematical formulas. Another explanation that I can get my arms around—one that is not so slippery to defend—is that students do not necessarily understand what it means to be a well-rounded and effective professional landscape architect or designer. So it is important, in the introductory grading course, to describe the context of grading in the continuum of academic preparation and professional practice. Students must be taught that grading is not an accessory but a key element in the design process, leading through design development, contract drawing preparations, and finally to the building of their projects. Grading can be the generative basis of arriving at a design concept. Given the generative potential of site grading, an introductory course in grading should be approached as a design activity. Like design, grading can be approached as a reiterative process and not a straight-line process with a beginning-to-end trajectory. Additionally, students should think of grading as the framework for design. Solving site-grading problems, like design, is a process grounded on in a body of knowledge that students must come to understand and master. Another parallel to design: Site grading involves the mastery of representational graphic skills necessary for clearly communicating a design intention, as well as for problem solving. Lastly, I alert students to the fact that in order to become licensed professionals they will have to successfully pass all portions of a landscape architecture licensure examination (a national examination administered by individual states) that tests for competency not only in planning and design but also in grading, drainage, professional practice, history, plants, and topics unique by state in some cases[1].

. . . .

1 Most states require an additional section to the LARE (Landscape Architect Registration Examination) to test the knowledge and competency of candidates in topics unique to the individual state. For instance, Alaska requires candidates to take and pass an arctic engineering course, while California and other Southwestern states test candidates for water management and plant selection considering drought conditions.

Site grading is typically taught as a stand-alone course in the technology stream of a landscape architecture or allied discipline curriculum. While this approach will most likely continue, there is a growing consideration for greater integration of site grading, and technology in general, with the design studio stream. This book is written to address the ambition to achieve a greater integration of design and site grading by placing emphasis on the design implications of site grading and presenting the material visually as well as textually. In considering how to approach writing this text, the author recognizes that students enter a program with an academic preparation and set of life experiences influenced greatly by computer and other technology.

A PICTURE IS WORTH A THOUSAND WORDS

Walking around a high school or college campus, one will quickly notice that most of the students' heads are tilted downward as they walk across campus or sit amongst their friends, with thumbs flying, either texting or doing Google searches. College students come into academic life well versed in and adept at a range of computer skills, and they expect the computer to be their primary means of doing their course assignments, including those in landscape architecture studio courses. While these students are highly computer literate, they may not have a sound grasp of the physicality of the world. I mean by this, that they may not understand concepts of scale or have knowledge of the physical attributes of the material world they pass through every day (such as its dimensions, construction materials and details, and design codes). This statement may not ring true for everyone, but it would benefit students to give them more hands-on experience of the materials they will be working with in solving for grading solutions. This text attempts to provide as close a hands-on experience as possible of the physical elements that a course in grading must address for the students. Actual examples, photographed in the everyday landscape, are integrated with the text (as in Figures 1.5-A and 1.5-B).

Figures 1.5-A and 1.5-B are examples of the type of diagrams that have been developed throughout the book. Photograph A shows an undulating grass area with hypothetical contour lines superimposed. Image B is the same location with just the contour lines, as might be found in a grading plan.

The information superimposed on the photographs is descriptive, to help the reader better visualize the information presented; it is not meant to be, in Figure 1.5-A for instance, the actual location or contours of the particular site photographed.

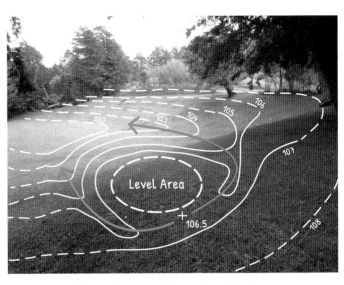

Figure 1.5-A Contour lines superimposed on a landscape

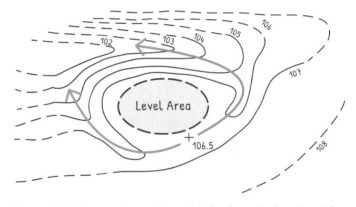

Figure 1.5-B Contour lines as they might be shown in plan view without the photograph

GAINING AN ESSENTIAL GRASP OF SITE-GRADING CONCEPTS

The impetus for this text is to present the technical material necessary to prepare students of landscape architecture and allied design professions in the art and science of grading and drainage, following a more accessible, visual approach. The goal is to provide students with an essential grasp of the material necessary to understand and master site grading. The students will also learn to solve simple as well as complex grading and drainage problems. The approach to achieving these goals emphasizes learning and understanding what is necessary through visualization, rather than relying on an approach that emphasizes problem solving through mathematical calculations. The primary approach of design education is an emphasis on a visually based problem-solving process, and this approach has its parallel in grading and drainage education. If the students are to believe the message on my "It's Time for Design" badge, then it seems a visual approach to learning site grading would be appropriate. At least the students would see the parallels between design and grading more readily. That is my hope and was the basis of developing the textbook Landscape Site Grading Principles.

The three images in Figures 1.6 through 1.8 were selected to present the range of public park spaces where site grading and design are integral to the projects. In all three projects, site grading was the generative force of these projects' success. They have become popular urban recreation and passive open space retreats in dense urban areas.

Site grading has become increasingly important, particularly in many specialized and emerging areas of site design. For instance, Figure 1.9, a skateboard park located in Albuquerque, New Mexico, represents a project type that has become very popular. Site grading is the foundation in the design of this kind of recreation venue. In golf course design, the more successful projects—those that challenge the golfer—are the result of carefully considered grading design. Athletic fields for all sports require the application of sound grading principles that not only contribute to the success of play but also facilitate successful ground maintenance.

Figure 1.6 Brooklyn Bridge Park, New York City
MICHAEL VAN VALKENBURG ASSOCIATES

Figure 1.7 Water Works Park, Phoenix, AZ
CHRISTY TEN EYCK, LANDSCAPE ARCHITECTS

Figure 1.8 Lucasfilm's Letterman Digital Arts Center campus, at the Presidio, San Francisco, CA
LAWRENCE HALPRIN, LANDSCAPE ARCHITECT

Figure 1.9 West Side Skate Park, Albuquerque, NM
MORROW REARDON WILKINSON MILLER, LANDSCAPE ARCHITECTS

Landscape Site Grading Principles was written for an introductory course in site grading for students in landscape architecture and architecture, as well as for majors in horticulture and landscape construction. Also emerging is a plethora of certification and two-year courses in landscape architecture from various providers, including community and technical colleges and nontraditional providers. *Landscape Site Grading Principles* can either serve as the primary required text for an introductory course in landscape site grading or be considered as a supplement to other required texts. *Landscape Site Grading Principles* has been written to serve both purposes.

WHAT THE STUDENT NEEDS TO KNOW ABOUT SITE GRADING

Site grading plans must not only solve practical requirements and meet various governmental standards but also create landforms that contribute to the aesthetic ambitions of overall landscape site design and architectural design concepts. *Landscape Site Grading Principles* will provide students with the necessary background knowledge and problem-solving skill set to develop site-grading plans that meet the standards of care expected of design professionals.

WHAT DOES THE STUDENT NEED TO KNOW ABOUT GRADING?

1. Be familiar with drafting conventions and the use of architectural and engineering scales.

2. Be able to read topographic maps and be able to identify landform features such as hills, valleys, steep and not-so-steep terrain, and drainage patterns. Also, the student should be able to determine elevations of any point or feature from a topographic map.

3. Be able to visualize three-dimensional landscape from contours given on a topographic map or map prepared by a land surveyor.

4. Be able to create a land surface, path, or built program feature that has a prescribed or intentional slope.

5. Be able to manipulate (change or modify) contours in order to create desired landforms and sloping surfaces. Also, the student must be able to manipulate contours so as to direct the flow of surface water in a desired direction, such as away from the entrance of a building.

6. Be able to assign spot elevations in plan and on sections.

7. Be able to calculate the volume of earth moved within a project site and determine the volume of earth or other soil or rock material that needs to be transported to or off the project site.

8. Be able to prepare (draw) grading plans following graphic conventions so that the contractor knows what to build. The grading plans must be of sufficient detail, and of course accuracy, that the contractor can prepare with confidence a cost estimate for doing the required work as depicted in the drawings and other contract documents.

9. Be knowledgeable about and understand various and pertinent design standards and legal requirements associated with grading. This knowledge base may include functional design requirements of minimum and maximum slope for various program elements such as recreation fields, parking and circulation, and handicap access (standards for persons with ambulatory and other physical disabilities).

10. Be able to develop grading designs that fall within project budget constraints, while meeting client program and functional requirements.

11. Be able to prepare grading plans that meet standards of care related to meeting public health, safety, and welfare design standards—that is, grading plans that limit and reduce the chance of public harm such as physical injury.

The eleven points in this list may appear daunting to the student taking an introductory grading course. Through the process of academic preparation, internship, and other forms of professional practice experience, students will achieve mastery of what a landscape architect is required to know and perform. Start with little steps, steps that build on one another, while acquiring the knowledge, skills, and tools necessary for preparing increasingly complex and challenging grading problems.

The building blocks for building competency in designing[2] (solving) grading plans for a project begin with being able to read topographic maps, including understanding scale and understanding various frames of survey reference such as datum terms of elevation and grids. After learning how to read a topographic map, one needs to learn principles of working with contours, spot elevations, and slopes to arrive at grading solutions. The student will also learn to visualize alternate grading design solutions, using and manipulating contour lines and calculating spot elevations toward creating landscape site-grading solutions. Finally, students should learn and follow the graphic conventions necessary for preparing the grading plans and drawings that provide the contractor with instructions. Grading plans and drawings are the landscape architect's instruments for conveying design intent, or what the contractor is expected to build, following the directions contained in the plans and support documentation.

. . . .

2 The word "solving" is commonly used to describe what a student does when given a grading assignment. The word suggests the use of mathematics and formulas and therefore may reveal why students find it convenient to separate grading from studio design. "Design," as a verb, is often used to mean solving a problem. The use of numbers and the employment of numerical calculations, while implicit to solving grading and drainage problems, is not implied in solving or creating design solutions. So, perhaps we should ask the students to develop a design solution for a grading assignment, as opposed to "solving" the proposed problems that make up the assignment.

Professional Relationships

The preparation of site-grading plans involves the collaboration of many disciplines. The typical team of consultants might include a landscape architect, civil engineer, land surveyor, architect, geotechnical engineer, and structural and electrical engineers. Professional land surveyors prepare the site survey and what serves as the base drawing for much of the site-grading work required. The base drawing prepared by a land surveyor documents existing conditions, including at a minimum:

- Property lines, servitudes, and easements
- Large trees and other significant vegetation
- Topography
- Structures
- Other on-site physical features requested by the client or the project prime consultant

Landscape architects, civil engineers, or both in collaboration, typically prepare site-grading plans. How the two collaborate will vary by project. It is common for the landscape architect to prepare a preliminary site-grading plan during the schematic and design development phases of a project. The landscape architect will have prepared a preliminary site design, then will develop a preliminary grading plan. These plans set the foundation of the landscape grading, including the earth forms, slopes, and critical elevations of hardscape areas and structures. The civil engineer may then take over in the design of storm water systems, principally sizing catch basins and belowground piping systems determined by runoff and infiltration calculations and the sizing of drainage channels. The civil engineer may also do the final site-grading design of roads and parking lots. Assignment of responsibilities is established during the negotiation of the professional services contract and may also be dictated by local or state laws that specify the responsibilities for "stamping"[3] the construction document drawings.

....

3 "Stamping" refers to professional licensure and the disciplines required to prepare various construction documents as defined by individual state licensure laws. By stamping or signing a technical plan, the individual or firm represented by the stamp becomes responsible for its accuracy and the health, safety, and welfare issues promulgated by the state.

Figure 1.10 is an example of a schematic design where grading is clearly an important element of the design. This plan was included in the review package submitted to the public client and was used to inform the park stakeholders at a public meeting.

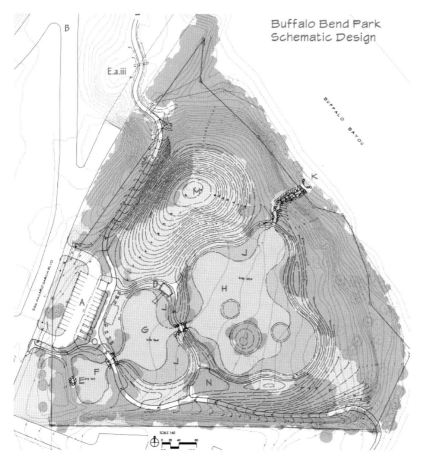

Figure 1.10 Buffalo Bend Park, Houston, TX
SCHEMATIC DESIGN PLAN COURTESY OF THE SWA GROUP

The Basic Structural Approach to This Book

The primary subject of this book is site grading: an introduction to the principles of landscape site grading for the visual learner. The first few chapters introduce background subject matter before focusing on the topic of site grading itself. Increasingly, as university-based landscape architecture and allied design programs have shifted emphasis from analog to digital representation, much of the material included in the early chapters of this book has dropped out of mainstream design curricula. For instance, drafting as a subject, together with documentation conventions, has for the most part been integrated into technology or early design courses. Map reading, drafting, and land surveying as stand-alone required course subjects have been folded into other courses and given, for the most part, cursory coverage. The content remains important, however, in considering the contents for this book it was felt that a basic introduction to the subjects of drafting or documentation conventions, map reading, and land surveying should be included, in order to better prepare students for the larger subject of site-grading principles. Students will increase their knowledge, understanding, and skills in all three topics as they fulfill internship requirements and as they advance their capabilities as part of their professional development.

Avoiding redundancy is one of the tenets discussed in Chapter 4, which discusses drawing and documentation conventions. The reader may notice that a topic is covered in more than one chapter, contrary to the tenet on avoiding redundancy. However, when this occurs, it is an effort to provide cohesion where crossovers between related subjects merit some repetition.

Let's get started!

2

SITE GRADING AND THE LEGAL REQUIREMENTS

In this chapter you will learn about:

- Site grading and why it is important

- The practical and aesthetic considerations of site grading

- How grading can be used to avoid or minimize various slope failure issues or area flooding

- The relationship between landscape architects, architects, and civil engineers as a team or collaborative enterprise

- Site grading as an integral component for achieving professional licensure

WHAT IS SITE GRADING?

Site grading is a process requiring a set of technical skills and understanding of a specific body of knowledge. The two are used together to guide the designer in modifying the existing topography of a project site to achieve functional objectives and accommodate program elements. Think of grading as land sculpture using the medium of topography to achieve a desired three-dimensional result. A sculptor might use clay, wax, or a whole range of materials to create three-dimensional forms. The materials or tools that landscape architects use to develop their design goals may initially involve clay, but eventually their three-dimensional explorations—regardless of the materials—must be transcribed into two dimensions: line drawings with notes. Although these drawings and notes involve mathematical calculations, in order to create the correct slope or elevation, this does not mean that aesthetics and the design process are not relevant.

The answer to the question "What is site grading?" or "What is the purpose of grading?" has four basic components:

1. Grading is a process for reshaping the topography of an existing site to accommodate programmed uses (such as a sport field or parking lot) and built structures (such as a residence, a school building, trails, or roads). The design of the pedestrian ramp and landscape in Figure 2.1 heavily relied on site grading. Grading is an essential component for all project scales involving properties as large as several hundred acres (in the case of a new residential subdivision) or as small as a half-acre (for a children's playground) or a 400-square-foot residential backyard.

Figure 2.1 Grand Park, Los Angeles, CA. Grading to provide wheelchair access connection from upper to lower park areas.
RIOS CLEMENTI HALE STUDIOS

2. Grading is necessary to reshape existing terrain not only to accommodate intended uses or built facilities but also to redirect surface water flow away from areas where the water is not desirable. Surface water can also be collected for some purposes, such as irrigation; allowed to infiltrate into the underground aquifer; or, as is more common, directed to a storm water system. See Figure 2.2.

Figure 2.2 Bioswale for recharging surface water runoff to aquifer, Phoenix, AZ

3. Grading and the creating of landforms can be employed to achieve an aesthetic goal and to help shape and create outdoor spaces as part of a complete design scheme. Such an outdoor design might include plantings, walls, water features, and hardscape. See Figure 2.3.

4. Grading and the creating of landforms can achieve specialized purposes such as water conservation and management or access control and site security. Figure 2.4 shows a small lake created by the landscape architect as a source of irrigation water, for aesthetic reasons as well as to provide a cooling effect in a hot, dry climate.

Figure 2.3 Stern Grove Concert Meadow Amphitheater, San Francisco, CA. Grading on sloping topography has provided visually attractive and informal seating for an outdoor amphitheater.

LAWRENCE HALPRIN, LANDSCAPE ARCHITECT

Figure 2.4 Private residence, Malinalco, Mexico

MARIO SCHJETNAN, GRUPO DE DISEÑO URBANO

AVOIDING GRADING PROBLEMS IN THE LANDSCAPE

Just as an architect must carefully design and detail a roof to avoid leaks, a grading designer must carefully analyze a site and develop a grading plan that will not result in slope failure, drainage into a building, or long-term maintenance problems such as the examples shown in Figures 2.5-A through 2.5-G. Figure 2.5-H demonstrates a properly designed and functioning parking lot grading solution where surface water is directed to an area catch basin. The photographic scenes in Figures 2.5-A thru G represent the equivalent of a leaky roof for the landscape. Such problems are the result of poor basic grading decisions involving the creation of slopes that are too steep relative to the soil condition, inappropriate user traffic, higher user traffic than anticipated, or allowing unwanted water to collect or flow into areas where it is not desired. The second failure conditions shown in Figures 2.5-C thru E were the result of inadequate subsoil preparation such as lack of proper compaction during construction or inappropriate installation of subbase material, or a combination of the two. Site-grading design and the selection and application of materials fall under the scope of work done in site grading. Instructions for communicating the design intent for grading are embodied in the technical drawings (grading plans, sections, and details) and the technical specifications (earthwork section).

Encounters in the Field of Grading: Problems That Could Have Been Avoided

Figure 2.5-A Ponding of storm water. This is the result of either ground settlement or an increase of storm water run-off with the installation of new pavement on adjacent areas.

Figure 2.5-B Ponding occurred as a result of either inadequate grading or subsequent ground settlement

Figure 2.5-C Inadequate design of the water diversion channel was exacerbated by lack of ground cover maintenance with highly erosive soil

Figure 2.5-D This steep and poorly maintained planted slope has resulted in soil erosion from the concentration of water runoff from the adjacent parking area

Figure 2.5-E Poor subbase installation has resulted in paving failure

Figure 2.5-F Erosion is seen on slope where unplanned foot traffic has occurred

Figure 2.5-G Caution, Flooding. Often, drainage problems such as those occurring in this parking lot are as much the result of poor planning as they are of poor design. In this case, a parking lot in this location should probably have been avoided and instead placed on higher ground or outside the natural flow of surface water.

Figure 2.5-H With a well-designed and executed grading plan, runoff water goes where it was designed to go: towards an area catch basin

SITE GRADING IN THE PROFESSIONAL PRACTICE OF LANDSCAPE ARCHITECTURE

The process involved in site grading fits into the continuum of what it means to practice landscape architecture. Practitioners of landscape architecture and its allied professions of civil engineering and architecture, together in teams, design and oversee construction of our built environments. The built environment may be an office or campus complex, a regional park or zoo, individual residences or a residential community, a public facility such as a library or museum, or a wetland restoration project. Working individually or together with other design consultants, landscape architects design places for living, working, and recreation, as well as a cornucopia of environmental restoration, remediation, and resource management project types, at a range of scale from a quarter-acre lot to parcels of thousands of acres. The landscape architect's role is generally defined as the leader in the site planning, design, and management of the areas outside the footprint of buildings and other structures such as roads and infrastructure. While the overlap between the responsibilities of the architect, civil engineer, and landscape architect is minimal (landscape architects are not licensed or trained to design buildings), the distinction between the work defined as engineering and that defined as landscape architecture may seem at times less clear, with significant areas of overlap. Where overlap may occur, discussion will ensue to define and assign responsibilities at the time of contract negotiations. For example, the landscape architect may set preliminary elevations and design for the built structures, preliminary site design of landscape and paved areas, and then carry out the full design for specialized site improvements such as fountains, pools, and outdoor uses areas. Preliminary site-grading design may also include setting the initial grades (elevations) of parking lots and areas adjacent to buildings, as well as a preliminary surface drainage plan in landscape and hardscape areas. Once this preliminary work is completed, the landscape architect will prepare site-grading plans for specified work, and the civil engineer will prepare the finalized technical plans, roadway alignments, and drainage infrastructure. This arrangement of shared responsibilities between the civil engineer and landscape architect is usually satisfactory to both; the landscape architect can fuss over and resolve the less clear considerations involved in the preliminary or schematic design phase of a project, then transfer the detail and specification preparations to the engineer, whose production processes are more efficient once key design decisions have been resolved in the earlier phases by the landscape architect.

This does not mean that the landscape architect stops at the preliminary phase of site-grading design. Very often the landscape architect's contract with a client will include a scope of work to prepare all aspects of a project's grading requirements. By education, followed with internship, professional experience, and licensure, a landscape architect is qualified to prepare grading plans for almost any situation; however, he or she may be limited administratively by state licensing laws that delimit scope of responsibilities of the design professionals. Landscape architects, for instance, can prepare the full set of grading plans for a 125-acre golf course, but may have limited responsibility on an interstate highway project that might include some grading associated with detail landscape planting or a special non-roadway feature (for instance, the design of a highway rest stop). Questions of professional liability (involving professional design or errors and omission insurance) may limit a landscape architect's involvement. The professional practice insurance industry often influences the design work and responsibilities of the various professions. In actual practice, the responsibilities of the various professions working together on a project are negotiated and defined during the contract negotiation phase, before the actual design work begins. These negotiations often are initiated as the project design team comes together, with the lead design firm managing if not dictating the responsibilities: shared or otherwise.

PROFESSIONAL REGISTRATION TO PRACTICE LANDSCAPE ARCHITECTURE

Courses in grading and drainage are a required part of any landscape architecture or other related curriculum. This requirement is for university landscape programs that seek and maintain accreditation status. One of the requirements to become a licensed landscape architect is for the candidate to have earned an accredited landscape architecture degree, either a four- or five-year degree in the case of a bachelor's degree, or a three-year master's degree. Each state registration law governing landscape architecture licensure may have other requirements, including a specified number of years working under a licensed professional. The Landscape Architecture Accreditation Board (LAAB) is a national board authorized under guidelines promulgated by the U.S. Department of Education. It is the body that establishes the requirements and criteria for achieving accreditation through an onsite evaluation process whereby a team of assigned evaluators determines if the standards for accreditation have been met. One of the requirements of accreditation[1] is that a landscape architecture curriculum (bachelor's or master's) offers instruction in grading and drainage, and that this instruction leads—in the evaluation of student work—to prescribed levels of mastery of grading and drainage topics.

Table 2.1 Steps toward Licensure

THE GOAL	HOW TO ACHIEVE THE GOAL
To be able to practice as and/or call oneself a landscape architect and to be paid for services rendered	1. A test called the Landscape Architecture Registration Examination (LARE) must be passed in order to be eligible for state licensure to practice. The LARE is developed and administered by the Council of Landscape Architectural Registration Boards.[2] Landscape architecture licenses are issued by each state.
To be eligible to take the LARE licensure exam	2. The candidate must meet the following requirements: 2.1 Earned an accredited degree in landscape architecture 2.2 Satisfied the minimum years of internship under an approved list of licensed professionals such as landscape architect, architect, or engineer 2.3 Have a satisfactory police record, such as not having committed a felony, and meet other legal criteria (e.g., no record of noncompliance to child support)

. . . .

1 Accreditation standards include the subject areas grading and landscape technology, design and planning, history, plant materials and design, and professional practice. There a range of subset subjects to each of these subject areas.

2 The LARE is a national examination administered by individual states but developed by the Council of Landscape Architecture Registration Boards. The examination contains a set number of sections that include: planning, design, grading and drainage, professional practice, history, and one or more specialized requirements specific to each state. For instances, Alaska requires the candidate to have successfully passed a course in arctic engineering, states in the West may require a section of specialized irrigation and plant material knowledge related to drought-tolerant conditions.

The questions and subject matter contained in the LARE test are selected to evaluate whether or not the candidate has the minimum level of knowledge, experience, and competency to prepare designs that protect the health, welfare, and safety of the public. This means that the successful candidate has the knowledge necessary to create designs that will not cause harm to individuals or the public. The LARE tests the candidate's knowledge of pertinent design standards, zoning and land utilization requirements such as structure setbacks, vehicular circulation requirements, national and state mobility standards (ADA), and other areas of knowledge considered standards of professional care. In other words, there is a body of knowledge including rules and design standards that every professional landscape architect must know, and must know how to apply when he or she prepares designs. The initial body of knowledge is learned in school in such courses as grading, design, and professional practice. A substantial amount of additional information is learned during the internship and pre-licensure phase of one's professional development and career. The necessary information is learned from teachers, professional mentors, and continuing education, and from experience working for and with others.

THE SECTION OF THE LARE EXAMINATION THAT TESTS GRADING COMPETENCY INCLUDES THE FOLLOWING ELEMENTS[3]:

- Prepare Existing Conditions Plan
- Prepare Demolition and Removal Plan
- Prepare Site Protection and Preservation Plans (e.g., soil, existing features, existing pavements, historic elements, vegetation)
- Prepare Erosion and Sediment-Control Plan
- Prepare Layout and Materials Plan
- Prepare Grading Plan
- Prepare Storm Water Management Plan

. . . .

3 www.clarb.org/Candidates/Documents/CLARB-LARE-2012-Exam-Specifications.pdf

Once the candidate has successfully passed the LARE and has acquired registration in one state, in order to practice in another state he or she must acquire registration in each additional state through a process of reciprocity. In the United States, professional licensure is required by each state to practice landscape architecture, engineering, medicine, law, contracting, and the like. In other countries, a national requirement enables one to practice in any province or region. An interesting development for the member countries of the European Union (EU) is close to finalization. Individuals who have graduated from the equivalent of an accredited university professional program in one EU member country will be able to practice their profession in any of the EU member countries. The legal and liability environment of these countries, unlike that in the United States, allows for the universal acceptance of a recognized professional degree. In our case, the federal constitution implicitly acknowledges states' rights to administer individual professional licensure and associated laws.

3

SITE PLANNING AND GRADING PROCESS

In this chapter you will learn about:

- The design process from a professional services contract basis
- How to prepare a slope analysis map
- How to make preliminary determination of best locations for program elements
- The meaning and significance of the term "due diligence": the expected performance of a licensed or practicing professional

INTRODUCTION

Site grading is one of many components in a landscape site design package. The preparation of a site grading plan generally occurs at some point after a preliminary site plan is prepared. When site grading is an important aspect of the design, a schematic grading plan is prepared and included in the design review process. The schematic site plan shows all proposed project program elements desired by the client. Each element is drawn to scale, and the plan shows the outline or footprint of all buildings and structures, vehicular and pedestrian circulation, outdoor use and landscape areas, and any other feature that will be built in a proposed project. Once a schematic site plan is prepared and approved by the client, a preliminary site grading is developed for several reasons, the foremost being to determine if the project can be accommodated within the existing topography of the project boundaries and can be accommodated within the project budget. The preliminary grading plan establishes the finish floor elevations of buildings, grades, and slopes of nonbuilding elements, including walks and roadway, surface drainage, and cut and fill estimates. These estimates are used for determining probable construction costs. Once the preliminary design package (schematic design phase of a professional services contract) is approved, the project design team proceeds to the design development phase of the contract, where more detailed design takes place. In the subsequent phase of construction documents, construction drawings, technical specifications, and other contract bidding documents are prepared.

THE DESIGN PROCESS

The design process begins with the client selecting a design firm, such as a landscape architecture firm, and then entering into a professional service contract with the firm. The professional services contract outlines responsibilities, schedule, deliverables and services, and compensation. The services of the designer are detailed in each phase of work to be carried out by the designer, beginning with schematic design and followed by design development, construction documentation and specifications, bidding, and finally construction administration. This chapter will present the process a designer would go through from the beginning of the project design process. Figure 3.1 provides a snapshot picture of the various steps of the process.

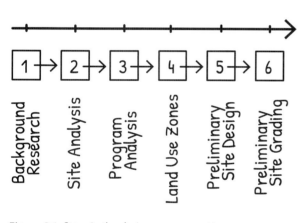

Figure 3.1 Steps in the design process continuum

STEPS IN THE DESIGN PROCESS CONTINUUM

Step 1. Background Research

"Due diligence" is a business term that involves the process of identifying the codes; design and safety standards; and zoning, permitting, and other governmental requirements that a designer would be expected to be familiar with, that are relevant to a specific project or project type. The applicable requirements would be researched at the outset of a project and would need to be addressed as part of the project programming prior to commencing the initial site design phase. It is understood that a professional landscape architect or other professional design service provider is knowledgeable about this process and capable of conducting the necessary background research appropriate for the design services being provided. In the case of a landscape architect, due diligence research would include a thorough investigation of (1) relevant zoning requirements, (2) design standards regarding the health, safety, and welfare of the public or users, and (3) other governmental regulations such as water quality, best management practices, and wetlands requirements. It is advisable that background research and site analysis be carried out when starting a new site design project.

1. Background research should also include verification of the project site legal description, including property lines, location of servitudes and existing on- and off-site utility services, rights-of-way such as roadways, and any other legal or physical encumbrances that may be attached to the project site. Much of this research is conducted in combination with the land surveyor and a land title company. The owner is normally responsible for providing the property legal description, although verification or due diligence by the landscape architect can be time well spent. For topography information, a USGS quad map or topographic survey prepared by a land surveyor should be consulted.

2. Background research should include a code review to identify relevant laws, rules, codes, and regulations governing the project site and proposed uses.

3. Further useful background information to gather at the outset of a project includes conducting an on-the-ground assessment of the site, including photographic documentation highlighting existing physical features and conditions. Soils, climate variations, sun angles, and slope are some of the physical features that should be documented and assessed for their potential relevance to or influence on site design. See Figure 3.2-A.

4. An aerial photograph (Google or other product) of project site and its context should be obtained, providing context information such as existing roads, buildings, tree and plant cover, and water features.

Figure 3.2-A Conduct field investigation to analyze the project site, document important features and landmarks, and identify opportunities and constraints. Record with notes and photographs.

Figure 3.2-B Making field notes on topographic map

Step 2. Site Analysis

The site analysis is useful to determine—among many considerations—the optimal location for various program uses (buildings and other structures), access and circulation, outdoor use and landscape areas, on-site drainage strategies, and other programmed requirements. A slope analysis would reveal patterns of steep to moderate, to level terrain on the site. The degree of steepness is determined by measuring the distance between contours. To be useful, the distances between contours are segregated into groups or zones. Each zone represents a range of slope where contours that are generally spaced farther apart have a slope less than 5 percent, contours generally spaced closer might have a slope range of 6 to 10 or 15 percent, and contours spaced close together are steeper, with a slope greater than 20 or 25 percent. Slopes greater than 25 percent are common in mountainous regions and can be as steep as 50 percent, 100 percent, and steeper. Through visual inspection, the designer segregates the topographic map into zones then calculates the average slope or range of slopes found within each zone.

For an example of how the process for preparing a slope analysis map begins with a topographic map, see the portion of a United States Geological Survey (USGS) map shown in Figure 3.3.

The first step is to make a visual assessment of the topographic map with the idea of grouping areas where the contours fall within a similar range of distance apart. Looking at Figure 3.4, you can see that the USGS map has been separated into zones: A, B, C, and D. The contours in zone A are generally spaced at a greater distance apart than the contours in the other zones. Zone B contours are closer together than those in zone A, and the contours in C are even closer together than those in B. The contours in zone D are generally the closest together, and indicate the terrain is steeper or at a greater percent of slope than in the other zones.

Figure 3.3 Portion of a USGS quad map

The contours in Figure 3.4 were first visually grouped into four categories. Category A contours appear to be the least densely spaced contours (that is, the contours are spaced farther apart than other groups of contours) in the topographic map, creating terrain that slopes from 0 to 5 percent. Group D contours are the most densely spaced and therefore result in a steeper average slope of over 20 percent. The zones shown as groups B and C fall somewhere in the middle of slope percentages, with the B area terrain averaging 5 to 10 percent and group C averaging 10 to 20 percent.

Figure 3.5 illustrates where the slope groups would occur in the field if each individual slope category were marked out on the ground. Figure 3.6-A shows another way to visualize the comparison between different degrees of slope in the landscape. The letter S noted on the triangles in Figure 3.6-A is the slope of the terrain expressed as a percent. Slope

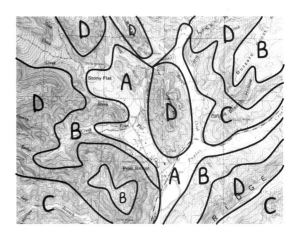

Figure 3.4 USGS map divided into four categories of slope from shallow (A) to steepest slope (D). Areas B and C are medium slope.

Figure 3.5 Photographic visualization of four different degrees of slope, with area A the least steep and area D the steepest slope in the landscape scene

A would have the least amount of slope, while slope C would have the greatest or steepest percent of slope. In Figure 3.6-B we can see another graphic means of visualizing the relative differences in slope steepness by how close or far apart the topographic contours are spaced. Area A in Figure 3.6-B has contours that are widely spaced apart, as compared to areas B and C. The contours in area C are relatively closely spaced, resulting in terrain that is steeper or has a higher percent of slope than areas A and B.

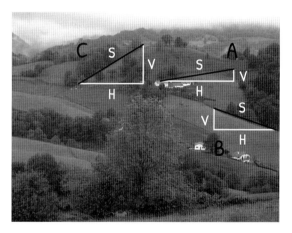

Figure 3.6-A Visualizing various categories of slope with different slope triangles

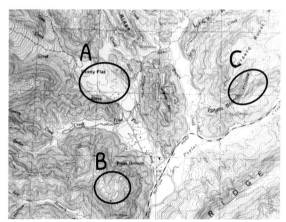

Figure 3.6-B Visualizing the difference of steep to shallow sloping terrain by the spacing of contours

To determine the actual slopes found in each area (A, B, C, D), the percent of slope would be calculated based on measurements taken from a topographic survey with contours. Figure 3.7 shows how slope is calculated using an engineer's scale and a USGS quad map.

For an example of how to calculate the average percent of slope of a given area, refer to Figure 3.7, taken from a portion of a USGS topographic quad map. The scale of the topographic map in the example is 1 inch equals 2000 feet. See Chapter 5 to learn how to identify the scale of a USGS topographic map. Using a 20 scale of an engineer's scale, the "0" tick mark on the scale is shown as A. The A tick mark is positioned on the 350-foot contour line. The B tick mark on the engineer's scale falls on the 300-foot contour line. The B tick mark is located on the 2500-foot mark of the engineer's scale. To calculate the slope between the 300 and 350 contour lines, use the formula S = V/H, where S or percent of slope is not known, V is the vertical distance between the 350' and 300' contours (50 feet), and the horizontal distance measured with the engineer's scale is 1500 feet. The calculation of slope is made as follows:

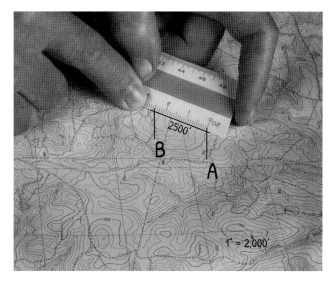

Figure 3.7 USGS topographic map with engineer's scale used to measure the horizontal distance between points A and B. The scale of this map is 1 inch equals 2000 feet.

$S = V/H$

$S = 50/2500$

$S = 0.02$ or 2%

In Figure 3.8 the contours are closer together. Using the same scale, the zero tick mark is positioned over the 400 contour, and the 300 contour is located at the 1100-foot mark. The slope percent is calculated as follows:

$S = V/H$

$S = 100/1100$

$S = 0.1$ or 10 %

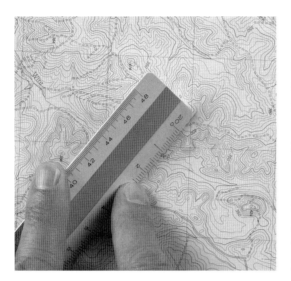

Figure 3.8 USGS topographic map with engineer's scale showing a distance of 1100 feet as the distance between 300′ and 400′ contours. The scale of this map is 1 inch equals 2000 feet.

In Figure 3.6-B the circled areas A, B, and C represent three slope categories, with area A being the more level terrain and area C the steeper terrain. Just considering terrain slope suitability, area A would accommodate uses such as sports playing fields or parking with minimum grading, as compared with areas B and C. Considerable grading, moving of earth, would be required in areas B and C to create a gently sloping area for sports fields or parking lots. Vehicular access to areas A and B would require less grading than area C. Cluster-type housing is a suitable use in areas A and B, with area B providing the opportunity for views, perhaps very desirable views that would increase the value of the property and economic return to the developer. Low-density use could be selectively accommodated in area C, but development would be minimal in order to retain the physical character of the terrain. Depending on the program requirements of a proposed development, utilization of areas A and B could accommodate a desirable site design offering diverse terrain to work with. Area C might be left undisturbed, perhaps serving as a watershed reserve or location for foot trails and low-impact activities needing only minimal grading, such as outdoor recreation uses.

The concept is to distribute land uses on the terrain where the least amount of grading (cut and fill) is required, thereby reducing construction costs. A football field or parking lot that normally would be sited on terrain of 3 to 5 percent could be placed on terrain that is steeper, for instance terrain that is 15 percent, 20 percent, and even steeper. However, considerably more grading would be required to create a level area to accommodate the field or parking lot than if the field and lot were located on existing terrain that was 5 percent or less.

Figures 3.9-A and 3.9-B Two alternative locations for a playfield, with option A resulting in less cut and fill than option B would require

Figures 3.9-A and 3.9-B compare the amount of cut and fill needed to locate a playing field on two different slope conditions. Figure 3.9-A positions the sports field on the more gently sloping terrain (5–10%) in the landscape. Figure 3.9-B positions the field on steeper terrain (10–20%). A diagrammatic section has been drawn for each option. On close inspection, one should see that there would be perhaps twice as much cut and fill required to accommodate the sports field in Figure 3.9-B than in Figure 3.9-A.

The slope analysis map, in essence, provides the designer with a guide to match the various program activities and use areas with the most suitable terrain for each use. There may be other considerations that necessitate locating program uses in less suitable terrain conditions, although doing so might require more grading and therefore increase construction costs. There are instances when the increased costs are acceptable in order to achieve the desired site design intent. For instance, a location decision may be based on exploiting outstanding views.

It is suggested that a preliminary site analysis be made at the outset of a project, certainly before doing a preliminary site design or grading plan.

Step 3. Program Analysis

Briefly, program analysis consists of meeting with the client with the goal of identifying the project program to be designed. The project program might include the facilities, structures, and outdoor use areas the landscape architect is responsible for designing. Programming under scope of work may also include such activities as wetland protection and storm water management, both important aspects of site development that the landscape architect may have the responsibility to consider and incorporate into a design solution, and later include as part of a site grading plan.

Once a program is identified, a diagram showing the desired physical relations between the design elements should be prepared. This diagram—which is also referred to as a program coordination diagram—groups together program activities that it is desirable to have adjacent to each other or in close proximity, and that might share certain functional elements such as parking or an outdoors common area. A circulation diagram would be superimposed showing access, vehicular traffic flow and sequence, and pedestrian circulation requirements.

One approach for deciding the best location for each program use area is to match each program with the most suitable percent of slope category prepared during the slope analysis. Recommended slope to land use activity pairings are shown in Table 3.1. The recommendations would cover most situations; however, in special circumstances (for instance in limited areas), the designer may consider adjustments. The exception is where maximum slope standards must be adhered to, as in the case of 8 percent slope for ADA (Americans with Disabilities Act) accessible ramps and where local codes dictate specific maximum-minimum slope standards.

Table 3.1 Suggested Slope-Grading Guidelines[1]

DESIRED SLOPE RANGE[2]	LAND USE	MAXIMUM SLOPE
0.5% to 1%	- Game courts such as tennis, basketball - Urban plazas (paved)	2%
1%	- Cross slope on sidewalk or paved walkway	
1% to 3% or 4%	- Parking areas (paved) - Grass or planted drainage swales[3] - Sidewalks	5% 25%
2% to 3%	- Sports field such as soccer, football - Mowed turfgrass	25%
1% to 8%	- ADA accessible ramps and walks - Public streets - Private streets - Access or service driveways - Walking/hiking trails	8% 12% 10% 10% to 12% 10% to 12%
1% or 2% to 10%	- Residential	25%+
1% or 2% to 10%	- Commercial	
Slope may vary	- Cut slope	33%
Slope may vary	- Fill slope	25%
2% to 25% Slope may vary	- Unmowed turfgrass slopes - Planted slopes	30% 40% to 50%

[1] Grading must meet local codes and requirements and, where applicable, state and federal guidelines. Applicable grading requirements must be identified before site design and grading work commences. This is considered a component of professional "due diligence" research and investigation.

[2] Maximum and minimum slopes may vary based on local climate and soil conditions, regional industry or governmental standards, and construction materials selected.

[3] The concern is to avoid erosion that can be caused when concentrated flows of surface water move down a swale.

Step 4. Land Use and Circulation Diagram

This next step requires the synthesis of the site analysis map with the program analysis. The goal here is to arrange the various program uses/activities—drawn to show their spatial or area needs (approximate square footages) and shape or dimension—in their optimum location, considering the information identified in the site analysis. For instance, the site analysis shows slope percentages by area. Program elements requiring less steep slopes would be located in these areas, while other program elements might be located on steeper slopes. The schematic design plan would be drawn to scale (20, 40, up to 100 scale depending on the size of the property) and would show:

1. Base information including property boundaries, existing roads, and existing vegetation or structures to remain

2. All activity use areas, buildings, and other structures or site features, drawn at the approximate shape and areal dimensions and showing key land use relationships

3. Site ingress and egress and internal circulation patterns for vehicular, non-vehicular, and pedestrian systems

4. Surface drainage patterns, setbacks for stream or wetlands located on or adjacent to project site (see Figure 3.10)

Other considerations for locating program elements include siting proposed structures and activity areas to take advantage of views or perhaps in areas that would provide for greater privacy or greater visibility from the street. See Figure 3.11 for an example of a circulation diagram and Figure 3.12 for a master plan site allocation diagram.

The land use and circulation diagram would be accompanied with a square footage or area analysis, and in the case of a residential or commercial project, unit densities such as housing units per acre, number of parking spaces, open space, and other use areas would be tabulated and included with the diagram. In the case of a park, numbers and types of playing fields and other park and recreation activities would be tabulated with their square footage calculations.

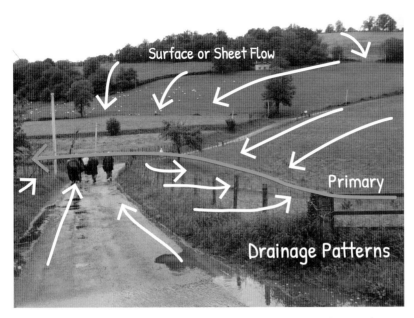

Figure 3.10 Arrows indicate direction of surface water drainage in the complex landforms that make up this rural landscape

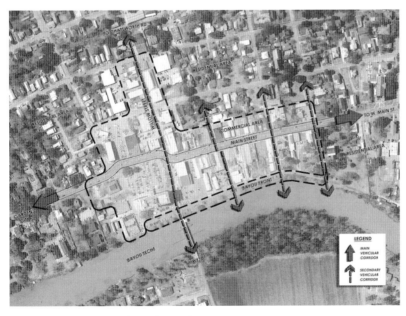

Figure 3.11 Program and circulation diagram

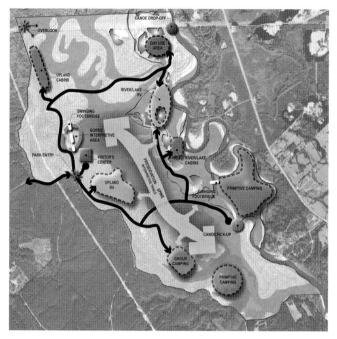

Figure 3.12 Master land use allocation diagram
COURTESY OF REICH ASSOCIATES

Step 5. Schematic Site Design

The land use and circulation diagram might be reviewed with the client
to obtain client input and approval. It is often customary to discuss with
the client the merits of one or more alternative land use diagrams. This
is a valuable strategy, allowing the client to identify a preference. The
preferred diagram might be a blending of portions from other diagrams.
From this client review, a final diagram would be prepared, serving as
the basis in developing a schematic site design.

Figures 3.13, 3.14, and 3.15 are examples of schematic design plans.
These types of plans transform the bubble-like diagrams of the land use
allocation and circulation plans into the actual shapes and dimensions
of the various program elements. Schematic design plans are drawn
to scale, as shown in the examples. Delineation of materials is shown
but not specified. For instance, the plan may show the location of trees
and shrubs but not their species or size. Different patterns of pavement
would be shown but not specified in terms of actual materials.

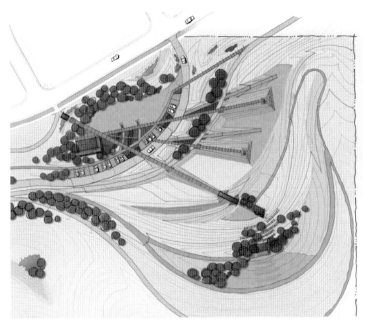

Figure 3.13 Schematic site design with preliminary grading
COURTESY OF DESIGN WORKSHOP, DENVER, CO

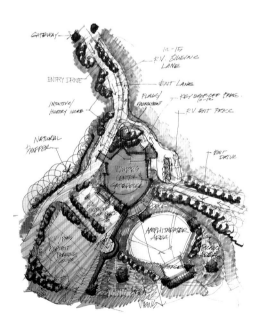

Figure 3.14 Hand-drawn plan of study area in preparation of schematic plan drawing
COURTESY OF REICH ASSOCIATES

Figure 3.15 Schematic park master plan
COURTESY OF REICH ASSOCIATES

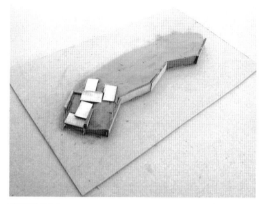

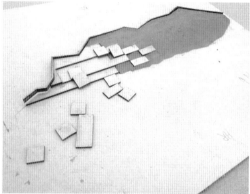

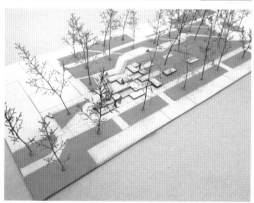

Figures 3.16-A, B, and C 3.16-A. Concept study model; 3.16-B. Development model; 3.16-C. Presentation model of for schematic design

An example showing how the designers develop preliminary design ideas using models is shown in Figures 3.16-A–C. Three stages of the development of a design can be seen, with Figure 3.16-A being the first study model, in this case a clay model created by the designer from a rough sketch. The designer used the initial model to better visualize the concept for a proposed landform in three dimensions (Figure 3.16-B), then constructed several iterations of the design, again using clay with cardboard to advance the design. Figure 3.16-C is the final study model, advancing this three-dimensional modeling design process. A schematic design plan was prepared to accompany the model for a presentation to the client, together with sections and several perspective drawings, and estimate of probable costs to complete the schematic design phase of the professional services contract.

Step 6. Schematic Design Grading Plan

As in design, think of grading as involving a deliberative process. In a deliberative process, the designer follows a purposeful path, a considered path that takes into account many factors, including: functional, aesthetic, environmental, climatic, and legal considerations. In Figures 3.17-A–D, we can follow a step-by-step process of considering alternate locations for a proposed structure such as a residence. In the left column a number of alternate locations are shown, and in the right column opposite each alternative a brief critique is given.

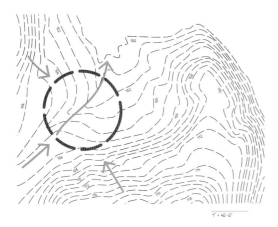

Figure 3.17-A Structure is located within a natural ravine. Unless the structure were designed to bridge the ravine or built over a culvert system, so as to allow surface water to flow beneath, a considerable amount of earth would need to be moved to divert surface water and not cause flooding into the structure.

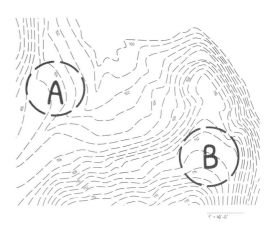

Figure 3.17-B Locating the structure at B would allow surface water to flow away from the structure by means of contour grading, without the costly bridge or culvert structure that would be needed in area A

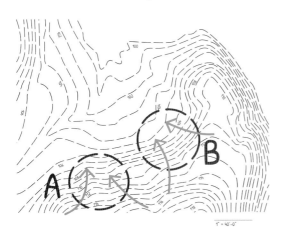

Figure 3.17-C Locations A and B are similar. However, the natural topography of A would tend to divert surface water to either side of the structure, while the topography of site B would tend to concentrate water toward the center of the structure location. More grading would be required to accommodate a structure at site B in order to divert surface water from the structure.

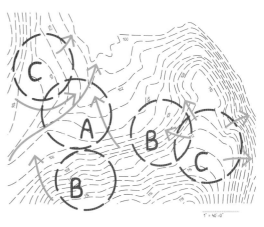

Figure 3.17-D The two site C locations would require less earthwork modification to accommodate a proposed structure than sites A, B, and C, and they are less steep than the two B sites

Figures 3.18-A through 3.18-C contain a second site with different topography. Four alternative locations for a building site are considered. Alternate locations A and D are more gently sloping than locations B and C and have desirable surface drainage patterns to more readily accommodate a structure or development.

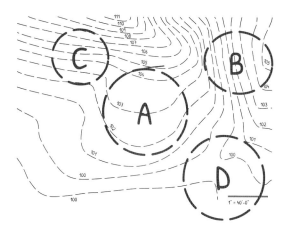

Figure 3.18-A Site evaluation and preliminary grading plan

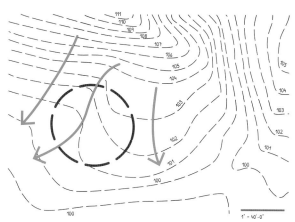

Figure 3.18-B The location was selected because it affords desirable views and has similar slope attributes to A in Figure 3.17-A. The location of A allows out-of-doors uses to be developed on the gentler slopes to the left and slightly downhill of the building site.

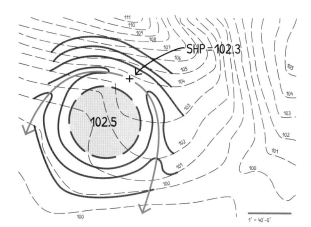

Figure 3.18-C The conceptual grading plan demonstrates how the topography can be modified to accommodate the proposed building area

PRELIMINARY SITE GRADING PLAN

A preliminary site grading plan is one of several drawings that is prepared as part of the schematic design phase of a professional service contract. Useful scales at which to draw a preliminary grading plan are 20 to 40 scale for sites less than five acres and 50 or even 100 scale for larger tracts of land, such as a regional park, residential subdivision, shopping complex, or business campus. Conceptual site grading plans should contain the following information:

1. Location of all proposed buildings and the first-floor elevation

2. The existing and proposed contours at a contour interval of two feet or less

3. The proposed elevations of the levels of land above and below retaining walls, as well as top wall elevations

4. The location of proposed vehicular facilities, including roads, drives, or parking areas, showing sheet flow and direction of parking areas, and location of drainage structures such as catch basins

5. The location of pedestrian and nonmotorized vehicle walks, trails, and ramps; location of steps, indicating number and riser height with spot elevations at top and bottom of each group of steps; spot elevations and top and bottom of walkways and ramps with percent of slope indication and cross slope

6. Grading limits and setbacks, including setbacks for stream, wetlands, woodlots, limits from property, and grading limits to protect existing trees, existing structures, or other features

7. Preliminary cut and fill quantity estimate

Just as a designer will advance the development of an initial design concept, the grading designer will also prepare a contour study model to help visualize and evaluate a preliminary grading design, as shown Figures 3.19-A and 3.19-B. A preliminary grading plan is first prepared after one or more exploratory grading plans are developed, as the designer works through the process of arriving at a grading solution. The contour model may be used as part of a presentation of the schematic design to the client. More importantly, the study model should help the designer assess the grading solution, primarily by evaluating its aesthetic merits.

The model could be taken outside to see the shading cast by the modeled landforms, to get a better idea of how the landforms created might look in the landscape.

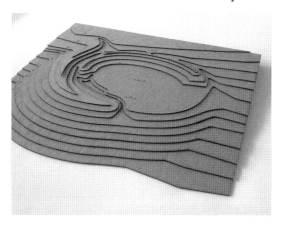

Figure 3.19-A Physical study models and computer 3-D modeling software used by the designer to visualize and evaluate proposed grading designs. An oblique view of an amphitheater study model.

JIESI LUO, MLA STUDENT AT RRSLA LOUISIANA STATE UNIVERSITY

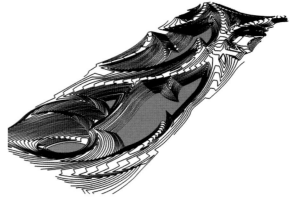

Figure 3.19-B A SketchUp model of a grading plan for Daybreak project

COURTESY OF DESIGN WORK SHOP, DENVER, CO

Figure 3.20 is included here for the reader to see a professional schematic grading plan. Figure 3.21 contains a photograph that was taken of the same site a year or so after construction was completed.

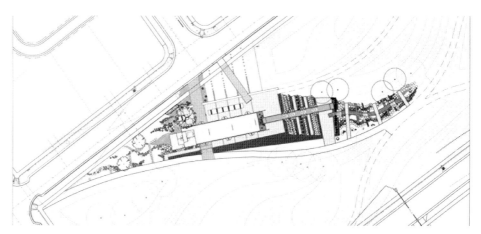

Figure 3.20 Daybreak project

COURTESY OF DESIGN WORKSHOP, DENVER, CO

Figure 3.21 Photograph of Daybreak project
COURTESY OF DESIGN WORK SHOP, DENVER, CO

DESIGN DEVELOPMENT AND SUBSEQUENT PHASES IN THE DESIGN CONTINUUM

Following the acceptance of the plans prepared during the schematic design phase, the project team will commence work on the design development phase. The work included in this phase advances the schematic design in considerably greater details. Drawings are drawn to actual scale and include selection and descriptions of materials, resolution of dimensions, and more detail in general. Developing design sections is important as a visual aid for the designer to resolve the physical landform of design elements, as close as possible to their final form, so that the client has a better idea of the grading design. Many of the sections are refined during this phase and become technical sections, included with other details in the construction drawing package. Other deliverable elements called for in the professional service contract, such as estimate of probable costs and materials and equipment catalogue descriptions, would also be included in the design development submittal package.

A design development grading plan includes a quantity estimate of earth to be moved, to determine the potential need to bring in additional material or to dispose of excess material. The earthwork quantities are used in developing an estimate of probable construction cost. After the submittal and acceptance of the design development phase documents, the project team prepares the construction documents and bid package. This package will be used in securing bids from contractors and used to guide construction. A final grading plan would be included, together with technical sections and details. Technical specifications and bidding documents would also be a part of this final construction bid package.

4

DRAWING CONVENTIONS

In this chapter you will learn about:

- The importance of drawing in accordance with established universal conventions
- Similarities and differences between graphic and analog drawing
- Guidelines for ensuring accurate and complete drawings
- The use of architect's and engineer's scales

DRAWING CONVENTIONS: LANDSCAPE DRAWINGS AND MUSIC SCORES

The application of what are described as graphic representation conventions is steeped in drafting traditions. Many years ago, drafting was considered a craft, practiced and cultivated by draftsmen—professional or semiprofessional trained employees who were prized for their skill and, in many instances, their artistry. The artistry for which the earlier draughtsmen were known was accomplished by hand, using a wide array of instruments and guides, drawn within and pencil on linen and later vellum paper and Mylar film. Presentation renderings were created using watercolor washes, colored pencils, conté crayon, and pastels. Some people refer to those as the "good old days," the days of analog rendering. Increasingly today, the physical materials involved in drawing by hand are being replaced by digital methods. We now draw "by hand" by manipulating the keys on a computer, navigating on a computer screen with a mouse or stylus. There are many advantages to digital drawing; it has increased productivity, facilitated a new way of communicating and sharing files, and yes, led to the creation of a wide range of artistic expression. Figure 4.1 is a recent image demonstrating the interrelation of analog and digital media in the production process at a professional landscape architecture office.

Figure 4.1 Contemporary landscape architecture office utilizing both digital and analog media

In the contemporary landscape architecture office in Figure 4.1, paper and electronic files have their place in the working environment. Professional employees are at their computer stations in the background. Paper printouts of current projects were laid out onto tables to be reviewed and marked up for later revisions that will be done on the computer.

DRAFTING AND REPRESENTATION

The word "drafting" is a carryover from days past. The term "representation" is becoming more widely used for what was called drawing or drafting. Graphic communication remains the primary means of communicating design and technical information. The words "drafting" and "drawing" will be used interchangeably here and will refer to either analog or digital graphic communication. When it is necessary to make a distinction, the word use will be clarified.

Drafting is the art of communicating complex design ideas in two dimensions. The drawings created by staff in design offices were done with pencil or ink on a variety of paper products, and later on Mylar film. Hand-drawn (analog) drafting makes use of a variety of tools, including a T-square, several types of triangles, French curves, a drawing compass, and variety of templates (such as a circle template). Drafting of the past is now referred to as analog representation (drawing by hand) and has been replaced by digital representation done on computers, applying an array of representation software such as AutoCAD.

The subject of drawing conventions is vitally important in site grading and justifies further elaboration. The lines, patterns, and symbols "drawn" by the designer are as necessary for successfully communicating design intent as the symbols, lines, and notations of a musical score that communicate a composer's intent. Musical symbols incorrectly written on a page of sheet music would produce a terrible sound in what otherwise might be a very pleasing musical composition. Likewise, a contractor could interpret a misused symbol or incorrectly drawn line in a site-grading plan with disastrous results.

Those practicing the professions of architecture, engineering, and landscape architecture communicate their design ideas to others following a set of drawing or representation conventions. These conventions consist of line width, patterns, numbers and text usage, and symbols that are universal to the extent that all professions involved at different stages in the life of a design project (from preliminary design through construction documentation, bidding, contract negotiation, and construction) understand these conventions and expect them to be followed. Grading plans contain a minimum of three layers of information: belowground surface, or subgrade; ground surface, or at grade; and aboveground, such as walls and other structures. The designer of site-grading plans needs to provide information for each layer, using spot elevations and contour lines for at grade, and spot elevations for below- and above-grade elements. Details, elevations, and sections are used to provide additional information to clarify the design intent for a site-grading plan.

The reader has a plethora of sources for researching the drawing conventions used in preparing landscape-grading plans, sections, and related graphic communication elements. It is not the intent here to discuss these conventions, although examples of grading conventions can be viewed in the professional examples in a later chapter.

THE CONCEPT OF DOCUMENTATION CONVENTIONS IN MUSIC AND DESIGN

Figure 4.2 is one page from a musical score. Like a grading plan, it provides a set of instructions to guide the activities of the reader: in the case of a score, the reader would be a musician, and in the case of a site-grading plan, the reader would be a construction contractor.

A good example of this idea of the universality of drawing and communication conventions can be found in music, starting out with the composer: the creator of musical compositions. (See musical score, Figure 4.2.) Composers,[1] regardless of the genre of music involved (e.g., opera, jazz, rock and roll, or hip-hop), use a standard music notation system. The music composed by the composer or artist is called the score. The composer first creates music in his or her head by some creative process. What is heard in the mind of the creator is transformed into marks on paper, using standard symbols and notation. When read by a musician, singer, or conductor, the score can be "heard" before the first note is played or sung. The drawings we produce to convey a landscape

· · · · · · · · · · · · · · · · ·
1 Music composers, principally from Western cultures and traditions.

Quartet No. 1 in E-flat Major, Op. 12

Figure 4.2 Felix Mendelssohn String Quartet No.1, Op. 12

design should follow accepted drawing conventions in order that the information can be readily seen or visualized by others: other designers, clients, government agency staff, and contractors. Thus, the graphic symbols of landscape architects are used to present instructions so that the client, contractors, and government plan reviewer can interpret the design intent correctly. A good set of drawings is particularly critical for the contractors, whose reading and understanding of the drawings should result in minimal misunderstanding while they prepare a competitive construction cost estimate and during the construction of the project. Similarly, when standard drawing conventions are applied, government agency reviewers will more likely be able to interpret the drawings submitted to facilitate approval of the proposed design.

Grading plans follow a set of drawing conventions that have strong similarity globally. If grading plans are drawn correctly following these conventions, contractors, agency reviewers, and others will be able to understand and see the designer's design intent, just as musicians and conductors can hear what the composer heard and wrote down in the form of a music score. One may, at first glance, recognize unique graphic representation styles in grading plans prepared by different landscape architects (see Figure 4.3). However, on a closer look, one will see that recognizable graphic conventions were followed. People's handwriting may look different, but the same conventions of composition and grammar are closely followed.

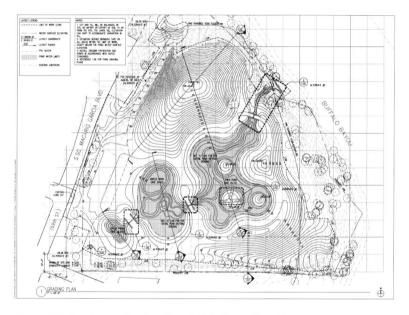

Figure 4.3 Landscape-Grading Plan: Buffalo Bayou Bend Park
COURTESY OF SWA GROUP, HOUSTON, TEXAS

In order for the reader to understand the importance of having and following graphic and documentation conventions, let's look at Figure 4.4 and consider the following questions.

1. What is the contour interval?

2. What is the horizontal distance from point A to point B?

3. What is the slope in percent between points C and D?

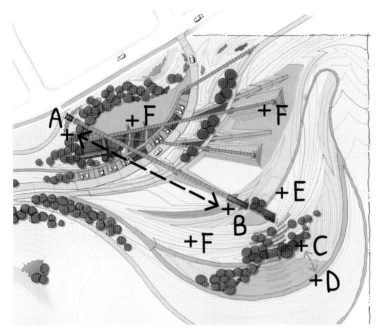

Figure 4.4 Design grading plan for Daybreak project
ADAPTED FROM PLAN COURTESY OF DESIGN WORKSHOP, DENVER, CO

4. What is the elevation of point E?

5. Where is the south side of the building?

6. What are the elements labeled F in the image?

The answers to these questions will be more fully discussed in subsequent chapters. However, the point to be made here is that the drawing is very professional looking and seems quite clear in terms of line work and attention to representing detail. But in fact the drawing is nearly useless, if not totally so, for the purpose of answering our list of six questions. To answer the questions, the drawing should have: (1) contours labeled in terms of their elevation, (2) a scale, such as 1 inch equals 40 feet, (3) a north arrow, (4) labels of key elements, and (5) a legend that identifies the various symbols and line patterns.

Knowing the contour interval for a topographic map, the designer is able to determine the degree of slope of different areas on a site and calculate elevations. If a drawing has a legend, then the meaning or significance of various lines, symbols, colors, and patterns will not have to be guessed at. The legend will also reduce labeling requirements while improving graphic clarity and communication. Having a north arrow on a drawing provides the designer with an analytical tool not only to provide orientation and direction but to project sun and shadow patterns useful in making site design decisions. By knowing the direction of north, the designer can prevent the sun from interfering with a baseball batter, or position a building so as to reduce solar gain. Scale makes a plan useful for the purposes of knowing distance and dimensions, calculating degrees of slope and elevation in concert with the contour lines, and calculating areas and the dimensions of any feature currently on a project site or being proposed.

FOLLOWING DRAWING CONVENTIONS PREVENTS MISCOMMUNICATION

The function of landscape-grading plans, in tandem with technical sections and details, is to communicate clearly, and with as little ambiguity as possible, the relation between existing site conditions (such as topography, vegetation, man-made features, and important context features), and the proposed designed site grading and landforms. The landscape-grading plans, together with the full set of construction documents, are, in essence, the directions used by the contractor to build the project. The contractor uses the construction documents to plan and develop strategies to build what is shown in the construction package.

We have described the importance of applying drawing conventions in landscape architecture in general, and specifically in the preparation of grading plans and drawings. There is room for personal graphic expression to convey the nuances a designer may want to use to communicate the grading information. There is room in the conventions of graphic representation for the designer to add shading, texture, color, and graphic composition (page layout) to make clear the nuances of the design. In some cases, graphic representation of grading information may have a more three-dimensional look, when the designer wishes to communicate specifics of sculptural form for which straightforward line drawing may not be adequate. A cautionary note: The nuanced aspects of a drawing should not overshadow and muddy the necessary information that followers of convention rely on for understanding a landscape-grading drawing or any other technical drawing.

Finally, there is a nearly universal application of graphic communication conventions in landscape architecture throughout the United States and other countries. As globalization becomes increasingly the norm in landscape architecture and related professions, drawing conventions become more universally applied, notwithstanding the use of metric versus imperial systems of measurement—yet another topic for the interested student to investigate elsewhere in the literature.

CONSTRUCTION DOCUMENTATION

Up to this point, the term "drafting conventions" has been used to describe primarily graphic communication principles and considerations. In professional practice, the term "documentation"—specifically "construction documentation"—is commonly used when describing graphic communication requirements. Design and construction documentation is integral to the design process. Design is a process involving critical thinking, incorporating a wide range of environmental, cultural, social, economic, and governmental topics. The result of the critical thinking must be effectively and clearly communicated in drawings and words, in order to be understood by others. The quality of the documentation has a significant impact on the design outcome and the process that develops into construction. Although appropriate documentation does not guarantee good design, it can contribute to the understanding of the design so that the intent can be successfully communicated to others, and lead to its successful implementation. Effective documentation can facilitate the process of collaboration between design disciplines working closely together. Effective design and construction documentation have following attributes in common:

1. They are accurate, with minimum conflicts and redundancies. The various components (graphic and written) do not contain conflicting information. Eliminating redundancies can minimize conflicting information. A guiding principle: Say it or draw it once.

2. They are complete, with a high level of resolution. A sufficient level of detail is provided to clearly communicate the design intent, so that the reader or reviewer has few if any questions as to what is intended.

3. They are organized in a consistent, accessible, and intelligible manner. There is an obvious organizational system that has been followed in presenting the information, in both graphic and written form, particularly for complex projects involving countless pages of drawings for a myriad of contributing consultants.

4. The information is presented in a predictable and consistent location. Everything has its place so that those looking for information know where to find what they are looking for on a page.

5. Information is organized using a hierarchical system. Drawing-line weights should be hierarchical, with heavier or darker lines assigned to the primary form or information, and lighter line weights used for more detailed information. The main subject items in text or drawings on the page should be the primary focus, with detailed or supporting information presented in smaller case or lighter line weights.

6. They utilize standard nomenclature and graphic standards in general use within the industry and design disciplines.

7. They are reviewed following a standard process of quality control implemented by the organization (firm, department, organization) and the need for following this process is understood by all staff within the organization.

8. All plan drawings in a documentation package are positioned with the same north orientation to the extent feasible. This will minimize confusion and reduce misjudgment. A corollary to this is that all drawing should have a scale.

ANOTHER WORD ABOUT SCALE

The word "scale," as used in map reading and landscape documentation, refers to the relationship between the distance or horizontal dimensions on a map and the dimensions or distance in the actual landscape. Topographic and land survey maps almost always use an engineer's scale. The units of measurement are expressed in whole numbers and decimal fractions. For example, forty-two and a half feet is written as 42.5 feet.

A grading plan or land survey map with a 20 scale means that one inch equals 20 horizontal feet on the ground. A 100-scale map means that one inch measures 100 horizontal feet on the ground. In the United States a second scale—architect's scale—is used. The units are divided into fractions of an inch. For example, a quarter- or half-scale drawing means that every ¼ or ½ inch equals one foot on the ground. Drawings prepared by building architects use an architectural scale. Most drawings that supplement the architect's drawings—such as the structural, electrical, and mechanical drawings—also use an architect's scale. Civil engineering, landscape architecture, and land survey drawings use an engineer's scale for design work and associated topographic and land surveys, roads, and utilities such as storm water systems. Site-grading plans are almost always prepared using an engineer's scale. See Figure 4.5.

Figure 4.5 Engineer's scale used to measure slope on a USGS topographic map

5

WHAT IS SCALE, WHY IS IT IMPORTANT, AND HOW IS IT USED?

In this chapter you will learn about:

- The many meanings of the word "scale"
- The reasons for scaled drawings
- How to choose the right scale for a drawing
- Principles for reading a topographic map

SCALE: A WORD OF SEVERAL MEANINGS

The word "scale" has at least three meanings in design. The wooden or plastic instrument we learned to call a "ruler" in kindergarten is referred to as a scale in landscape architecture, engineering, and architecture. In its first meaning, the word "scale" refers to the device we use for measuring, to guide the designer in creating a plan or detail on paper or computer. The second meaning of the word "scale" refers to proportions—that is, a means of representing the actual dimensions of say a building by a drawing that fits on a sheet of paper. A third meaning of "scale" refers to the size of an object relative to the size of a person. In this case, when we use the word "scale," as in "the wall height is in scale with people," we mean that the height of the wall is not overwhelming relative to the space and the people using the space.

The pattern of the campus walkway shown in Figure 5.1, located in the central quad on the UCLA campus, was designed by early twentieth-century landscape architect Ralph Cornell, with the intent of incorporating selected architectural details from the surrounding buildings. The buildings are all faced with brick, using both standard (3⅝ × 2¼ × 7⅝) and Roman (3⅝ × 1⅝ × 11⅝) sized bricks. The basic module that underlies the size, shape, and pattern of the walkway is based on a Roman brick. The walkway was designed with a sufficient width to handle the traffic of large numbers of students. The walkway was subdivided into units representing individual personal space. The larger intersection that can accommodate 16 to 20 students is given a personal scale by subdividing the width into smaller units. The designer for the original drawing used an architect's or engineering scale, prepared at 20 or perhaps 40 scale. One can critique the design by saying that the designer brought the scale of the broad walk, built to carry a large number of people, down to human scale by establishing a detailing module that roughly approximates the personal space of a single student. The term "relative scale" is the meaning of the word "scale" used here.

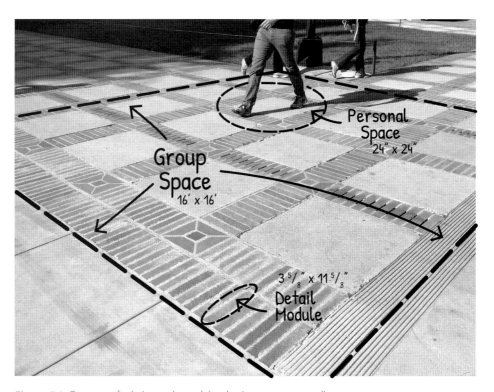

Figure 5.1 Concept of relative scale explained using a campus walk

THE NEED FOR SCALED DRAWINGS

While it is possible to build a landscape design without any drawings—and in some special cases it may be a reasonable approach—in the litigious world we live in, it is probably not a good idea. One could build a garden, play area, or any other landscape design on-site using shovels, picks, and possibly earth-moving machinery without a set of drawings. The opportunities of doing so are limited, in large part due to the complex nature of our lives in the context of governmental requirements and legal constraints. You could create, say, a small garden following a design in your head, and a "build as you go" approach—for instance, your own garden or the garden of a friend or relative who is confident of your design sensibility and skills. However, grabbing a shovel and proceeding to construct an urban plaza or wetland restoration project without first going through a design process that follows a paper trail of reviews and approvals is next to impossible in today's world of regulation and contracts. The practice of landscape architecture consists of a series of formalized steps following a paper trail whereby preliminary designs are first developed and presented for client feedback and governmental approval.

Drawings and sketches, either drawn by hand or using computer software, are involved in a process consisting of a sequence of steps. Each step requires refining and developing more detailed plans, with technical details, sections, and technical written specifications. At the close of each step, the client and governmental units having jurisdiction for design and plan review will evaluate the drawings. The design review process often involves, in addition to governmental review, a requirement for scheduling and conducting public hearings and outreach to gain public input and approval. A number of governmental authorities are tasked with reviewing landscape designs—including grading plans—to assess their conformity to a range of public safety and health standards. Examples of governmental entities having review and approval authority would include municipal government departments, state public works and environmental quality agencies, federal government resource managers such as U.S. Department of Wildlife and Fisheries, and additional agencies having jurisdiction over water quality and wetlands management.

SITE GRADING IS INTEGRAL TO THE PHASES OF DESIGN

The process of landscape architecture design generally follows standard steps or phases of work similar to the steps followed by architects and engineers. The process is detailed in a professional service contract under the heading of scope of work. The scope of work consists of a number of phases: first, consultation with the client, followed by developing one or more design solutions, each of which is accompanied by a budget analysis. Subsequent steps in the process lead to the preparation of what are called bid documents. These documents contain a set of plan drawings, details, written technical specifications, and other contractual and bonding documents that make up the complete bid package. Contractors prepare and submit their bids based on their review of the plans, detail drawings, and technical specifications prepared by the landscape architect.

Now that we have established the broader context of the design process, we should appreciate why design involves many steps and the preparation of many documentation types, graphic and written. A documentation package specific to the requirements of each phase would include preparation of plans, details, and other graphic representation drawings for client and governmental reviews.

A site-grading plan is a representation of a portion of the earth, such as the project site. The project area is drawn to fit on a sheet of paper or within a computer file that is viewed on a screen. The distinctive characteristics of a site (topography, tree cover, circulation, and structures) are represented with lines, symbols, contours, and elevations supplemented with notes and dimensions. These graphic representations are of course smaller than the real areas they represent. The lines, dimensions, contours, and other graphics are drawn such that each dimension and length on paper represents an actual dimension or length on the ground. Two-dimensional representations of the physical world are drawn at a prescribed scale. Further explanations of the concept of scale are found in the following section.

USING AND CHOOSING THE RIGHT SCALE

Where this explanation is leading us is to concepts of drawing conventions (covered in Chapter 4) and scale (to be covered here). The design services of a landscape architect involve (1) developing design ideas, (2) refining these ideas according to input from the client and others, then (3) resolving the refined ideas into their final form of construction-ready plan drawings and details. The drawings are a representation of both what is on the ground (existing conditions) and what is projected to be built on the ground, usually by a third party such as a landscape and building contractor. In order for the contractor to build what the designer intends, the drawings must contain sufficient detail and an accurate representation of existing site conditions. The graphic information must be organized around a graphic system that the contractor and the land surveyor can transpose from hand-drawn or digital information to the ground. The use of scale, in a graphic representation sense, allows the designer to transfer ideas to paper, then allows the contractor to transfer them from paper to the ground.

Scale is the relationship between measured distances on the ground and the dimensions of a three-dimensional physical element that is drawn as a plan or as a series of details and sections. The drawings represent the physical reality of the project site and a scaled facsimile of the designed elements to be built. A plan scale represents a fraction or a ratio whereby a unit of measurement shown on a plan, such as an inch or fraction of an inch, is equal to a prescribed number of feet on the ground. For instance, a drawing prepared at 20 scale means that an inch on a ruler represents 20 feet on the ground. So if a playing field is designed to be 100 feet wide and 300 feet long, it would be drawn—on a piece of paper or using a computer—5 inches wide by 15 inches long. Simple enough, but the decision of which scale to use to prepare the needed plans and details has as much to do with the level of detail to be included as with the sheet size of the drawings, in the context of the actual size or area of the project site.

A golf course, which could be 150 to 200 acres, might require a drawing scale of 1 inch equals 100 feet (100 scale) in order to fit on a standard drawing sheet size, while a residential backyard having dimensions of 75 by 120 feet could be drawn at 10 or 20 scale. In the case of the golf course, two sets of drawing scales might be used: an overall general plan layout of the course at 100 scale with a minimum of detail, then several drawings representing portions of the golf course drawn at 20 or 40 scale so that required detail and accuracy are possible. Individual greens that require considerably more detailed grading information might be drawn at 10 or 20 scale. When a project—such as a golf course—is subdivided into a number of plans, a referencing system is required to ensure that the information of one plan can be seen in relation to adjacent portions of the project.

The decision as to which scale should be used when preparing to draw a plan or detail considers several factors: the size of the project area, the complexity of the designed elements, and the level of detail required to communicate the design intent to contractors. At an early phase of the design process—when drawings are made to inform the client and gain approval to proceed in the design development and contract document phases—a scale might be different than the ones used in subsequent work phases. As a general practice, an attempt is made for all the major plan drawings to be drawn at the same scale. This depends on the areal size of the project site and the level of design detail required. The drawings might include: site demolition, grading, staking and layout, planting, irrigation, lighting, and other construction components.

REFERENCE PLAN AND MATCH LINES

The reference plan showing the project subdivided into individual smaller areas is shown in Figure 5.2. The reference plan might be drawn at 50 or 100 scale, with the individual subplans drawn at 20, 30, or 40 scale. Notice the darker lines outlining each sheet beginning with L3–01 thru L3–14. The dark lines "match lines" that are used to make the locational relation between each individual sheet visually apparent. Each subsheet from the reference plan is contained within the system of match lines. While there might be some overlap of the sheets, this is done to assist the contractor to coordinate the work shown in adjoining sheets. A minimum of detailed information should be included within the overlapping areas. It is advisable to avoid significant overlap to avoid information conflicts or discrepancies. Each subplan is assigned a sheet number (for instance L3–01). If the subject is landscape and the plan is divided into five areas, then the subplans might be identified as Sheet L-1 through L-5. If the subject is grading and the same subdivisions are used as in the landscape plan, then the grading sheets might be identified as Sheet G-1 through G-5.

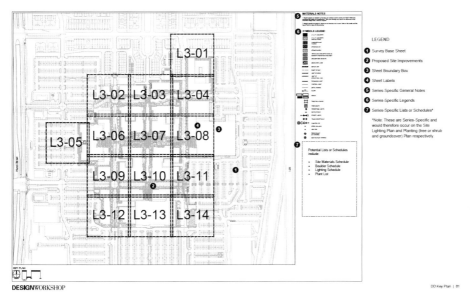

Figure 5.2 Sample plan with match lines as dark lines defining each plan sheet beginning with sheet L3–01

COURTESY OF DESIGN WORKSHOP, DENVER, CO: DW DOCUMENTATION: STANDARDS AND BEST PRACTICES, P. 61

Many areas have been mapped at different scales. The most important consideration in choosing a map is its intended use. A city public works engineer, for instance, may need a very detailed map to locate precise sewer lines, power and water lines, and streets. A commonly used scale for this purpose is 1:600, or one inch equals 600 inches (600″ / 12″ = 50 scale, where 1 inch on the map represents 50 feet on the ground). This scale is sufficiently large that many features—such as buildings, roads, and railroad tracks—can be drawn to scale instead of being represented by symbols as in a USGS 1:24,000-scale quad map.

ARCHITECT'S AND ENGINEER'S SCALES

Grading plans, sections, and profiles are drawn using an engineer's scale. Buildings designed by an architect use an architectural scale. Grading plans prepared for a residential garden or small property might be drawn at 10 or 20 scale, while a city park could be drawn at 40 or 50 scale. Grading plans prepared for a several-hundred-acre residential subdivision or campus would employ two or more scales, similar in concept to the golf course discussed in the section "Using and Choosing the Right Scale." The subdivision might be divided into a number of blocks of lots so that each block fits on a standard sheet size of, say, 240˝ by 360˝. The convention is to use standard scales, scales that are found on an engineer's scale. For example 10˝ equals 1250´ is not found on an engineer's scale, although when using computer-aided software it is possible to produce a drawing at 125 scale. The professional convention is to use a standard scale such as those found on an engineer's ruler. It is imperative that anything drawn at each phase of the design leading to contract document preparation be drawn at a standard scale. Others who may have use of or access to the drawings need to know the scale of a drawing in order to figure out the dimensions or measurements.

One might think that making a drawing smaller or larger to fit on a piece of paper and relying on a bar graphic would be acceptable. However, the resulting drawing can be a cause of misinterpretation if it is not sized at a known or common scale. Yes, relying on a graphic bar scale may be sufficient for certain purposes, but the drawing that has only a bar scale of an unknown—or worse, unknowable—scale is nearly useless to contractors who are trying to transfer measurements from the drawing to the ground. The standard of care in professional practice is that drawings are drawn and published using standard scales: engineer's or architect's scale, depending on whether the content of the drawing involves primarily civil engineering (such as for earthwork, drainage structures, and roads) or buildings (including residential, commercial, or governmental structures).

TOPOGRAPHIC MAPS ARE USEFUL PREPLANNING TOOLS

Just about everyone uses a map in his or her daily life. Maps are available in many forms: printed in books or on sheets of paper, or brought up on one's computer screen, smart phone, or tablet. Google (the verb) the name of a restaurant or auto repair shop, and a website will pop up with a map marking the location of the business with a street address. We can glean an amazing and diverse array of information about our world from maps, from directions to the location of hot spots to visit. Landscape architects use maps for nearly every facet of what they do, to better inform them about a project site. Maps represent the Earth in two dimensions. The maps commonly used by landscape architects have topographic information. Topographic maps (ones prepared by a land surveyor or published by the United States Geological Survey) provide three-dimensional information such as elevation and landform, represented graphically in two dimensions. From a topographic map—that is, a map with contour lines—one can determine the level or steep areas on the ground, and identify the aspect of landforms such as areas that are in shade (north side of a hill) or predominantly in sun (south side of a hill). The ground on the north side of a hill is generally wetter, with deeper soils. Soils having more moisture support more diverse and lush plant cover, as they are often in shade during the daylight hours. The ground facing the south is generally drier, with thinner soils and therefore might support drought-tolerant but less diverse plant species. As one becomes more familiar with topographic maps and skilled at using them, a treasure trove of useful information can be mined to give one a better understanding of the physical and temporal aspects of a site, and to assist one in making important early site-planning and later design decisions.

Topographic maps published by the United State Geological Survey (USGS) are often the first maps landscape architects and other design professionals go to, in the early stages of a project. These maps are available for free in the form of PDF files online from www.USGS.gov or can be purchased as hard-copy maps. Local surveying supply, drafting supply, and outdoor outfitter stores often maintain a supply of local USGS maps. Each USGS map is assigned a unique name, usually selected from a local prominent geographical feature or place name. For example: the USGS map Mt. Tamaulipas is named after a prominent landmark located in Marin County, north of San Francisco, California. USGS quad maps are useful for doing early research on a prospective project site; for instance, when one needs background information for developing an A/E[1] professional services proposal, and then later when one is preparing a scope of work and fee proposal to the client. A topographic map is useful in the early planning stages of a project in a number of ways, including:

- Identifying potential locations for the project program elements, such as the best location for buildings, roads, and outdoor use areas.

- Creating a very useful preplanning and site design map for making a preliminary site analysis and inventory of key landscape features, including existing conditions on-site and in the surrounding context.

- Delineating the limits where design surveying is necessary and potential areas where geotechnical information about soils will be needed. It is not always necessary to survey an entire project property, particularly large parcels of land. As survey and geotechnical investigations can be expensive, limiting the area surveyed would reduce costs (a saving to the client).

The USGS publishes approximately 57,000 different topographic maps covering the United States and its territories (see Figure 5.3). USGS

. . . .

1 Architectural and engineering professional service firms including landscape architecture firms

topographic maps are beautiful, having a graphic aesthetic that presents the information clearly and precisely. USGS topographic maps show and name prominent natural and cultural features. The maps contain a wealth of accurate, varied, and detailed information, including landform, vegetative cover, hydrologic systems, road and utility systems, cultural features (including individual buildings, urbanized areas, and cemeteries), and governmental boundaries. From these maps one can make early determinations about elevation and land use suitability. As a project progresses from preliminary to schematic design phase, the detail represented by the contours and other physical features is usually adequate for making good design and planning decisions that can later be refined with more detailed and accurate topographic information prepared by a land surveyor.

Figure 5.3 Portion of a USGS Quad Map. Go to www.usgs.gov for USGS maps and other map products.

MAP SCALES AND CONTOUR INTERVALS

USGS maps come in several scales. Scale is the relationship between distance on the map and distance on the ground. A map at 1:24,000[2] (1 inch = 2000 feet) shows considerable detail useful for planning and design purposes. The maps follow a standard graphic representation format, a format established early in the twentieth century. Older maps provide useful historical information, snapshots of land development over time when earlier maps are compared with more recent ones.

Map contours graphically represent the shape and elevation of the terrain. The contours represent a system of elevations, with the elevation difference from one contour to the next being equal throughout the map. The elevation difference is called the contour interval. Contour intervals vary, depending on the terrain and the scale of the map. For instance, the contour interval for a 1:24,000 map, where there are considerable elevation differences, such as in a mountainous region, the contour interval might be 20 feet. For example, a sequence of contours in steep terrain might be 140′, 160′, 180′, and so forth. The contour interval is printed in the margin of each U.S. Geological Survey map. In the example that follows, the terrain is gently rolling, so the contour interval is 10 feet. Where the topography of an area is relatively flat, such as in the Central Plains or coastal wetlands, the contour interval might be 5 or 10 feet, so that a sequence of contours might be 120′, 130′, 140′, and so forth.

Topographic contours on a USGS map are shown as brown lines of different widths or opacity. To aid in more easily determining elevations, index contours (such at 100-foot intervals) are darker and wider, with lighter, thinner lines for intermediate 20-foot contour intervals. Elevation values are printed in several places along these lines. The narrower intermediate and supplementary contours found between the index contours help show more details of the land surface shape. Contours that are very close together represent steep slopes. Widely spaced contours or an absence of contours means that the ground slope is relatively level. The elevation difference between adjacent contour lines, called the contour

. . . .
2 To convert a USGS quad map to an engineer's scale, consider a USGS map of 1:24,000 scale, where one inch equals 24,000 inches. Divide 12 into 24,000 to get feet. The result is 1 inch equals 2000 feet.

interval, is selected to best show the general shape of the terrain, including prominent hydrologic features such as rivers and valley streams.

RECOGNIZING LANDFORM PATTERNS

A topographic map is a representation of a small area of the earth's surface. The distinctive characteristic of a topographic map—as opposed to a treasure or city road map—is that the shape of the earth's surface is shown by contour lines. Contours are a way of showing elevation and landform graphically in two dimensions. Contour lines are derived from points of equal elevation in the landscape. The shapes of the contours convey to the viewer the sculptural form of the terrain. In Figure 5.4 contours were created using elevation data surveyed on the ground in combination with aerial photography. Their elevation is based on a reference surface, such as mean sea level. The reference information, together with the date of the original or updated survey information, is shown at the bottom of each USGS topographic map.

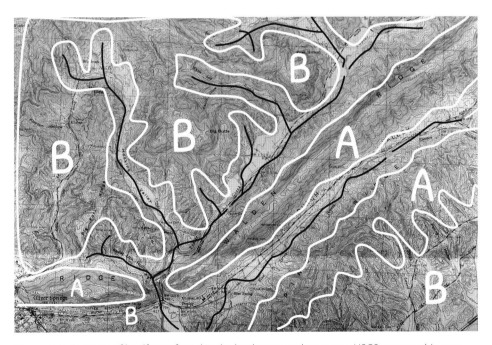

Figure 5.4 A variety of landforms found in the landscape as shown on a USGS topographic map

Contours make it possible for the user of a USGS quad map to determine the height of mountains, depths of the ocean bottom (bathymetric maps), and steepness of slopes. A topographic map shows more than contours. The elevations of tops of mountains are often shown, elevations of ponds or borrow sites, and of key cultural features of interest. A USGS map includes symbols that represent such features as streets, buildings and other structures, infrastructure (power and pipelines), streams, vegetation, and other made-made and natural features.

THE INFORMATION CONTAINED IN TOPOGRAPHIC MAPS

If you like reading maps and have experience doing so, you may find that with little to no instructions you will be able to understand most of the graphic content shown on a topographic map. For the most part, interpreting the lines, areas, and other symbols will be easy. The system of colors and line weights used will also help make the features represented more obvious. For example, areas shaded in green indicate the presence of vegetation, usually forest. Features colored in blue represent water, lines of blue represent small streams, and amorphous shapes can be lakes and ponds. You will easily understand what you are looking at, and if not, refer to the legend when in doubt. The various map features are shown as points, lines, shading, and text. The width of lines and intensity of colors graphically help to distinguish between higher and lower levels of importance, depending on the size and extent of the feature. For example, individual houses may be shown as small, uniform black squares, while the actual shapes of larger buildings are shown. In densely built-up areas, most individual buildings are omitted, and the area is shaded in light gray or perhaps standard urban land use colors. On some maps major public buildings such as post offices, churches, city halls, and other landmark buildings are outlined using a set of symbols that can be found in the legend. Features such as cemeteries, airports, and athletic facilities also follow a standard set of symbols.

The first features usually noticed on a topographic map might be the contour lines, shown in brown. Other major features such as vegetation (green), water (blue), and densely built-up areas (gray or red) are easily recognized. A grid also overlies the entire map. The grid generally represents a one-mile-square unit. This unit is an administrative land parcel system referred to as a section. Geodesic lines will also be evident, a universal land system established throughout the United States by the U.S. Geological Survey.

Both natural and man-made features are shown by lines that may be straight, curved, solid, dashed, dotted, or in any combination. The colors used generally indicate similar types of information: topographic contours (brown); lakes, streams, irrigation ditches, and other water-related features (blue); land grids and important roads (red); and other roads and trails, railroads, boundaries, and other cultural features (black). Again, refer to a map's legend, or go to the USGS website for legend clarification.

Names of places, including cities, towns, counties, and other places or prominent landscape features, are shown in a color corresponding to the feature type. Many features and place names are identified with labels, such as Old Faithful Village, Mississippi River, Los Angeles, Substation, or Golf Course.

U.S. GEOLOGICAL SURVEY AND SCALES OF OTHER COUNTRIES

Most countries of the world have established a national map system similar in many ways to that of the United States. While the maps produced by various countries have much in common graphically, unique variations do exist. One should refer to the map legend to better understand the information presented. One of the distinguishing features of various countries' map systems is whether maps use the metric system of measurement or the imperial (feet and inches) system. The United States is one of the few countries still using the imperial system.

The U.S. Geological Survey publishes maps at various scales. The scale used for most U.S. topographic mapping is 1:24,000. USGS maps at this scale cover an area measuring 7.5 minutes of latitude and 7.5 minutes of longitude, and are commonly called 7.5-minute quadrangle maps. Map coverage for most of the United States has been completed at this scale, except for Puerto Rico, which is mapped at 1:20,000 and 1:30,000, and for a few states that have been mapped at 1:25,000. Most of Alaska has been mapped at 1:63,360, with some populated areas also mapped at 1:24,000. For countries where the metric system is used, map scales follow the same proportional system, whereby 1:10,000 means one unit, (such as one centimeter) equals 10,000 units (e.g., centimeters), or one meter equals 10,000 meters. With practice and a degree of curiosity one can quickly become conversant with such maps and effective at using maps of all types for a variety of professional purposes.

6

WHERE ARE YOU?

In this chapter you will learn about:

- How to accurately locate features on a site using a referencing system
- How to apply a coordinate system, including longitude and latitude
- The appropriate components of a property and topographic map for landscape site-grading and design projects
- The use of a grid system to locate spot elevations and design features for a site

THE LANGUAGE OF MAPS

Maps are as much a form of communication as pages of written words. Both utilize a language consisting of a set of symbols organized by a set of rules so that those who know the rules can arrange or sequence the graphic symbols to communicate an intended purpose. Likewise, a person knowing the rules can read and understand what is contained in a map. The rules used in map making derive from geographic and cadastral systems and graphic conventions. If you learn and understand the systems, symbols, and graphic conventions that are used in making maps, you will generally be able to read a map and mine a wealth of information from it.

Just as there are different languages, each with its conventions of syntax, there are many different types of maps, each having its unique set of purposes. Depending on the purpose for creating a map, there are many graphic symbols and conventions that map types might apply. Each map type may have symbols and conventions that are unique and contain a graphic language to represent a specific place in the world and its physicality. Maps and the written word are both used to convey ideas, descriptions, attitudes, and values. Maps have the added quality of noting and conveying measurable values with the capability to represent a three-dimensional world as well. Just as we talk about reading text, maps are also read. From the symbols, lines, and numbers that are used to create maps, we can "see" and determine dimensions and distances, elevations, physical features including landform, and a multitude of natural or cultural features. The preparer of a map may also provide directions or record what is on a piece of property or tract of land.

HOW TO FIND AND LOCATE PLACES IN THE LANDSCAPE, OR: WHERE AM I?

To answer the question "Where am I?" posed in Figure 6.1, look for the answer represented in Figure 6.2. Your location, or that of some feature of a site such as a building or water fountain, is linked to a horizontal control referencing system generally utilizing coordinates or a grid. The elevation is tied to a vertical control system, generally a system based on ocean high tide and a system of bench marks placed throughout a given governmental jurisdiction, such as a city, linked to a topographic survey.

Figure 6.1 A photo simulation to help the reader visualize the difficulty in answering the question "Where am I?" Without any visible or known reference features or reference system, there is no way of communicating your location to others.

The title of this chapter is: "Where Are You?" It is a question that may seem to have an easy answer. One could answer, "Well, I am here!" But where is here? Gertrude Stein, an important early twentieth-century American author, famously stated, in referring to her home town of Oakland, California: "When you get there, there is no there, there." In most instances, the answer of here or there requires one to elaborate more precisely, for example: "I am the one with a blue baseball cap, standing on the south-west corner of 35th Street and Broadway." To limit any possible misunderstanding, you could add, "in New York City." Most people should be able to locate you and pick you out of the crowd with such a descriptive answer.

The photograph in Figure 6.3 provides a vivid example of another complexity in finding an appropriate answer to "Where is here?" The concrete column in the center of the photograph was installed in a field a couple of hundred years ago, along with several hundred similar columns installed elsewhere throughout the Netherlands. The top of the column is where the ground originally was when the column was installed. The columns serve as witnesses to the extent of ground subsidence at each location. The elevation difference, or extent of ground subsidence in this instance, is just over six feet. This photograph serves another purpose. It graphically demonstrates the ephemeral nature of landscapes and of places. Ground subsides in some regions, and it shifts laterally in others. It also is washed away or eroded in other locations. Change, or even erasure, occurs across the landscape, sometimes very slowly (such as ocean level rise), sometimes dramatically (e.g., slope failure caused by an earthquake).

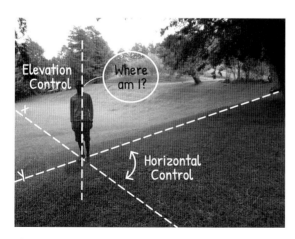

Figure 6.2 Elevation and horizontal control

Figure 6.3 Elevation marker in a farm field near Delft, the Netherlands. The distance from the ground to the top of the marker indicates the extent of ground subsidence at this location.

Consider the information included in Figure 6.2. A grid is projected on the ground, shown as an x/y-axis. This information is useful in the sense that it would be possible to retrace the location of the grid on the basis of a known reference system by which the grid coordinates are a part of such as one established by the United State Geological Survey or a state coordinate system. The grid provides a means of establishing horizontal control. Also in the photograph is a vertical line that represents elevation control. So, if there was an established horizontal and vertical referencing system in the vicinity (such as a city) that one could research (to find the control systems), it would be possible to reestablish the grid system—in this example, to locate the person asking where he/she is on the subject property, and the elevation where the person is standing.

Maps are drawn for many purposes. In the case of the map in Figure 6.4, the purpose was simply to provide directions using roads, landmarks, and physical features to guide a traveler to a destination. The map in Figure 6.4 represents one of the most common types of two-dimensional maps used to convey information and accomplish a particular purpose. The map was hand-drawn providing directions to Chum's Fishing Camp. Obviously it was drawn by hand, perhaps on a handy piece of scrap paper or napkin, with little concern about scale and proportional accuracy. To be useful, the hand-drawn map needed to be accurate in arranging the important physical features of the immediate area (roads, trees, building, and bridge). Mileage indicating the distance from the Highway 92 turn-off to Dalton Road is the only numerical reference provided. The person who drew the map included only the most relevant physical information, north not being considered important and probably of little direct use to the traveler.

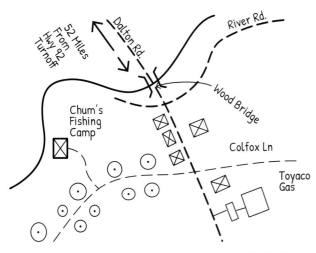

Figure 6.4 Directions sketched on a piece of paper for finding Chum's Fishing Camp

The three treasure maps shown in Figures 6.5-A through 6.5-C were originally drawn by hand and, like the map in Figure 6.4, were created with the purpose of providing directions to a desired location (the X, as in X marks the spot where treasure was buried). The person looking for the treasure would not be able to succeed with only the information included in Map A. Map A does not give any indication in what hemisphere of the earth the islands are located, just their shapes and relation to north. Map B is significantly more helpful in that it includes latitude and longitude. Now the traveler knows in which part of the earth's surface to begin to search for the treasure. Map C includes a scale so that horizontal distances can be determined. The larger island where the treasure is buried shows contour lines. The elevation of the contour lines, while not shown, would provide the traveler with a fair idea of the topography and landform, allowing him or her to set out in the right direction to the top of the hill at the southern end of the island. Presumably by the probing of a sword and a few test holes, the treasure would be found. Minus the horizontal control provided by longitude and latitude, mileage scale, and topographic contours, finding the treasure with Map A would be impossible unless, as in Map C, the person drawing the map included additional graphic clues such as contours and graphics or provided a written description of the physical features where the "X" is shown.

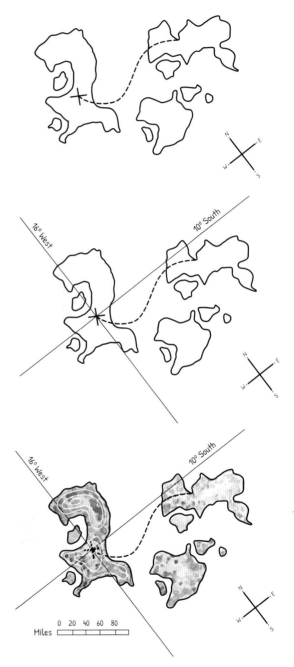

Figures 6.5-A–6.5-C A series of treasure maps with increasing degrees of useful information and clarity

MAPS SERVE A VARIETY OF PURPOSES

The illustrations provided by Figures 6.4 and 6.5 serve to underline the idea that maps are made for a purpose and will require a range of information types and detail depending on the circumstance. Depending on a map's purpose and the circumstance in which it is made, a prescribed set of data references will make it significantly more useful in carrying out an activity such as locating a specific point on the earth or for way-finding. In the case of Figure 6.4, the critical information making that map useful was the inclusion of pertinent landmarks and their relative positions and order. The quality and accuracy of drafting was not important for the map in Figure 6.4 to be useful. Important information to make Map C in Figure 6.5-C useful was the inclusion of scale, a known horizontal reference system, topographic contours, and the shape of the islands, to allow the treasure hunter to locate the buried treasure. The accuracy of the outline of the island was not critically important, but a fair approximation of the landform shapes made the map useful.

Translating what was just presented to the activity of site grading, a set of conventional information is necessary in order to create a useful site-grading plan. A plan is a map of sorts, as it is intended to represent a set of spatial information in a two-dimensional format. The information requirements for creating a site-grading plan are described in earlier chapters. Also, a site-grading plan utilizes a set of drawing conventions, as discussed in Chapter 4.

COORDINATE SYSTEMS

Latitude and Longitude: A Geographic Coordinate System

A common system for locating points on the earth is called the geographic coordinate system. This system uses degrees of latitude and longitude to describe a geographic location or feature on the earth's surface. Latitude lines run parallel to the equator. Lines of latitude divide the earth into 180 equal portions between the North and South Poles. The equator is the reference or starting latitude line and is identified as zero degrees (0°). As you travel north toward the North Pole latitudes are designated so many degrees north such as 20° north, 56° north, all the way to 90° north when you reach the North Pole. Traveling south, below the equator, the latitude designations are 20° south, 56° south, until you reach the South Pole positioned at latitude 90° south. See Figure 6.6.

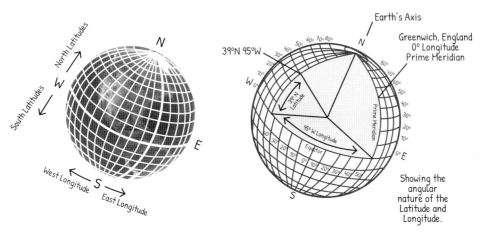

Figure 6.6 Longitude and latitude

Lines of longitude run perpendicular to the equator and converge at either pole. The reference line established for longitude is a line that runs through Greenwich, England, and is designated as zero. Traveling west, longitude lines are designated 0° to 180° west; conversely, those traveling east from the Greenwich meridian are designated 0° to 180° east. So referring back to Figure 6.5-C, the buried treasure is located in the Southern Hemisphere, noted by its 10°S latitude coordinate, and is close to the opposite side of the earth from Greenwich, England, with its 162°W longitude coordinate.

While the system of geographic coordinates is in common use for crossing oceans, other systems are used to facilitate the work done by civil engineers, land surveyors, and landscape architects. Longstanding systems have been established for use in locating and describing property lines and subdivisions, and for just about any situation involving land ownership, land surveying and topography, and site design and site grading. These land surveying systems have much in common with the geographic coordinate system in that they all are based on a base reference. In the United States the base referencing system includes a base line and principal meridian (equivalent to a longitude line) called a meridian (similar to latitude lines running parallel to the equator). The next level of grid subdivision established by the U.S. federal government utilizes a grid of township and range lines called the Public Land Survey System (see Figures 6.7 and 6.8). The U.S. Geological Survey and the U.S. Bureau of Land Management manage this system. With each acquisition of land territory (California-Arizona, Washington-Oregon, or Alaska) a base reference or meridian was surveyed with physical markers (surveying monuments) placed in the ground as permanent markers, in the form of a brass disk mounted on concrete or hard stone, or in some cases placed on what are called witness trees (see Figure 6.9-A, a USGS survey monument, and 6.9-B for a Chinese example). The markers and their location were entered in a national registry, making them traceable for future surveying activities such as establishing property lines, road and railway rights-of-way, and municipal and county boundaries.

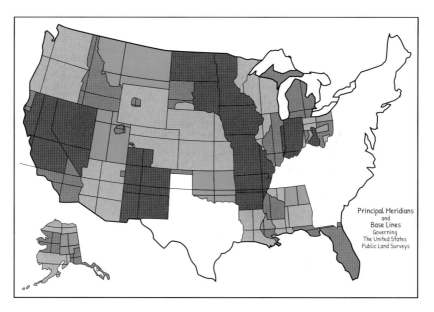

Figure 6.7 Township and range: the Public Lands Survey System

The property lines for all parcels of land—such as an urban residential lot, subdivision, farm, or school site—are established and referenced to a federal or state land survey system. Each land parcel and its property lines can be researched in public records, such as a municipal land office or public works department, and are described according to the operating set of bench marks and the land survey grid system. For the most part, the local land survey system is a finer-grained grid tied in to the township and range system. The corners of a set of property lines that define an individual land parcel are tied to this system, with one corner based on the nearest bench mark located in the vicinity of the property. This bench-mark system is maintained by the local governmental jurisdiction. Any one bench mark can be researched at the appropriate land records office of a city or county, depending on where the parcel is located.

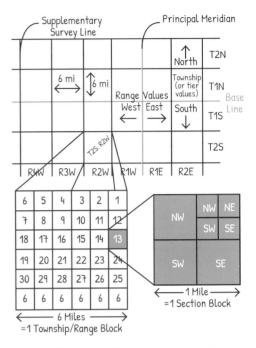

Figure 6.8 There are 36 sections (section dimensions are 1 mile by 1 mile) in each township block

Figure 6.9-A USGS survey marker

Figure 6.9-B Chinese survey marker

REFERENCING SYSTEM FOR A LAND PARCEL

Figure 6.10 is an example of an individual property map. The map was prepared by a land surveyor and shows the property lines, their length, and their direction (bearing), area in acres or square feet, various physical features such as a road, and other pertinent information as described in the legend and notes. Often a land survey property map will indicate the initial property corners established from their closest reference or bench mark. This map is a legal document, recorded at the appropriate land office of the jurisdiction in which the property is located. At a later date, when the owner of the property decides to construct improvements (a house or other structure), construct a driveway or system of roads, and make other constructed improvements, a land surveyor will be hired to prepare a topographic survey. The topographic survey would also be tied to a referenced topographic system with contours and elevations based on a topographic bench mark.

This system of referenced property lines and topographic information is used for locating or establishing the elevation of all features within a property. This information is part of the legal description of the property. All the information related to the preparation of subsequent drawings, such as site-grading plans, is referenced to a comprehensive municipal, county, or state land survey system. That means the plans the designer prepares—the lines on the paper—can be physically and accurately located on the ground by a contractor to build what was designed, including the grading plan. A similar land and topographic referencing system can be found in nearly any other city, state, or country in the world. The systems have many similar characteristics such as being tied into an established national land or geospatial referencing system.

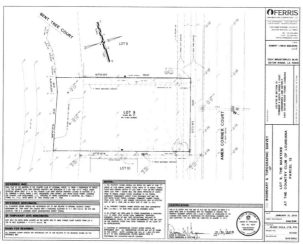

Figure 6.10 Property plat map
COURTESY OF RONALD K. FERRIS, BATON ROUGE, LA

LICENSED LAND SURVEYOR

A licensed land surveyor does the preparation of a property or topographic survey similar to the one shown in Figure 6.10. Landscape architects, civil engineers, and architects use the surveys prepared by the land surveyor as a base for their own work. A civil engineer or landscape architect will use a topographic survey to develop and prepare grading and drainage plans. All constructed site features, such as buildings and other structures, roads, walks, paved areas, pools, plazas, and other constructed elements, are located and referenced to the property lines and property corners drawn up by the land surveyor. The package of construction documents are considered legal documents prepared by licensed professionals who follow established conventions of plan preparation and geospatial referencing systems. The work of each professional is assumed to have followed the pertinent design health and safety standards, codes, and rules, including zoning, fire and safety, ADA access, and other regulations established to protect the health, safety, and welfare of the public.

The landscape architect prepares a site-grading plan in order to provide the best and most accurate information for a contractor on how the existing site topography within project boundaries is to be modified to accommodate a desired end result. For a grading plan to be useful it should provide scale, precise location of project boundaries or property lines, accurate topographic information, and a system of horizontal and vertical control. Horizontal control has to do with having an established and clearly marked datum, such as the property corners, from which the contractor can accurately locate and establish dimensions for any point on the ground—including old and new structures and designed program elements (such as paved surfaces, walks) to be built—and their specific elevations. The designer or contractor often will establish a grid (25, 50, or 100 feet) and overlay that grid on the property. The grid would first be drawn in plan and then would be recreated on the ground with stakes placed at each grid intersection. The contractor uses the grid to provide horizontal control, which assists him or her to establish the locations of plan elements (structure, driveway, parking, landscape area, and other elements). The grid would serve a secondary and equally important function as the basis for transferring the elevations shown in the grading plan to stakes on the ground. The vertical control for the earthwork is provided by the topographic survey, with proposed topographic contours supported and refined with proposed spot elevations.

LOCATING A BUILDING OR OTHER ELEMENT ON THE GROUND

Using the grid in Figure 6.11, the building contractor can locate the corners of a proposed building or group of buildings and other structures. This is done by first noting that the first horizontal line at the bottom of the drawing is labeled North, Zero or N0. The grid is set up in 50-foot increments. One corner of the building is situated between S100´ and E112'. If you measure the distance below the O gridline, the corner of the building falls on the 10´-foot mark. Now notice that building corner is located between the E100´ and E150´ vertical lines. If you measure the distance from the E100', the building corner is located 12 feet east (to the right) of the E100´ grid line or E1120´. The precise location of the building corner is S100´, E1120´. The contractor would continue locating additional building corners using the grid system. The architect or landscape architect would show the grid coordinates for all corners of the building or buildings in the staking and layout plan, a plan that is part of the construction document package.

Sharing stories from the field with students often provokes the occasional laugh and more often the look of disbelief. One story I often share is the instance when the contractor called asking where I wanted the parking lot to be located for a project

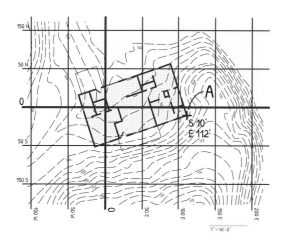

Figure 6.11 50' × 50' graphic grid overlaid onto a land parcel. The grid is referenced to existing property lines, survery marker, or governmental referencing system.

my firm designed. My immediate response was to say to look at where the parking lot was positioned on the plans, and locate it as shown. As it happened, there was not adequate room to place the parking lot as shown on the drawing between the building and the property line. Once out on the site with the contractor, we measured the distance between the building and the property line, revealing a discrepancy. The building was built closer to the property line than shown on the staking and lay-out plan. Why was that? Several explanations come to mind, but in the end the building was not built on the site as thought, thus requiring me to return to the office to come up with a solution modifying the parking layout with the new dimensions taken into consideration.

One explanation for the discrepancy is that the original survey may not have located the property lines accurately. There could have been a mistake in the location of the property corners in relation to the local bench mark or local property records. The building location may not have been staked accurately, so that it was laid out differently than shown by the landscape architect's site layout and staking plan. What I intend students to understand from this story is that it is not always so easy or straightforward to locate points on the surface of the Earth. Errors are possible with property maps or any drawings given to us by others. As professionals, we must always check the work done by others for accuracy as part of professional due diligence. Errors are made because people are in a hurry, or caused by some form of mis-communication. For example, a property measurement could have been researched as 2498 feet then recorded as 2489 feet—reversal of the numbers 9 and 8. Reversal of numbers happens, especially when people are in a hurry, tired, or under stress.

The parking lot story is not an isolated occurrence; this sort of thing happens more frequently than one would think. To avoid a similar experience, one should always field-check critical dimensions before beginning the design process. This is particularly prudent when you are handed a plan showing a building already constructed on a site. Make sure the building is shown on the plan as it actually is on the ground.

Time spent verifying the location of a building or other structures will help you avoid a costly embarrassment later during construction.

So, the answer to the question "Where are you?" in terms of landscape site design and site grading can be found using the USGS or local jurisdiction referencing system. Once one or more property corners are identified, these corners can be tied to the jurisdictional system. From there, any point or series of points, lines, or objects existing within the property can be precisely located based on a grid system overlaid on the property. Proposed design elements such as a building or parking lot or driveway are dimensioned using the grid reference system, to establish property line corners based on nearby governmental bench marks that can be researched at a local municipal, county, or state public works or planning department.

7

CONTOURS

In this chapter you will learn about:

- The graphic conventions for representing and communicating landforms using contour lines
- How to manipulate contour lines in creating a variety of landforms
- How to determine slope and precise elevations of any feature in the landscape
- How to establish the slope of a land or paved surface using contours

INTRODUCTION

The focus of this chapter is the use of contour lines in site grading; a later chapter will concentrate on the use of spot elevation. Together, contour lines and spot elevations are the basic tools of the designer in creating the slope, three-dimensional forms, and ultimately site-grading plans. Contours are especially useful to the designer in helping him or her visualize the forms to be created in the landscape, while spot elevations provide more precision to guide the detailed site-grading design. Contour lines in a grading plan fill in the gaps, providing critical information in transitional areas between hardscape features and areas of pavement and walls. For instance, where dimensions and spot elevations establish the height of walls, contours transition from the wall to the adjacent landscape areas. Contours provide a similar transitional function in the design of roadways, walks and trails, and paved areas, with spot elevations providing the precision a contractor needs, in order to establish grades. Our basic tools for providing grading instructions to a contractor are contours, spot elevations, and slope designations. Together these three elements are used to create a site-grading plan used by the contractor to build what we have designed.

The photograph of the Getty Museum Garden in Figure 7.1 illustrates where contours and spot elevations can work together in developing a

site-grading plan. Basically, the designer would articulate critical elevations for the construction of the low walls and paved areas shown in the image. The grades for the landscape areas would rely primarily on contour lines for establishing both the landform for the lawn and raised landscape areas, with the possible use of spot elevations for critical high and low points. Contours would have most likely continued through the paved areas to articulate the design intent for transitioning from pavement to grass and landscape areas.

Figure 7.1 Getty Museum Garden, Los Angeles, CA

Reading the Landscape

Reading the landscape is made possible by visual clues, some revealed by natural processes and others that are the result of human activities. Geologic history is visually evident when the exposed structure of geologic strata is manifested as layers, sometimes seen as books stacked

Figures 7.2-A and 7.2-B A cultural landscape can reveal its contour topography

horizontally or tilted upright like books in a bookshelf. In Figure 7.2 patterns of land ownership and agriculture management are revealed in the patterns of tree hedgerows marking property boundaries or pasture plots. The hedgerows seem to follow lines of equal elevation or contours.

CONTOUR LINES: A LANGUAGE FOR TWO DIMENSIONS

Contour lines are a human invention used just as are letters and numbers to communicate and describe the world. The word BREAD consists of a selection of symbols—letters in an alphabet—to communicate a physical object or an idea. The letters B – R – E – A – D when seen on a piece of paper by an English language reader are understood to represent a loaf or piece of bread. Both contours and numbers, when applied following a set of rules, can communicate something of meaning and can also allow the reader to visualize the shape or a landscape.   However, the same symbols applied without a framework of rules will not produce understandable results. A writer who knows the conventions for assembling individual letters can create words, and by following sentence structure conventions—syntax—is able to create sentences that convey ideas or descriptions, emotions, and images of places, among other purposes. Like sentences, contours can be thought of as communication devices. In the case of contours lines, they are used to portray the three-dimensional shape of a landscape or designed outdoor environment. Contour lines are a graphic device used by designers to visualize or see landform (which is three dimensional) in two dimensions on a piece of paper or computer screen. The two-dimensional contour or topographic plans created by a designer are used to communicate the design intent—in the case of terrain modifications—to others such as clients, government design review boards, and contractors.

Contour lines, together with spot elevations and a range of standard symbols and numeric and alphabetic annotations, are used to create site-grading plans. Contractors are guided by the grading plans in performing the required earth moving on a site to create the desired earth forms, building pads for the various structures, outdoor use areas, and hardscape, including walks and roads.

Contour lines are created by land surveyors and compiled in a topographic and land survey map. Land surveyors prepare topographic maps either by a photometric process that uses aerial photography or on the ground with crews using surveying instruments. In both cases the information (data points) collected from the aerial photograph or survey instruments is analyzed, and through mathematical modeling the points are converted to what we know as contours, lines representing elevation. Converting the landscape into contours gives us a visualization tool for making modifications such as for building roads or creating level areas for building structures.

Contours not only help us understand elevation variation, they also serve as an aide to visualizing natural landform and, in the built environment, sloping planes and three-dimensional forms such as walls and steps. The contours shown in Figure 7.2-B were drawn to help the viewer visualize the relation between the two-dimensional construct of contours and the forms they represent in the three-dimensional world.

WHAT THE LANDSCAPE WOULD LOOK LIKE WITH CONTOURS

Figures 7.3 through 7.6 are further examples of what contours might look like if they existed in the real, three-dimensional world. In these examples the contours help the viewer better understand the ups and downs and the undulations of the ground surfaces. In Figure 7.3 the sculptural form of the steps is exaggerated by the contours, while in Figure 7.4 the sharply defined drainage swale of the rolling landscape becomes more evident. The drainage swales in Figures 7.4 and 7.5 are enhanced by the added contour lines, giving greater emphasis to the sculpted landform. In both Figures 7.5-A and 7.5-B, the viewer can readily see the direction of surface water flow toward a culvert. The water continues to flow in the culvert under a drive via the drainage swale. The drainage swale parallels the road in Figure 7.6, conveying rainwater or runoff to a culvert located under an entry drive at the far end of the image.

Figure 7.3 Stepped access to lower-level food court and public space, Los Angeles, CA

Figure 7.4 Natural drainage swale in an Oak-Savannah region in Portugal

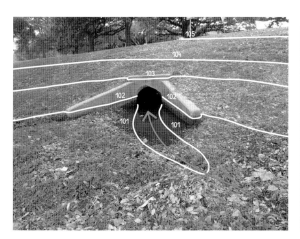

Figures 7.5-A and 7.5-B Road culvert with contour signature similar to that of the drainage swale in Figure 7.4

A contour study model of a proposed site-grading design based on a scaled drawing is shown in Figure 7.7-A. The model was constructed with stacked cardboard, with each level representing a contour, which makes it easy to see where the contour lines are, as well as the shape the contours take in creating the undulating landform. Figure 7.7-B shows the photograph of an urban plaza with amphitheater seating. Although these are projects from different parts of the world, the model-like look of the two amphitheaters is apparent. In the two cases, the stepped or terraced seating roughly parallels what could be actual contour lines.

Figure 7.6 Swale with contours along a university access road

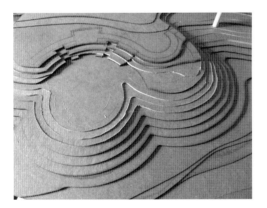

Figures 7.7-A Visualizing proposed grading design by constructing a scaled study model
COURTESY OF JIESI LUO, MLA STUDENTS, RRSLA, LSU.

Figures 7.7-B Amphitheater space, Tavira, Portugal

The spacing of the lines—lines drawn close together or far apart—indicates the relative steepness of slopes in a landscape. Contours also represent the sculptural, three-dimensional shape of the land, such as a hill, a valley and river, and plateau and level areas. Contours can also be thought of as a graphic tool for designers to manipulate a landscape—much as one might do working with clay. By shifting and arranging existing contours, one can achieve a design intent or purpose such as creating a ball field, earth-formed amphitheater, or bike trail. Just as one uses lines to outline a tennis court, plaza, or building, lines representing contours are used to create the three-dimensional or elevation aspect of outdoor use areas, including paved areas and walls, drainage swales created to carry water from one location to another, and berms constructed to block unsightly views or for the moderation of off-site traffic sound.

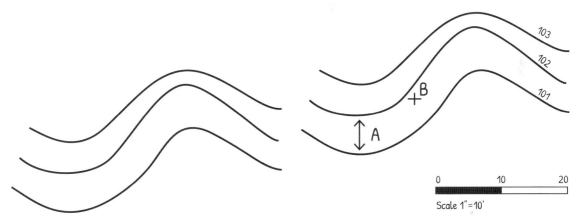

Figure 7.8-A Three, wavy lines: Are they contours or something else? What additional information is needed for the same three wavy lines to represent contours?

Figure 7.8-B The same three wavy lines but with added information, making it impossible to mistake the lines for anything but a set of contour lines

The three lines in Figure 7.8-A are meant to be contour lines, but if one is not told what they are, they just look like three wavy lines. If one is to recognize them as contour lines, additional information is required to make it more obvious what the lines represent. First, each contour line needs to be labeled with its elevation, as shown in Figure 7.8-B. For example, the lower line is labeled 101 (101 feet above a known datum), the middle line is 102, and the top line is 103. Next we need to know the scale of the drawing. With scale we can then make a variety of calculations, such as calculating the degree of slope between contour lines 101 and 102, as shown in location "A." Spot elevation B, located between contours 101 and 102, or any point located between any pair of contours, can be calculated once we know the scale of the drawing.

N

50' 100'   200'   300'   400'

Figure 7.9 Example of a topographic survey prepared by a professional land surveyor

Contours are more than lines on a piece of paper. A contour represents a continuous line of the same elevation. Each contour on a map represents an elevation. A contour map is created by a land surveyor from information collected on a project site using surveying equipment or a process involving aerial photography. A topographic survey is a map created by a land surveyor and includes contours and spot elevations representing the existing terrain or landform. In addition to showing contours, a topographic survey also includes property lines, existing features such as vegetation and structures, utilities, utility or other right-of-way designations, and other above- and belowground features of importance. Figure 7.9 is an example of a topographic survey prepared by a professional land surveyor for a specific client. The surveyor in Figure 7-10 is gathering elevation data in an existing parking lot. The information will be used to prepare an as-built topographic map, later used during the re-design of the parking lot, perhaps to correct an existing drainage problem.

The benchmark in Figure 7.11 is located near the city of Chicago, Illinois, in Cook County. The bench mark is contained in the Chicago Loop USGS quad map, 1997. The data sheet containing information on this bench marker can be found at this URL: http://www.ngs.noaa.gov/cgi-bin/ds_mark.prl?PidBox=ME1633.

The benchmark image shown in Figure 7.11 is at 598.95 feet above mean sea level. The elevation and other information related to the marker can be retrieved at the National Geodetic Survey archives using the E 134 reference on the marker. The marker was given a unique catalogue number of E 134 that was stamped in the center of the marker with the date on which the marker was placed in the ground. The following description of the physical location of the marker was taken from the NGS Datasheet:

Figure 7.10 Surveyor gathering elevations on an existing parking lot that will be later modified to correct reoccurring surface rainwater drainage problems

Figure 7.11 USCGS bench mark
SOURCE: WIKIPEDIA CREATIVE COMMONS: FILE USCGS-E134.JPG.
(HTTP://EN.WIKIPEDIA.ORG/WIKI/FILE:USCGS-E134.JPG)

Described by Coast and Geodetic Survey. Located 5.8 miles NW from Chicago. About 2.35 miles north along Michigan Avenue from the Illinois Central Railroad Station at Chicago, thence 0.7 mile north along Lake Shore Drive, thence 2.7 miles west along W. North Avenue, 116 feet west of the west curb of N. Milwaukee Avenue, 8 feet north of the north curb of W. North Avenue, set vertically in the south face and 4.3 feet west of the west edge of the west door for building number 2018, 4.8 feet east of the southwest corner of the building, and about 3 feet above the level of the sidewalk.

CONTOURS EXPLAINED

Landscape architects and civil engineers prepare site-grading plans similar to Figure 7.12 using base information from fieldwork performed by a professional land surveyor in creating a land or topographic survey map. Contours with spot elevations are the graphic means for communicating to contractors the required landform or earthwork modifications of an existing site to accommodate the structures or activity areas to be built.

The elevations shown on a topographic map are referenced to the average elevation of the ocean's surface. The average sea level elevation is determined as the halfway point between mean high and mean low tide. Sea level elevation is considered the zero contour line. The dashed line labeled 0 in Figure 7.13 represents mean high tide, or zero elevation. The dashed line labeled 1' Contour represents a one-foot elevation above the sea level. Contour 2 and Contour 3 represent one-foot elevation increases. The intent of the photograph

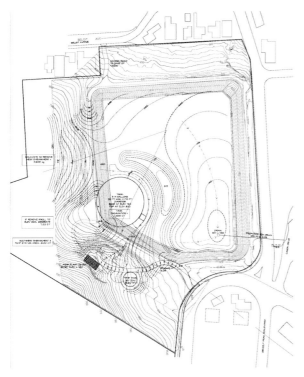

Figure 7.12 A preliminary site-grading plan
COURTESY OF DILLINGHAM ASSOCIATES

with the contour markings is to help the reader visualize the concepts that established elevation and contours.

Figure 7.14 shows a steep constructed embankment with dashed contour lines superimposed on the face of the slope. The contours represent three-foot contour intervals; that is, the elevation difference from one contour to the next is three feet.

Figure 7.13 Layers of waves along a Pacific Coast representing contour lines. Each dashed line represents a hypothetical contour line.

Figure 7.14 Sloped embankment with contours at 3-foot intervals

Figure 7.15 consists of three diagrams that will help you visualize the relation of contour line spacing to steep and gentle slopes. The diagrams show how close the contour lines in plan are drawn for each slope condition. Contour lines on a topographic or grading plan that are close together represent a steep slope; contour lines spaced farther apart are less steep.

The closer contours are spaced together, the steeper the slope, as depicted in contour plan and section in

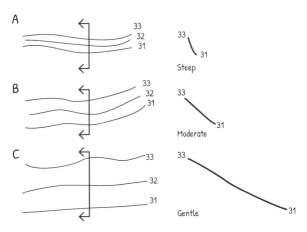

Figure 7.15 Example of steep (A) and less steep (B, C) slopes represented by the spacing of contours and their corresponding sections

Figure 7.15-A. Contours that are spaced farther apart, as shown in Figure 7.15-B and C, have slopes that are less steep. Compare the horizontal spacing of the contours of a less steep slope with the contours that are closer together in the same figure. Slope in site grading is described as a percentage, so two contours that are a horizontal distance of 100 feet apart represent a 1% slope, as in: 10′/1000′ = .01 or 1%. Contours with a one-foot contour interval that are 10 feet apart represent a 10% slope: 10′/100′ = .1 or 10%. The slope for a parking lot can vary from as low as 1% to as steep as 3% or 4%. A tennis court should be graded so that the maximum slope is 2%, with 1 to 1.5% slopes preferred to facilitate comfortable play. An urban plaza might be designed with 1% to 1.5% change of slope variations, and in some situations can be graded less than 1% for smooth concrete surfaces. A plaza surface graded to 3% or 4% will feel "steep" and uncomfortable, when in fact the slope would in other situations feel like an acceptable, gentle sloping surface. In situations where the existing terrain is highly varied, in that the elevation difference from one end of the property to the other has a 100-feet elevation difference, steeper slopes might be necessary to accommodate a walk or trail between two buildings or between a building and a parking lot or outdoor use area. In this case the walk might be graded to 4% and 5% to a maximum of 8% to accommodate ADA mobility standards, as shown in Figures 7.16-A and B.

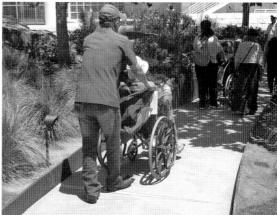

Figures 7.16-A and 7.16-B Wheelchair access provided on steep hillside slope leading from a lower garden to upper museum buildings at the Getty Museum, Los Angeles, CA

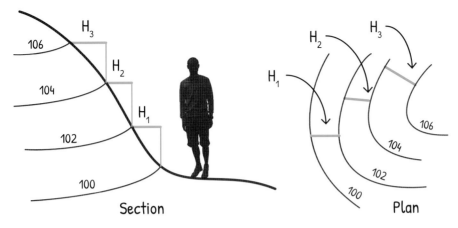

Figure 7.17 An embankment shown in section and plan

Section and plan views are shown in Figure 7.17, with the horizontal dimension between contours identified by the letter H. When calculating the slope of a surface (level or inclined), divide the elevation difference between two points or series of contours in a plan by their horizontal distance. For instance, if the horizontal difference between contours 100 and 106 (as measured on the plan, if it were drawn to scale) is 20 feet, then the slope in percent is 6/20 = .0333, or 3.3%

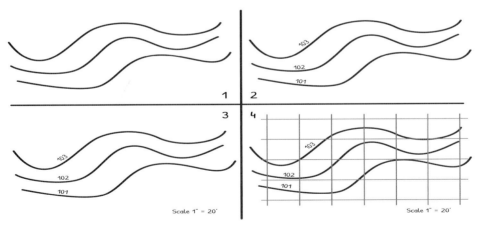

Figure 7.18 Three wavy lines increase their usefulness with each additional set of information: contour elevation, drawing scale, and reference grid system

Figure 7.18 presents a sequence of diagrams, each with the same set of three contour lines but different additional information. Diagram No. 1 in Figure 7.18 has simply three wavy lines but is absent of any additional graphic or alphanumeric information. Without any additional information, we can only guess what the three lines represent. For these contours to be useful or even recognizable as contour lines, additional information is required, as shown in diagram No. 2. The contours in diagram No. 2 include an elevation above each contour. Now we can see that the contours represent a partial slope with elevation 101 as the low point and elevation 103 two feet higher. With the addition of a scale (in this case 10˝ = 200´), the percent of slope can be calculated (see diagram No. 3). The steepness or degree of slope can be determined by dividing the vertical elevation difference between the contours (for instance, contour 101 and 102) by the horizontal distance between the two contours.

In diagram No. 4 of Figure 7.18 a grid has been overlaid on the contour lines. The grid is useful in a several ways. Assuming the grid is referenced to site property lines, a contractor would be able to pinpoint the exact location of any existing or proposed object or feature, including a precise elevation at any intersection within the grid. The contractor would place stakes in the ground with the desired elevation for each grid intersection. This grid pattern of stakes would guide the earth-moving operations to achieve the grading shown in a site-grading plan prepared by the designer. The method used to calculate spot elevations and slope will be covered in the Chapter 10, "How to Calculate Spot Elevations."

SLOPE IN PLAN AND SECTION

One of the tools used in developing a site-grading plan is a section drawing. A section drawing aids the designer to quickly visualize existing terrain under study, as well as to see what one or more proposed grading strategies look like before deciding which design alternative is the better solution. A section should be drawn to show relations of the terrain with other elements as the proposed shape of the land or series of paved surfaces between buildings. Sections are useful when structures are involved, to allow the designer to better see how the structure meets the ground and then transitions to the adjacent landscape. Section drawings are usually included in a construction drawing package. Sections are drawn to provide greater detail not easily accomplished in the plan view of a grading drawing and to guide the contractor. Sections can often explain the designer's grading intent to a contractor and others more clearly than the grading plan view alone. Although both the plan and section are two-dimensional drawings, the section helps to better visualize the three-dimensional aspects of the grading plan.

Construction of a section drawing is a multi-stepped process. Refer to Figures 7.19-A–7.19E to follow the process.

STEP A REQUIRES TWO ACTIONS

First, draw a section line (sometimes referred to as a section cut line) over the topographic or grading plan and label it *Section AA*. The plan should be at the same scale the designer is using to develop the grading plan.

Next, draw a series of contour lines that will have the same horizontal scale as the topographic plan; however, the vertical scale is usually exaggerated by three times the horizontal scale. So if the plan were drawn at 20 scale, the vertical scale would separate each contour line by the equivalent of three feet shown on the 20 scale. The contour lines shown below the topographic plan are drawn so that each contour is separated by three-foot intervals on a 20 scale with each contour labelled.

STEP B

Go to Section AA on the topographic map, and at each point where the Section AA line intersects a contour on the plan, draw a perpendicular line down to the equivalent contour line stacked below the plan. In this case we have started in the middle of the topographic plan at the 350-contour line and dropped two perpendicular lines to the 350-contour line below. Normally, the designer would start the process going from left to right rather than starting in the middle.

STEPS C AND D

The process continues moving across the Section AA line along the plan and dropping a perpendicular line where the cut line crosses a plan contour line. Once all the contour lines corresponding to the contour lines on the plan have been located below, a line that will represent the section view is drawn by connecting the "dots," as shown in Figure 7.19-D. In this case, the section constructed shows the existing terrain with a hill shape in the center and valleys to either side

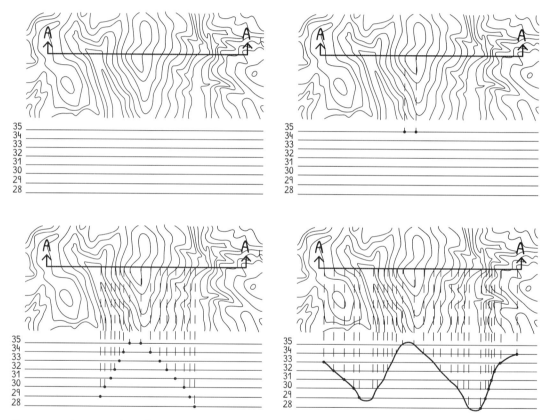

Figure 7.19-A–7.19-D Steps for creating a section from a topographic map or site-grading plan

STEP E

The next step would be to alter the existing contours in the plan view, to create, say, a level or gently sloping area for a building site. To create this level area, the contours would be repositioned to reshape existing topography, creating areas for a building site, road, or other land use area. The contour reshaping process will be covered in a later chapter. Once the repositioning of the contours was done, a new section would be prepared using the same section cut line, then projecting the new contour locations as they intersect the section line down to the contour lines that will make up the section. Typically, the new section will be drawn as a solid line and the existing terrain with dashed lines (see Figure 7.19-E). Where the solid line is now positioned on top of the dashed existing line, fill material would be required. Where the solid line falls below the dashed line, cut would be necessary.

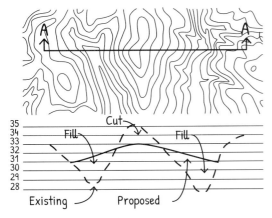

Figure 7.19-E The section is this figure shows existing terrain as a dashed line and the proposed reshaping of the terrain as a solid line. The use of dashed and solid lines is a convention used to graphically distinguish existing and proposed contours and landform. NOTE: for clarity, the contours on plan above were not revised to represent the proposed section below.

8

SIGNATURE LANDFORMS

In this chapter you will learn about:

- The concept of landform signatures and the correlation between landforms found in nature and the creation of site-grading solutions

LANDFORM SIGNATURES

Contours on a topographic map have very specific shapes or forms. Each landform has a recognizable arrangement or pattern of contours in plan. Each landform has a plan arrangement of contours that is often described as a contour or landform signature. Four contour signatures can be seen in Figure 8.1. Area A is a signature for a mound or hill, B is the signature for a valley, C is the signature for a concave or crown-shaped landform, and the nearly parallel contour lines of D form the signature of a sloping, uniform plane.

A mound or mountain form is shown in plan as contours arranged in concentric or irregular concentric circles, as shown in the circled area labeled A in Figure 8.1. A valley landscape (area B in Figure 8.1) has its unique signature with the contours arranged with a "V" bottom, indicating a sharp, incised valley shape formed by the erosive action of a river or drainage swale. Contours with a wide, flat bottom represent a valley formed by the

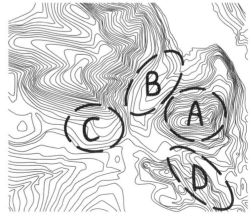

Figure 8.1 Four distinct landforms found in nature

glacial action of erosion. Area C is a convex-shaped hillside, and area D is a steep slope embankment. Each of the basic and more common landform contour signatures is described in the following material.

 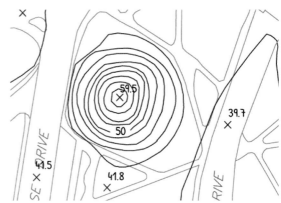

Figures 8.2-A and 8.2-B Hill landform signature

Contours have been superimposed over the photograph in Figure 8.2 of a small hill or mound (called the Indian Mounds) on the Louisiana State University campus. The contours are drawn to illustrate what the contours might look like in the landscape. The same landform is shown in plan with the actual contours taken from a topographic survey.

Hypothetical contour lines have been superimposed on the driveway shown in Figure 8.3-A. In 8.3-B, the same driveway is shown in plan

Figures 8.3-A and 8.3-B Convex landform signature

view with the actual contours. Notice that the contours bow downhill along the driveway, indicating that the driveway was constructed with a crown. The crown directs water to the outer edges of the driveway surface toward the curb.

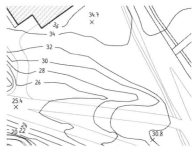

Figures 8.4-A and 8.4-B Valley, ravine, or swale landform signature

In the photograph in Figure 8.4-A the contours are oriented uphill, creating a swale or valley landform, while the contours in the road bow downhill to form a crown landform. Figure 8.4-B is a plan view of the same general area where the photograph was taken. You can readily see how the contours create a swale condition along the north side of the road, as well as a crown along the centerline of the same road.

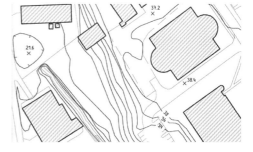

Figures 8.5-A and 8.5-B Uniform slope landform signature

Figure 8.5-A illustrates what contours would look like on a slope where the contours are parallel to one another. In the center of Figure 8.5-B, you can see what contours that fall on a similar planar slope look like in plan. A simple level or flat area is shown in Figure 8.6-A. The central level area is bordered by a sloping embankment that appears fairly steep, as shown by the closely spaced horizontal distance separating the contour lines in Figure 8.6-B.

 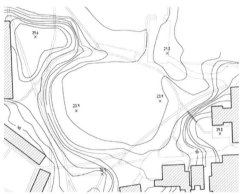

Figures 8.6-A and 8.6-B Level landform signature

WATERSHED LANDFORM SIGNATURE

Watersheds come in all shapes and sizes. A watershed can be as small as a couple of hundred square feet or many millions of square miles, like the Mississippi River watershed. Figure 8.7 is an aerial view of a Southern California mountain range with three sub-watersheds outlined. A designer may create a watershed in developing a grading solution in situations where surface waters are collected within a semi-enclosed landform to then flow downhill in the direction of a pond or stream similar in concept to a watershed. An example of how a designer applied the watershed concept for a paved landscape is shown in Figure 8.8.

Figure 8.7 Aerial view of a Southern California outlining watershed and sub-watershed units

A watershed is simply an area of land that is bounded by a ridge-line or continuous embankment line of higher elevation; rainwater that falls within this defined high-ground boundary flows to a central low point such as a lake, stream, or catch basin. Water that falls outside of the ridge boundary flows to an adjacent watershed and its lowest central point. In Figure 8.9-A, you can see the outline of a watershed where all rainwater that falls within the ridgeline then flows downhill to a river. In Figure 8.9-B, three additional watersheds abut watershed A and are indicated as B, C, and D, with arrows indicating primary drainage flows.

Figure 8.8 The catch basin in the center of the walk is the lowest point in this example of a watershed-like solution for collecting surface water in a paved area

Figure 8.9 Watersheds delineated on contours adapted from a USGS quad map with arrows showing direction of surface water flow

In Figure 8.10-A is a rural pond created by the farmer to impound (store) water for irrigation and farm animals. The pond was formed by the construction of an earthen dam across the valley floor to capture rainwater. In effect, the farmer created a watershed that is utilitarian and provides a convenient water source. The rainwater previously flowed down the valley in a slow-moving stream into a larger stream several miles away. Hypothetical contours have been drawn of the same pond scene shown in Figure 8.10-A to help the reader visualize what the contours might look like in a topographic map.

A watershed is considered a topographic and hydrological phenomenon; however, the concept of creating a closed catchment surface is commonly used in site grading. The concept of a watershed has been used in devising a way of collecting and disposing of surface rainwater on the university campus plaza shown in Figure 8.11. All rainwater that falls within the dashed outline of the watershed flows to a central catch basin. Rainwater that falls outside the dashed line flows to other catch basins or to landscaped areas where the water is collected, or perhaps allowed to percolate into the soil or be carried by a swale or sheet flow to some other nearby area.

Figures 8.10-A and 8.10-B A farmer's pond located in the Alentejo region of Portugal

Figure 8.11 Campus quadrangle composed of a series of watershed-like shallow cells, each with a catch basin located at the lowest elevation within its cell

PUTTING IT ALL TOGETHER

Site grading is as much an art as it is an analytical process. Typical landforms were reviewed in this chapter, presented as an idea, like colors of paint or a kit of parts. The kit of the designer for creating site-grading plans is a variety of landforms woven into a well-organized and seamless site-grading design. The parts in the kit are landforms found in nature and adapted to the needs of a site-grading design scheme. The landforms can be applied in solving site-grading problems and thus creating a new landscape. In Figure 8.12 the various contour patterns that translate into landform signatures are outlined, demonstrating how a grading plan as a whole composition is the sum of its parts. The parts compose the assemblage of a variety of contour patterns, resulting in a cohesive site-grading plan. Figure 8.12 is a diagram—a three-dimensional drawing—to help readers visualize the grading design and storm water management concepts. Figure 8.13 is the actual site-grading plan. Area A in Figure 8.12 is the application of the watershed landform described earlier, used to create a storm water detention pond. The areas outlined as B1 and B2 are sloping planes, area C is a swale, area D is a driveway with a crown forming a concave landform, and areas E make up a series of terraced parking lots with slightly sloping or tilted planes.

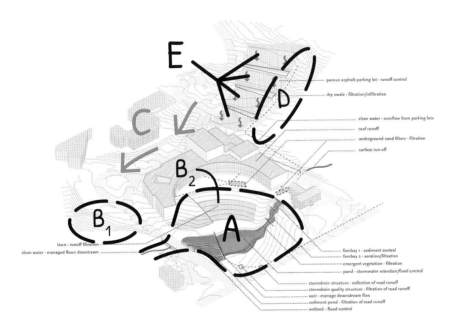

Figure 8.12 Storm water management concept, Hamilton College at College Hill Road

ORIGINAL IMAGE PROVIDED BY REED HILDERBRAND ASSOCIATES

Putting all the landform tools together to create an aesthetically inspired and functional grading plan is more than assembling a kit of parts. A process for creating a grading plan is presented in Chapter 12.

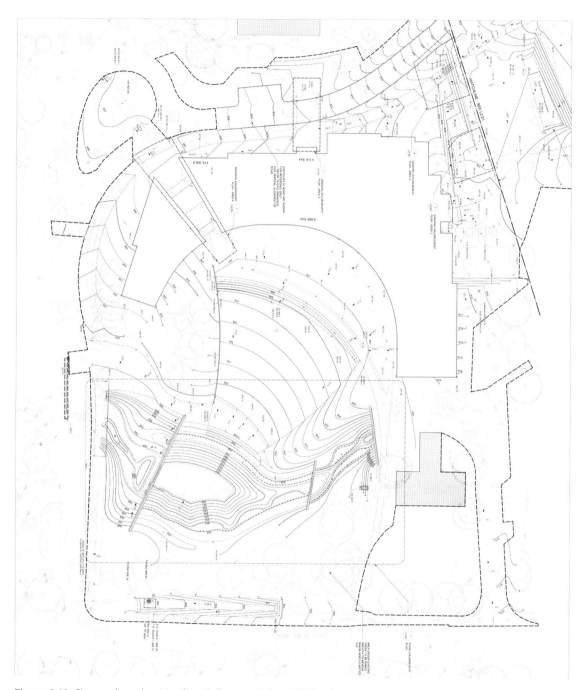

Figure 8.13 Site-grading plan, Hamilton College, at College Hill Road

ORIGINAL IMAGE PROVIDED BY REED HILDERBRAND ASSOCIATES

9

CALCULATING SLOPE AND OTHER GRADING CALCULATIONS: TOOLS FOR GAINING MASTERY IN GRADING

In this chapter you will learn about:

- How to employ one simple equation for calculating slope, horizontal distance, and elevation
- How to calculate the slope of a paved or landscape surface
- How to place contours to achieve an intended percent of slope
- How to determine the elevation of a point or object in the landscape
- How to create slope using spot elevations

This and the following chapters will together take the reader step by step through the site-grading process. Each chapter has its emphasis for presenting the tools for preparing site-grading plans and for making necessary calculations. Grading involves a number of operations; some involve making mathematical calculations and others drawing lines to create forms or areas for some purpose such as creating a level area that will accommodate a building or perhaps a tennis court. In other chapters there is discussion on drawing in scale, establishing a project's location or boundaries, and reading topographic maps. In this chapter a kit of tools will be presented with examples of how to use the tools. These tools are the means for a designer to solve landscape-grading problems and create competent grading solutions. You will not only gain experience at harnessing your creativity to create credible landscape grading solutions, you will also learn how and when to apply the various tools. The more you use these tools, the more your capability at solving site-grading solutions will increase—increase in speed and accuracy. In time, you will become increasingly adept as you gain confidence through practice and by challenging yourself to discover more aesthetically exciting and innovative site-grading solutions.

Figure 9.1-A A pen mirrors slope of a steep embankment

Figure 9.1-B A landscape that was altered by a farmer with a variety of slopes, from steep to level

Slope in site grading refers to the angle or degree of the surface of a landform (such as the side face of a hill or the steepness of a river valley or drainage swale) or a paved surface (such as walkway or tennis court). The drawing pen in Figure 9.1-A is tilted so as to mirror the sloping surface of a constructed earth embankment. As you can see, the face of the embankment is quite steep; probably impossible to walk straight up on without considerable difficulty. The degree of steepness is expressed as a percent of slope, with slopes of 25 or 30 percent following in the steep range. Slopes of 2 or 5 percent are considered shallow or even almost level of surfaces that are 1 percent. In Figure 9.1-B the terrain is highly varied with steep to shallow sloping earth surfaces and everything in between. More on slope and angle of slopes will be discussed below.

INTRODUCING CALCULATION OF SLOPE

Contour lines and spot elevations are the primary tools to modify the terrain of an existing project landscape. Used in combination, the manipulation of contours and establishment of spot elevations are the primary means to create level areas for buildings and sloping areas to direct water runoff, and to sculpt project terrain to accommodate safe circulation for pedestrian and vehicle movement. We also modify the existing landform to provide a visual barrier in the form of berms or depressions, or to achieve some other aesthetic purpose. We use contours and spot elevations to indicate our intended modifications of the existing topography. When we draw two or more contours, the measured distance between the contours determines the steepness of the slope. Percent of slope can also be calculated between two spot elevations. Slope is expressed as a percent, which is the inclination of the sloping ground plane or embankment. For instance, an entry walk to a building might be sloped at 2 or 3 percent, which is a comfortable slope adequate to direct surface water away from the building. Figures 9.2-A and 9.2-B provide concrete examples of two slopes (S).

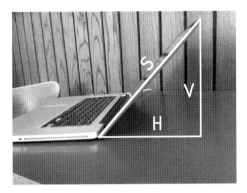 

Figures 9.2-A and 9.2-B The angles of the computer screens in the two photographs represent different slopes. When you want to calculate the slope of a surface, you divide the vertical height V by the horizontal distance H as in S = V / H.

In Figures 9.2-A and 9.2-B, the computer screen is shown at two different inclinations. The slope of the computer screen relative to the table in Figure 9.2-A is not as steep as the computer screen slope in Figure 9.2-B. The slope of the computer screen is labelled S. In grading, slope is described as a percent that is the relation between the vertical elevation difference of two points divided by the horizontal distance between the two points of interest. Referring to Figure 9.3-A, the line labelled V represents the vertical elevation difference from point b to point a. Line H is the horizontal distance measured between points c and b. Mathematically, this relation is expressed in the formula:

S = V / H

With this formula and an understanding of the relationship of the three elements (slope, vertical elevation difference, and horizontal distance), one can determine the slope of a landscape (e.g., Figure 9.3-B) or pavement plane and establish spot elevations for buildings, walls, paved and unpaved surfaces, and just about any existing or proposed physical feature in the landscape.

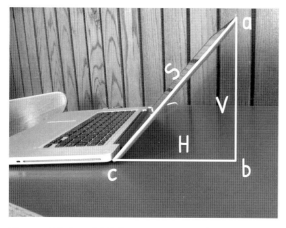 

Figures 9.3-A and 9.3-B Two examples of sloped surfaces: laptop computer screen and grassy slope embankment. The process for calculating the slope or percent of incline is the same.

Figure 9.4-A Trekker walking up a trail with a slope of 10 to 15 percent

A FEW SLOPE CONVENTIONS

What is slope? If you have ever gone on a hike and walked up or down a mountain, you have experienced slope. Mountains that are easy to walk up have a shallow slope or degree of inclination. A mountain that is difficult to walk up is described as having a steep slope (see Figures 9.4-A and 9.4-B). Slopes are expressed in percent; slope percents of 2 percent, 5 percent, and 8 percent are easy to walk up, while slopes of 20 percent, 30 percent, or more increase in difficulty as the number increases.

Obviously, one can walk up as well as down a mountain slope. Slopes that we walk up are defined as positive slopes (see Figure 9.5-A). The experience of walking up a steep slope may not be described as a positive experience, but in grading, uphill slopes are mathematically expressed as being positive. The converse of going up a slope is going down one, and a trail where a hiker is working his or her way down a mountain is described as a negative slope (see Figure 9.5-B). Water, of course, flows downhill, therefore the slope might be described a negative (or minus), say, 5 percent. When a contractor is studying a grading plan and sees -2% or just plain 2% on a walk or parking lot, the contractor knows that the walk or parking surface needs to slope downhill so that the water flows in the direction the slope arrow is pointing. Where a +2% is shown on a grading plan, the contractor knows to slope a surface uphill. The use of + and – may seem confusing at first, but the use of these symbols is one of the common conventions in landscape architecture and civil engineering. The use of the plus or minus symbol becomes mathematically important when preparing drawings in the design of roadways or bicycle trails. The convention when using slope arrows in grading plans is that the arrow is pointing in the direction the designer wants surface water to flow (see Figure 9.6).

Figure 9.4-B Trail with slopes varying from 1% to 12%

Figure 9.5-A Positive slope going uphill: +15%

Figure 9.5-B Negative slope going downhill: –15%

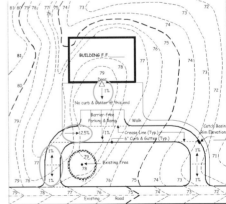

Figure 9.6 Note the use of arrows with percent of slope indication in this preliminary grading plan. In all cases the arrow is pointing in the direction the designer intends surface water to flow.
COURTESY OF SADIK ARTUNC

SLOPE EQUATION: PRIMARY TOOL FOR MOST CALCULATIONS REQUIRED IN GRADING

How to calculate slope has been introduced together with several conventions that are familiar to all designers in landscape architecture and civil engineering, as well as contractors. A complete explanation of how to calculate slope is presented here.

Slope can be calculated using a simple right triangle equation (see Figure 9.7). The right triangle equation is written as: S = V / H. S is slope, and V is the elevation difference from point C to B. H is the horizontal distance from point A to point B. In the case of Figure 9.7, the incline of the embankment is sloping at some percent perhaps greater than 50 percent. V, the elevation or vertical measurement (BC in the figure), is calculated by subtracting the elevation at the point marked A (the foot, or toe, of the incline) from the top marked B. If the toe of the incline is 120 feet above sea level and the elevation at the top of the slope is at the elevation of 132, then V would equal 12 feet. With a tape measure you could measure H, the horizontal distance from points A and C. If that distance were 15 feet, then you could calculate for the slope by dividing V by H, and you would have:

$$S = V / H$$

$$S = 12 / 15$$

$$S = 0.8 \text{ or } 80\%$$

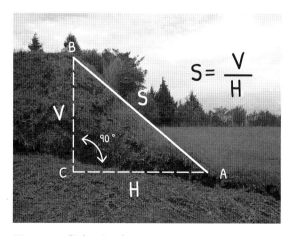

Figure 9.7 Right triangle equation

80 percent is a steep slope, one that would be very difficult to climb straight up from the toe of the slope. A slope of 25 percent is more easily traversed, and certainly would making mowing the grass much easier than the slope shown in the Figures 9.7 and 9.8-A and B.

In Figure 9.8, the slope of the embankment can be determined by measuring the vertical elevation difference from the bottom of the slope to the top, then dividing by the horizontal difference between the top and bottom of the slope elevations.

Figure 9.8-A A review of the elements used in the slope equation: S=V/H

Figure 9.8-B Diagram of the slope equation where S = slope (as a percent), V = elevation difference (measured in feet), H = horizontal distance (also measured in feet)[1]

Slope, or S, equals the elevation difference between two contours or spot elevations, or V divided by the horizontal distance, or H. The equation S = V / H is the most useful and most often used equation for making most of the calculations necessary for creating grading plans. It is used not only to make slope calculations, but also to determine horizontal distance when slope and elevation difference is known. The equation is also used to determine the elevation difference when slope and horizontal difference are known. See Figure 9.9.

To determine slope between two points	$S = \dfrac{V}{H}$
To determine horizontal distance between two points	$H = \dfrac{V}{S}$
To determine elevation difference between two points	$V = S \times H$

Figure 9.9 How to apply the right triangle equation

. . . .

1 V, or elevation difference, may be referred to as "rise," and H, or horizontal distance, may be referred to as "run," as in slope = rise / run.

For instance, with two contours that are spaced 20 feet apart where the vertical difference between the contours (the contour interval) is one foot, the resulting percent of slope created is 5 percent.

S = V / H

S = 1 foot / 20 feet

S = .05 = 5 percent

Notice while looking at the contour lines in Figure 9.10 that they are not uniformly drawn the same distance between contours. The spaces between various portions of contours vary, with some contours having a narrower space between them, while other sets of contour lines are farther apart. Each set of variations can be measured with an engineer's scale. The distance measured is the horizontal distance, or H in the slope formula: S = V / H. The percent of slope can be calculated using the S = V / H formula between two contours or sets of multiple contours such as C and E in Figure 9.10. The two contour lines indicated by the letter E are closer together and therefore the degree of slope is steeper than for the two contour lines labelled C, which are a further distance apart. The calculation for determining the slope between contour lines 23 and 24 for the space E is shown in Figure 9.11.

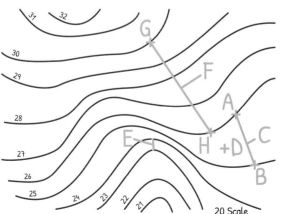

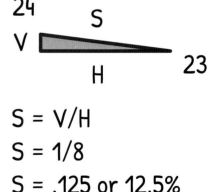

Figure 9.10 Contour map with three sets of contours to use in determining their percent of slope

Figure 9.11 How to calculate the percent of slope between two contours

Figure 9.11 shows how to calculate slope E between contours 23 and 24 in Figure 9.10. The horizontal distance between contours 23 and 24 is 8 feet. The vertical or elevation difference between the two contours is one foot. Slope E is:

S = V / H

S = 1 / 8

S = .125 or 12.5%

Figure 9.12 shows how to calculate the slope F created by the contours shown in Figure 9.10. In this example we are going to calculate the average percent of slope between points G and H. The horizontal distance between points G and H is 40 feet. The vertical or elevation difference between contours 26 and 30 is four feet. Slope E is:

S = V / H

S = 4 / 40

S = 0.1 or 10%

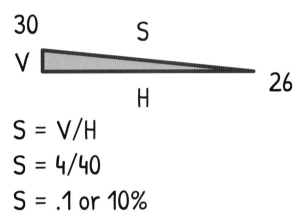

30

S

V

H

26

S = V/H

S = 4/40

S = .1 or 10%

Figure 9.12 Finding the slope between the 26 and 30 contours

Figure 9.13 shows how to calculate the slope C created by the contours shown in Figure 9.10. The horizontal distance of 25 feet separates the two contours. The vertical elevation distance between the two contours is one foot. Slope C is:

S = V / H

S = 1 / 25

S = .04 or 4%

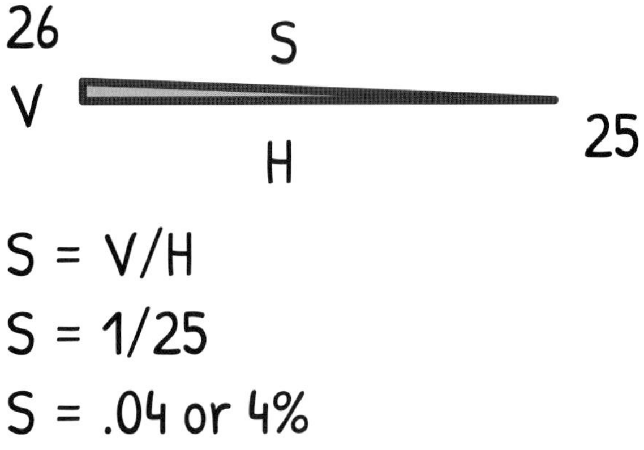

26

S

V

H

25

S = V/H

S = 1/25

S = .04 or 4%

Figure 9.13 Finding the slope between the 25 and 26 contours

How to Show Slope in Plan:

A FEW EXAMPLES FOR CALCULATING SLOPE

Referring to Figure 9.14, we will calculate the slope between three sets of contours. The drawing was prepared at 40 scale, where 1 inch = 40 feet.

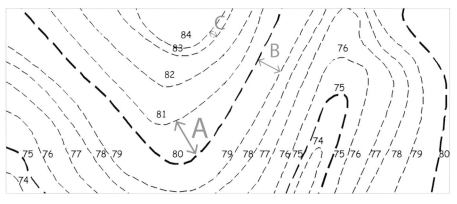

Figure 9.14 Portion of a topographic survey, Scale: 1″ = 40′

Set A contours are 80 and 81. The measured distance (plan was drawn at 40 scale) between them is one inch or 40 feet.

S = 1′ / 40′
S = .025 or 2.5%

Set B contours are 79 and 80. The measured distance between them is .5 inch or 20 feet.

S = 1′ / 20′
S = .05 or 5%

Set C contours are 83 and 84. The measured distance between them is .25 inch or 10 feet.

S = 1′ / 10′
S = .1 or 10%

In Figure 9.15 the elevation of the sidewalk pavement at point A is 34.5 feet. If we wanted to know the elevation of point B, we would use the S = V / H formula to make the calculation. In order to calculate the elevation of point B, we need to know two components of the slope formula. From the figure we can see that the slope is 5 percent, and the horizontal distance from point A to point B is 35 feet. Now let's calculate the elevation of point B:

S = V / H
.05 = V / 35′
V = .05 X 35′
V = 1.75 feet
Subtract 1.75 from the elevation of point A to get the elevation of point B
35 − 1.75 = 33.25   The elevation of point B is 33.25 feet.

Figure 9.15 Considering the slope of a sidewalk from point A to point B

How to Calculate Slope between Two Spot Elevations:

In Figure 9.16 there are two spot elevations: point A and point B. The horizontal distance H between the two points measures 120 feet. The vertical distant V is calculated by subtracting the elevation of point A from point B, and equals 1.2 feet. What is the slope between points A and B?

S = V / H

S = 1.2 / 120′

S = .01 or 1 percent

The example of a tennis court shown in Figure 9.16 is generally not the preferred approach for grading a tennis court. Typically tennis courts are graded so that the net is set at a higher elevation (essentially creating a crown) with the playing surface sloped downward at 1% from the net to the back of each side of the court.

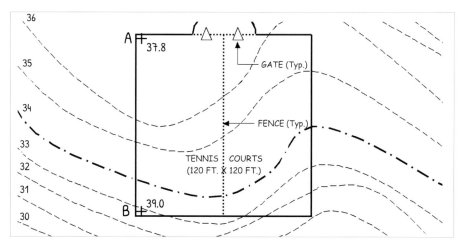

Figure 9.16 Proposed tennis court layout with spot elevations A and B
COURTESY OF SADIK ARTUNC

Now let's calculate spot elevation B in Figure 9.17. What do we know in looking at the figure? The slope is 2 percent, and the horizontal distance between points A and B is 120 feet. Now let's calculate the elevation for point B:

S = V / H
.02 = V / 120′
V = .02 x 120′
V = 2.40′

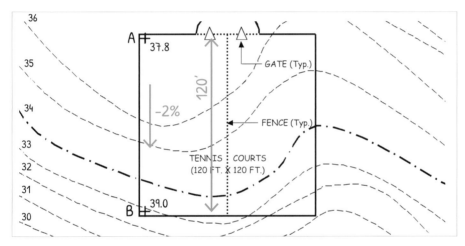

Figure 9.17 Tennis court

Referring to Figure 9.18, we will determine the horizontal distance between points A and B. What do we know looking at Figure 9.18? We know the slope, and we can calculate the vertical elevation difference between points A and B. With this information we can calculate the horizontal distance between points A and B.

S = V / H
S = .03
V = A minus B or 36.5 – 32.2 = 4.3′

.03 = 4.3 / H

H = 4.3 / .035

H = 122.86′

One more example of how to use the formula S = V / H. Suppose you want to locate an elevation of a point between two known points. Look at Figure 9.19: you know that point A is at elevation 56.8′ and point B is at elevation 55.2′. Now let's say that you would like to know where the elevation of 56′ would be along a straight line drawn between points A and B. Two questions come to mind: What do you know, and what do you not know, in order to solve the puzzle? You know H and V but you do not know S yet. If you first solve for the percent of slope from point A to point B you could next locate the elevation of 56′, which should be some distance between points A and B.

Figure 9.18 Considering the horizontal distance between points A and B

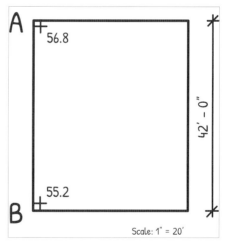

Figure 9.19 Determine slope in this example

To determine the slope in Figure 9.19 first ask: "What do you know from looking at the figure to use in solving the formula?" You do not know S, but you can calculate the slope because you can figure out the elevation difference between points A and B. You also know the horizontal distance between the two points.

S = V / H
To determine V subtract the elevation of point B from A = 1.6 feet
To determine S divide 1.6 by 42 feet = .038 or 3.8%

Now using the same figure and the information you used to calculate slope, next locate the 56 elevation between points A and B. See Figure 9.20.

To find the location of the 56 spot elevation on a sloping surface in Figure 9.20, you first need to ask: What do you know?

S = .038 (3.8%)
H = is what you need to calculate, using the formula S = V / H
V is the 56.8′ elevation of point A minus 56′ = 0.8′

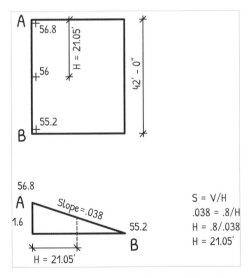

Figure 9.20 Locating spot elevation 56 in this diagram

Now plug what you know into the formula and solve for H, the distance the 56′ elevation is from point A, or 56.8′:

S = V / H
.038 = 0.8″ / H
H = 0.8′ / .038   = 21.05′

Measure 21.05 from point A to locate the 56′ spot elevation.

Referring to Figure 9.21, find the location of the 96′ spot elevation. What do you know?

Slope = .05 (5%)
V = 1′ which was determined by subtracting 96′ from 97′
H = is what you want to calculate
S = V / H
.05 = 1 / H
H = 1 / .05
H = 20′

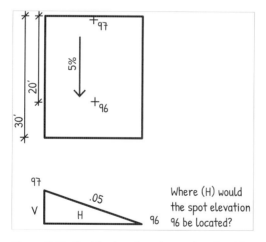

Figure 9.21 Find the location of spot elevation 96

The 96′ contour is located 20′ downslope from the 97′ contour in Figure 9.22. Using an engineer's scale, measure 20 feet from the 97′ contour line to locate the 96′ contour line in the figure.

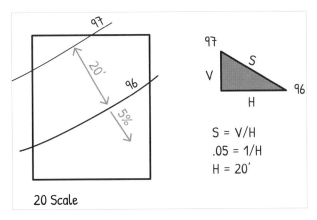

Figure 9.22 Diagram for determining the location of contour 96

The formula S = V / H can also be used for locating contour lines. Referring to Figure 9.22, how would you locate the 97′ contour line, assuming that it will be parallel to the 97′ contour line shown as a dashed line in Figure 9.23? Again ask: What do you know from the figure?

Slope is .05 or 5%

Vertical distance is 1′, determined by subtracting the 96′ contour line from the 97′ contour line.

Horizontal distance between the 97′ and 96′ contour lines is what you want to determine.

S = .05 or 5%
V = 1′
H = you want to calculate

$S = V / H$

$.05 = 1 / H$

$H = 1 / .05$

$H = 20'$

Using an engineer's scale, measure 20 feet in Figure 9.22 from the 97´ contour line to locate the 96´ contour.

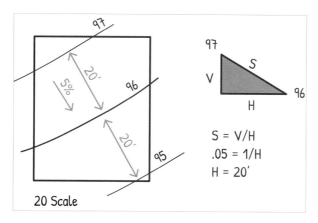

Figure 9.23 Locating one-foot contours on a 5 percent sloping surface

Suppose you wanted to create a uniform slope using contour lines. Refer to Figure 9.23. Assume you were starting from the 97´ contour line and wanted to create a 5 percent slope using contour lines. You have already calculated the horizontal distance between the 97´ and 96´ contour lines in Figure 9.23. Since you are continuing with a uniform slope of 5 percent, the horizontal distance of the next contours 95´, 94´, and further down-slope would also be 20 feet. Thus, to create the 5 percent slope, you would measure a 20-foot distance from the 96´ contour to the 95´ contour and from the 95´ contour to the 94´ contour, and draw the lines for creating a uniform 5 percent slope.

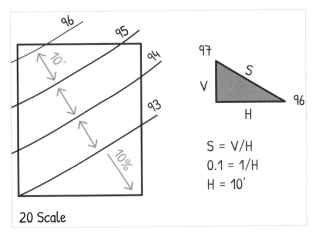

Figure 9.24 Locating one-foot contours on a 10 percent sloping surface

In Figure 9.24 is one more example of how to create a uniform slope using contour lines. In this example the slope is 10 percent, so to find the horizontal distance between successive contour lines, you need to solve for H in the formula S = V / H.

S = 0.1
V = 1′
H = is what you want to determine
S = V / H
0.1 = 1 / H
H = 1 / 0.1
H = 10′

You can now measure and space the distance of 10 feet between 95′ and 94′, through 90′ contours. The contours are evenly spaced 10 feet apart on the plan to create a surface sloping at 10%.

Referring to Figure 9.25, you will determine the slope indicated by the arrow between points A and B. Applying the formula S = V / H:

S is what you are going to determine

V is the difference between point B and point A = 3.7'

H = 128'

S = 3.7' / 128'

S = .0289 or .03

S = 3%

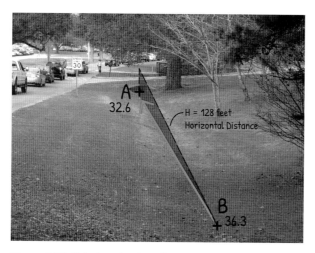

Figure 9.25 Calculate the slope from point A to point B

In the next chapter we will consider calculating spot elevations for different situations called for in developing landscape site-grading plans.

10

HOW TO CALCULATE SPOT ELEVATIONS

In this chapter you will learn about:

- How to locate where spot elevations are needed in a grading plan
- How to use spot elevations to communicate grading intent to contractors
- How to calculate spot elevations
- How to apply spot elevation conventions

INTRODUCTION

If you look at a grading plan and technical section, you will notice they contain both contours and spot elevations. The contours graphically represent sculptural landform design intent, while spot elevations communicate precise elevations at critical locations on the plan and in the sections. Think of contours as two-dimensional visual clay. The shape and flow of the contours and the distances between them help us visualize the landforms they represent.

WHEN ARE SPOT ELEVATIONS NEEDED?

The number of spot elevations that are needed in any one plan is not a fixed number, nor is the number based on any calculation. Generally spot elevations are needed to provide greater elevation specificity on sloping paved surfaces, and to set the height of walls and other built landform elements, such as the top of earth forms and the bottom elevations of depressions such as ponds. The designer considers where to place spot elevations to clarify the grading design intent, particularly in critical areas such as where the direction of slope must be maintained on paved or landscape surfaces. Spot elevations provide greater control to prevent the flooding or ponding of storm water. Spot elevations take precedence over contours in a site-grading plan.

Most firms have established rules about the placement of spot elevations. Spot elevations are the primary means of communicating grading design intent on hardscape surfaces, walls, fountains, and other constructed features. Contours are the primary means of communicating grading design intent on nonpaved surfaces including landscape areas and nonpaved surfaces. Technical sections are also used to augment contours and spot elevations. Sections provide the construction contractor with greater elevation accuracy in situations where the designer feels it is necessary—for instance, heights of walls and structures with complex elevation changes or roadway or bicycle paths.

Spot elevations are shown on the grading plan in a set of construction drawings. Spot elevations may appear in other locations when details and sections are placed on other sheets in a set of construction drawings. Avoid redundancy; that is, avoid multiple spot elevations for the same element in more than one location. If for some reason the designer makes a spot elevation change on one sheet, there is a 50/50 chance that the change will not be made in the other locations, and this discrepancy can cause a cost overrun for the contractor—or worse, that could be considered a design error with potential legal consequences in the eventuality of someone getting injured as a result of the error. Contractors generally use spot elevations to construct both hardscape (paved surfaces) and soft-scape landscape areas. In areas of the grading plan where contours are primarily used, the contractor will establish a grid and interpolate spot elevations at the grid intersections. The grid will be established on the ground with surveyor's stakes, with spot elevations surveyed and marked on each stake.

Figures 10.1-A and 10.1-B The J. Paul Getty Museum at Getty Center, Los Angeles

For the plaza shown in Figure 10.1-A, a project at the Getty Museum in Los Angeles, a grading plan would require the use of spot elevations entirely. Spot elevations would be needed to guide the construction for all the elements of this upper museum plaza, including elevation of all walls, paved surfaces, steps, fountain, handrails, and any storm water collection points (catch basins or French drains). For the area in Figure 10.1-B, a grading plan would include both spot elevations and contours—contours primarily in the lawn and landscape areas, with supplemental spot elevations where the softscape adjoins hardscape. Spot elevations would be the primary means of communicating design grades (elevations) for the walls, ramps, fountain, and hard surface areas. Technical sections would also be prepared to show the elevation relationships where there are changes of grade and structural elements, such as for a fountain, walls and steps, and terracing. The following paragraphs provide general guidance about where and how to use spot elevations for the various component parts or elements in a grading plan.

WHERE SPOT ELEVATIONS ARE NECESSARY

Spot elevations should be the primary information provided in site-grading plans to establish elevation for the following site design elements:

1. Stairs
2. Ramps
3. Walls and fences
4. Rim elevation of drains
5. Beginning and ending of swales
6. Finish grade elevations of hardscape elements and structures
7. Existing trees to be saved
8. Finish grade of elevation of special landscape elements

1. Stairs: Top and bottom of group or run of stairs with a note indicating the number of stairs in the run and the height of stair rise.

The + symbol is used in grading plans to note the location of a spot elevation. In Figure 10.2 two spot elevations are noted as spot elevation A and spot elevation B. Typically, spot elevations are given at the bottom and top most steps. A note on the plan would indicate the number of steps plus the riser height of each step indicated by C in Figure 10.2. A note would be added in the plan indicating the number of steps (in the case) between spot elevations A and B and the riser height: 8 Steps with 12´ tread and 6´´ risers.

Spot elevations A and B designate the top and bottom of each flight of stairs shown in Figure 10.3 Spot elevations are needed at the bottom of each flight of stairs as well as the top step. Normally a note is also included noting the number of stairs for each flight and the height of the riser (five steps with 5½-inch riser, or height). Technical details would further articulate other critical dimensions and details for the stairs. A more complex design incorporating stairs, terraces, and ramps is shown in Figure 10.4. The letters stand for the following elements in the figure:

A = Slope of the paving surfaces shown as a percent. A spot elevation is given at the start and end of each similarly sloped surface.

Figure 10.2 Stairs connecting lower with upper terraces at Teotihuacan, Mexico

Figure 10.3 Multiple flight of stairs at a Louisiana State University student housing complex

B = Critical spot elevation on the paved surface. In the grading plan for this design there would be numerous B spot elevations.

C = Spot elevation at the beginning of the ramp leading into the gathering area

D = Elevation of the top of the catch basin

E = Elevation of each terrace step

G = Elevation of the top of wall or TW

2. Ramps or uniform sloping surfaces: Top and bottom of the ramp supplemented with the percent of slope of the ramp.

Needed spot elevations are shown in Figure 10.5, indicated as A, B, C, and D. Typically spot elevations are required at the beginning and end of a sloping surface, or where the degree of slope is changed. For instance, where a ramp might begin with a 3 percent slope, a spot elevation is given at the start of the ramp and at the point where the designer has changed the slope of the adjoining surface or the continuation of the ramp, from 3 percent to 5 percent. S1, S2, and S3 in Figure 10.5 indicate where slope indications are needed along the ramp.

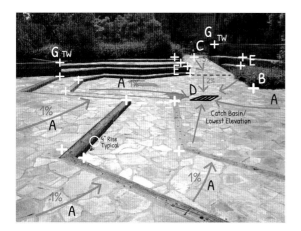

Figure 10.4 Stairs used as terraces in an informal student gathering area on the Cal Tech campus in Pasadena, CA

Figure 10.5 A wheelchair-accessible walk at the UCLA campus, composed of several ramp sections with landings spaced no greater than 20 feet apart. This ramp was designed before handrails were required. A similar ramp built today would include handrails.

Figure 10.6 shows a more complex ramp design providing access by means of a switchback ramp from an upper garden area to a lower plaza and walkway. The items marked with an A indicate where spot elevations are necessary; B items are arrows showing the direction of slope and also noting the percent of slope; and items marked C approximate landing sections that would be sloped at 1 percent and are required and spaced at intervals to meet wheelchair-access design standards.

3. Walls and fences: The finished elevation of the top of walls, with spot elevations shown at top and bottom of each stepped wall section. In the case of walls or fences that are meant to slope at the top, a spot elevation should be noted at the beginning and end of each sloping surface.

Spot elevations were used to establish the height of walls shown in Figure 10.7. Typically spot elevations are provided at the top and bottom of a wall. In addition to the grading plan prepared for this Scottsdale terrace garden, technical elevations were included in the construction documentation, showing all dimensions of the walls, with key wall heights and their elevations indicated and coordinated with the site-grading plan. The location and dimensions of the light fixtures (item B) and the window cutout (item A) on the back wall also were shown in

Figure 10.6 Wheelchair-accessible ramp recently constructed at Grand Park in the Los Angeles, CA, Grand Park, Los Angeles Civic Center

Figure 10.7 Upper terrace of a residential landscape
STEVE MARINO, LANDSCAPE ARCHITECT, SCOTTSDALE, AZ

the technical elevation. Spot elevations were provided in the grading plan for the steps, hardscape paving (item C), and landscape areas (item D). The grading plan included spot elevations in several locations where there are landscape plantings. Handrails would generally be required for steps and the upper terrace where a difference in elevation between the terrace and the ground below is greater than 18 inches. The technical elevations and sections for this design would include critical elevations as well as dimensions to work in combination to guide the construction of the walls and other design elements.

Spot elevations are found on grading plans to establish the height of walls. In the example shown in Figure 10.8, the wall is stepped and the top of each step is kept level, while the ramp below is sloped. Spot elevations should be given at every elevation change or the beginning and end of each wall step section in the grading plan. Item A indicates the need for a spot elevation at the top elevation of the wall at the beginning and end of each wall step section. Item B indicates the need for a

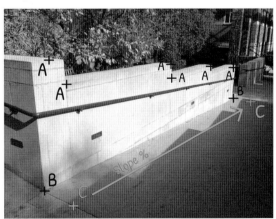

Figure 10.8 Stepped wall along sloping ramp, UCLA campus in Los Angeles, CA

spot elevation at the bottom of the wall where the wall meets pavement, or the ground, in the case of a planting area. Where walls with sloping top surfaces are designed, a spot elevation is given for the start and end of each sloping section of a wall. If a sloping wall is not divided with stepped sections, then a top-of-wall spot elevation is provided at the start and end of the wall. Spot elevations are given at the beginning and end of the sloped ramp (item C). Detailed sections and elevations would accompany the site-grading plan to provide the contractor with greater detail of the wall and ramp design intent of the designer.

The image in Figure 10.9 shows the critical grading documentation features of a wall and step combination. Item A is the bottom elevation of the stairs, item B is a note indicating number of stairs and riser height, and item C is the spot elevation at the top of the stairs. Item D gives the height of the wall, with the second item C giving the elevation of the top wall, and item F the elevation of the lower wall. TW is a common abbreviation meaning "top of wall."

4. Rim elevations for drain inlets (catch basins or French drains): Catch basins and French drains are shown in site-grading plans. Several elevations are associated with the detailing of these drainage elements. A spot elevation is given for the rim elevation of each catch basin and the drainpipe where the water is being carried away underground. In addition, technical details are provided giving the dimensions and construction details of the entire catch basin unit, including sections showing inlet and outlet pipes that take water from a catch basin or drain in the system to the municipal storm water system, or, in the case of on-site disposal, to a detention/retention pond. See Figure 10.10.

5. Beginning and ending of swales: With intermediate spot elevations when slope changes occur.

Spot elevations are provided at the beginning and end of drainage swales. Intermediate spot elevations may be needed when the slope along the swale changes (becomes steeper or more shallow). In Figure 10.11, point A represents the beginning of the drain swale in the lawn area, and the arrow indicates the direction of water flow with a percent of slope provided. At point B there is a change in percent of

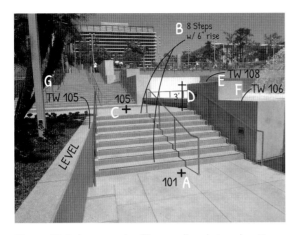

Figure 10.9 An example of how wall and step elevations are coordinated through the use of spot elevations for paving, steps, and walls. Grand Park, Los Angeles, Civic Center.

Figure 10.10 A catch basin was installed at the lowest elevation in this grass area, with spot elevation A for rim elevation of the catch basin

slope, so a spot elevation is given. Point C is a spot elevation, and it is also the rim elevation at the top of a catch basin where surface water is collected and drops to an underground pipe that is connected to the storm water infrastructure system.

6. Finish grade elevations in the landscape: Finish grade elevations or spot elevations are required to communicate critical elevations such as earthen mounds or embankments, finish grade of landscape areas at corners and entrances of buildings or other structures, and finish grades of hard surfaces for complex urban plaza areas.

Figure 10.12 is an annotated photographic diagram showing typical locations where spot elevations are needed in a grading plan for a plaza with fountain and other hardscape features. In addition to spot elevation, a grading plan will include slope indications represented in Figure 10.12 by the arrows. The arrows

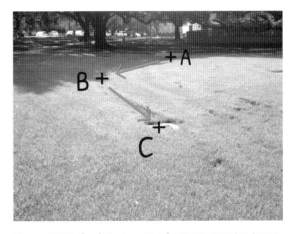

Figure 10.11 Swale in a campus lawn area terminating at area catch basin

indicate the direction surface water is to be directed by the sloping surface, with a percent of slope accompanying each arrow. The number and locations of spot elevations and slope arrows shown in this example are illustrative and not meant to be comprehensive.

A = Spot elevation at building entry. Yellow arrow indicates direction and percent of slope of pavement to direct water away from entry.

B = Spot elevations at critical points of paved surface, with blue arrows indicating directions and percent of slope to direct water

C = Spot elevations of pool water heights and bottom of pools

D = Elevation of seating benches

E = Elevation of stepping units across pool

F = The rock sculpture in the middle of the fountain would include many elevations showing heights of major elements supplemented by one or more sections detailing rock forms and elevations

G = Elevation of finished grade soil in planting areas

H = Elevation of handrail

The rock sculpture in the middle of the fountain would include many elevations showing heights of major elements supplemented by one or more sections detailing rock forms and elevations.

Figure 10.12 Upper terrace fountain at the J. Paul Getty Museum at Getty Center in Los Angeles, CA

Figure 10.13 Detailing finished grades at a building entrance on the UCLA campus in Los Angeles

The photograph in Figure 10.13 provides another example of the use of spot elevations for a site-grading plan.

A = Finish grade at building entry. Entry landing is sloped away from building toward steps.

B = Spot elevations at top and bottom of steps, key points at corners of paved surfaces or where there is a change in paving slope.

Arrows indicate direction of slope of pavement surfaces. In addition to arrows showing the direction of pavement is to slope, a percentage would normally be included, with a percent provided with each arrow. In this example, the primary slope directs the water away from the building and steps. The second arrow indicates a cross slope to pitch surface water toward the grass area, eventually to a catch basin in the lawn.

7. **Existing trees to be saved:** Spot elevations are necessary and should be provided at the base of the tree trunk and within the drip line, to control the finished grade at the base of tree trunks when earthwork involving cut and fill is critical to saving the trees. In Figure 10.14, item A is the existing elevation at the base of the tree. Item B is the elevation of the top surface of a partial tree well.

8. **Finish grade of landscape features:** Such as ponds; detention/retention basins; earth forms such as earth mounds and athletic play surfaces; and sculpted hardscape forms such as skateboard ramp forms.

The pond in Figure 10.15 was constructed by the farmer to retain water runoff from surrounding slopes for farm use and as a backup water supply for farm animals. Item A in Figure 10.15 indicates the highest elevation on the island. Item B is the designed water level, and item C is the lowest elevation in the pond. Item D is the elevation of the pond outlet, if one were to be provided. This elevation may be for the top of a weir or other water control height structures.

Figure 10.14 The existing tree trunk had a partial tree well installed to protect existing roots

Figure 10.15 Retention pond on an old dairy farm in Costa Rica

OVERVIEW FOR THE GRADING CONDITIONS DISCUSSION

The list of typical site design elements just reviewed is provided to give the grading designer an idea where spot elevations are needed in site-grading plans. It is possible to have too many spot elevations; however, their use should be considered wherever the grading designer wishes to provide specific elevation instructions and to clarify where confusion may be possible. The goal is to provide the contractor with a clear road map of what is expected. As a general rule of thumb: Use spot elevations to direct the contractor in the construction of all hard surfaces and constructed elements. Contours are primarily used to direct the contractor in grading all softscape areas, with spot elevations placed at critical high and low points. Provide spot elevations where changes of grade occur and for critical elements such as rim elevation of catch basins, tops of created landforms, or bottoms of ponds and depressions. Provide spot elevations at the beginning and end of sloping surfaces such as swales and ramps, and to control the heights of walls and fences. When in doubt, provide a spot elevation.

HOW SPOT ELEVATIONS ARE USED BY CONTRACTORS

Construction contractors rely on spot elevations in establishing and guiding most if not all their work. Typically, a contractor will set up land-surveying equipment at the construction site, then set up a system of stakes marked with desired spot elevations to guide earth moving or setting the forms for hardscape and other work. The contractor may also lay out a grid in areas where the grading plans contain contours, then establish subgrade and finish grade spot elevations at each grid intersection to guide construction. In the eyes of most contractors, spot elevations have priority over contours. This does not mean that contours are not utilized. Contours do establish the design intent of the designer; however, they may be converted through interpolation into a grid of spot elevations, or they may establish key elevations to guide construction of the project.

HOW TO CALCULATE A SPOT ELEVATION

The same formula used to calculate the percent of slope of a ground or paved surface is also used to calculate spot elevations: $S = V / H$ (see Figure 10.16). To use this formula in making a spot elevation calculation, a reference elevation is needed. A reference elevation is simply a known elevation on a project site such as a bench mark, existing building floor elevation, road centerline elevation, or any other existing physical feature, including property line corners or elevation information contained in a surveyor's topographic survey.

The best way to learn how to calculate a spot elevation is to start out with an example. In Figure 10.17 the elevation (spot elevation) of point A is 32.5. It is located at the entrance to a building. Let's say that we want to determine the elevation for point B in the figure.

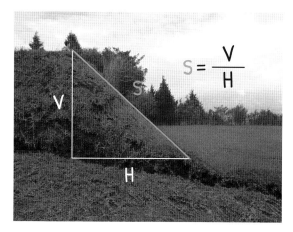

Figure 10.16 A reminder of the formula for calculating slope and spot elevations

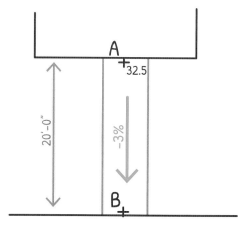

Figure 10.17 Use the information in the figure to determine the elevation of point B

Using the formula S = V / H, write down all the relevant information referring to Figure 10.17.

S is 3% or .03 (the slope of the walk)

H is 20 feet (horizontal distance from point A to point B)

V is what we will determine, to find the elevation of point B

Plug the numbers into the formula, then perform the calculation:

S = V / H

.03 = V / 20'

- V = .03 × 20'= 0.6'= the elevation difference between points A and B
- Subtract 0.6' from the elevation of spot elevation A to find the elevation of point B (note: the percent of slope above the arrow shows that the direction of the slope is minus 3%)
- Elevation A is 32.5' so subtract 0.6' to find the elevation of point B = 31.9'

Referring to Figure 10.18, calculate spot elevation B knowing the slope of the surface and the measured horizontal distance between points A and B.

To start, ask yourself: What do I know to apply to the formula $S = V / H$?

- You know the slope is 5 percent, sloping down from point A to point B.
- You know the horizontal distance between the two points is 35 feet.
- What is the elevation of point B?

$S = V / H$

$.05 = V / 35'$

$V = .05 \times 35'$

$V = 1.65' =$ the difference in elevation from points A and B

Elevation of point B is $34.5 - 1.65 = 32.85'$

Calculate the spot elevation of B in Figure 10.19 knowing that there are three steps, each with a 6-inch riser, between A and B. Ask yourself: "What do I know?"

- You know there are three steps, each with a 6-inch rise.
- 3 steps $\times .5' = 1.5'$
- The elevation of point A is 36.5' so subtract 1.5' from this elevation to find the elevation of point B = 34.0'

Figure 10.18 Use the information in this figure to determine the elevation of point B

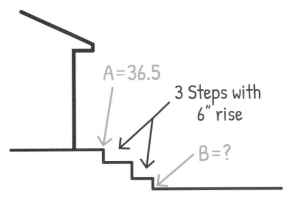

Figure 10.19 Use the information in this figure to determine the elevation of point B

THE STEPS FOR ESTABLISHING SPOT ELEVATIONS ON A SLOPING SURFACE

In Figure 10.20 is a paved surface that is to be constructed with a 2 percent slope, sloping down from point A to point B. From the information contained in the figure it is possible to calculate the spot elevations for many points on the paved surface. We will begin by determining the spot elevations of points A and C.

To start, ask yourself: What do I know to apply to the formula $S = V / H$?

- Slope is 2 percent, as indicated by the line drawn between points A and C.

- Using 40 scale measure the horizontal distance from A to C.

- The elevation where the 34' contour intersects the slope line indicated between points A and C is 34. (point E)

- The elevation of point A would be higher than points E and C

Let's continue: Switch to Figure 10.20-B to calculate the spot elevation of point A. What we know is that point E is at the intersection of the diagonal slope line with the 34-contour. The elevation of E is 34'.

- Measure the horizontal distance between points A and E = 20 feet.

- We know the percent of slope is 0.02.

$S = V / H$

$.02 = V / 20'$ $V = .02 \times 20'$ $V = 0.4"$

Point A elevation = 34' + 0.4' = 34.4

The elevation of point C can be calculated considering that we now know the elevation of point A, and we know the surface is sloping down at 2 percent toward point C. Now measure the horizontal distance from point A to point C, which let's say is 68'.

$S = V / H$

$.02 = V / 68'$ $V = .02 \times 68'$ $V = 1.36'$

Point C elevation = 34.4' − 1.36' = 33.04

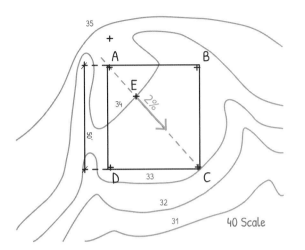

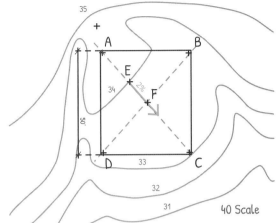

Figures 10.20-A and 10.20-B

Now let's calculate the elevation of points B and D in Figure 10.20-C.

Consider for a moment that the paved surface is sloping at a uniform 2 percent from A to C, so that we could calculate the elevation of any point along the diagonal connecting the two points A and C. Draw a line connecting points B and D. Assuming the line is perpendicular to the AC line, any point along the BD line would have the same elevation. To calculate the elevation for points B and D, knowing that any point along the line between B and D is the same elevation, including point F, let's calculate the elevation of point F from point A.

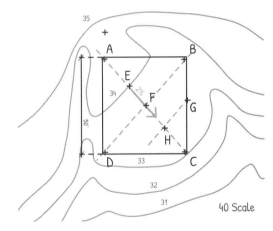

Figure 10.20-C

$S = V / H$

H or distance from point A to point F = 34'

$.02 = V / 34$ $V = .02 \times 34$ $V = 0.68$

The elevation of point F $= 34.4 - .68 = 32.64$

So the elevation of points F, B, and D are the same = 33.72

Now let's calculate the elevation of point G (for practice, as there is no significance to this point). To solve this, draw a line starting from point G so that it is perpendicular to AC. The point where the line intersects AC is noted as point H. If we find the elevation of point H, it is the same elevation as point G.

$S = V / H$

H or distance from point H to point A = 50'

$.02 = V / 50'$ $V = .02 \times 50'$ $V = 1.0'$

The elevation of point H $= 34.4' - 1.0' = 33.4$

The elevation of point H is 33.4'. It is also the spot elevation for point G.

USING THE RISER HEIGHT OF STEPS TO CALCULATE SPOT ELEVATIONS

Each of the seven steps has a 4" rise

$7 \times 4" = 28$ inches or 2.33 feet

Elevation of point B is 32.4'

Elevation of point A is $32.4' + 2.33' = 34.73'$

Figure 10.21 Steps leading to a campus administration building

Use of Spot Elevations in Grading Plans

Site-grading plans contain a variety of information used to communicate to the contractor the desired elevation and landform for a project. The contractor uses the information to lay out and to establish the basis for guiding his work. Spot elevations provide specific detailed elevations for key locations throughout paved surfaces; heights of walls and other structures to be constructed; and tops and bottoms of flights of stairs, catch basins, drainage swales, and ponds. Spot elevations also augment landform generally shown as topographic contours. Spot elevations will be given at the start and end of slope lines along pedestrian ramps or within a paved surface or drainage swale. Those preparing grading plans decide where best to provide spot elevations, generally giving the contractor specific elevation instructions to ensure that adequate drainage is provided, for instance pitching a walkway so as to direct surface drainage away from a building entrance.

Spot elevations on walls are supplemented with sections and elevations that include wall dimensions and additional spot elevations for use by the contractor in constructing the forms (in the case of poured in place concrete wall), building modular masonry walls (see Figure 10.22), or constructing timber walls.

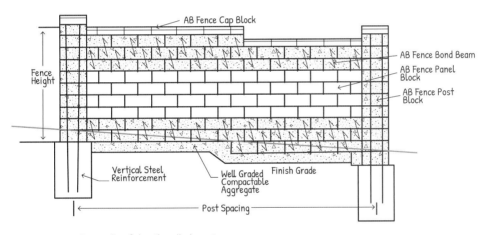

Figure 10.22 Example of detail wall elevation

Coordination of Spot Elevations with Other Elevation Conventions

Spot elevations are used with other symbols and notes for indicating precise elevations when needed on a grading plan. In Figure 10.23 the various ways of indicating elevation and grading design intent are shown.

Spot elevations are coordinated on a grading plan with direction of slope arrows and percent of slope. The slope arrows indicate the direction where the designer wants to direct surface water flow on paved surfaces, along swales, or on sloping ground. Referring to Figure 10.23, item A indicates the direction and degree of slope to direct surface water in this campus outdoor gathering area. Spot elevations are indicated by the + symbol. Further items in the figure include:

A = Slope arrows

B = Percent of slope

C = Spot elevation at entry to gathering area

D = Spot elevation at the rim of the catch basin

E = Place for a note indicating there are three steps, each with a 4" riser

G = Spot elevation at top of wall (normally, a spot elevation at the bottom of the wall would also be given)

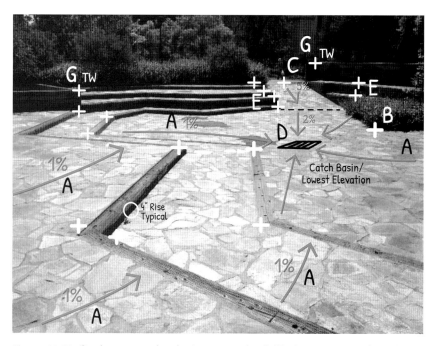

Figure 10.23 Outdoor terraced gathering area at the Cal Tech campus, Pasadena, CA

Notice that contours are not shown or used in the grading plan for the hardscape area shown in Figure 10.23. Contours could have been included in the original grading plan to provide coordination of this gathering area with the grading of the surrounding campus landscape areas and adjacent access walks.

HOW A CONTRACTOR USES SPOT ELEVATIONS SHOWN ON A GRADING PLAN

The four photographs in Figures 10.24-A through 10.24-D were taken at several construction sites and were selected to show how a contractor uses spot elevations from a site-grading plan to construct concrete work. Figure 10.24-A shows the wood forms a contractor constructs in preparation for pouring concrete for an entry drive. A surveyor marks each corner stake with the elevation shown on the grading plan. The contractor fastens (usually with nails) the form boards, first lining up the boards with the surveyor's elevation mark. Figure 10.24-B shows the concrete pad with the wood form boards still in place soon after the concrete was poured and the concrete surface was finished. The contractor will remove the forms, usually within a day after the concrete has set up or begun the hardening process.

Figure 10.24-C shows the manner in which the contractor makes sure the wood concrete forms are square and are set at the elevation specified in the grading plan. In this case, carpenter's string is used to guide the squaring of the wood form. Note that one end of the string is tied to a nail. The nail was set by the surveyor at the prescribed elevation shown on the grading plans. Figure 10.24-D provides a bird's-eye view of the forming layout for a circular driveway and drop-off. After all the forms are in place and secured, a concrete pour will be scheduled, followed by a finishing crew to complete the finishing of the surfaces per the technical specifications.

Figures 10.24-A–D Photographs A thru D show typical methods used for preparing a site for concrete work

FROM SCHEMATIC DESIGN PLAN TO GRADING PLAN

The following examples (Figures 10.25 and 10.26) taken from recent professional work are included here to show how all the elements described in this chapter are applied in actual site-grading plans. Prior to preparing a site-grading plan, the designer prepares a schematic design plan, similar to Figures 10.25-A and 10.26-A, to be approved by the client. Schematic design plans, supporting drawings, and written information (perhaps in the form of a progress report) are used to review the design with the client. The schematic design drawings may also be used to inform and solicit input from appropriate stakeholders, including user groups and government agencies having review or permitting authority. After the schematic design is approved and notice is given by the client to proceed to the design development phase of the project, the designer will prepare a site-grading plan, as shown in Figures 10.25-B and 10.26-B.

In the next chapter, the focus will be on contours and their use in developing site-grading plans.

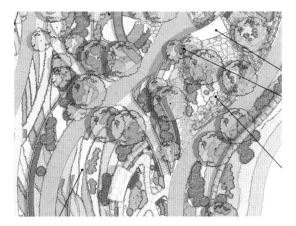

Figure 10.25-A Portion of the schematic design rendering for Red Butte Garden, Salt Lake City, Utah
COURTESY OF STUDIO OUTSIDE AND 3 FROMME DESIGN

Figure 10.25-B Portion of the grading plan for Red Butte Garden, Salt Lake City, Utah
COURTESY OF STUDIO OUTSIDE AND 3 FROMME DESIGN

Figure 10.26-A Tarrant County College District, Downtown Campus, site schematic design plan
COURTESY OF STUDIO OUTSIDE

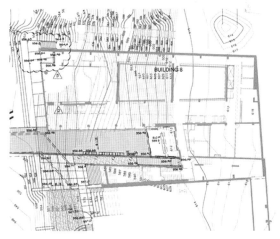

Figure 10.26-B Tarrant County College District, Downtown Campus, site-grading plan
COURTESY OF STUDIO OUTSIDE

11

WORKING WITH CONTOURS: CREATING LANDFORMS WITH DESIGN IN MIND

In this chapter you will learn about:

- How to create or alter topography to accommodate specific design elements, using contours

- How to create level or sloping landscapes and hardscape surfaces, using contours

- How to establish elevations in the form of spot elevations

Figure 11.1 The sloping central lawn increases visual interest and enhances the apparent scale of the landscape spaces at Teardrop Park, New York City

MICHAEL VAN VALKENBURGH ASSOCIATES, INC.

CREATING LANDSCAPES USING CONTOURS

This chapter will incorporate what was presented in previous chapters to advance our understanding of site grading and refine our skills. We will explore how to modify a project site using contours as our initial means of representing grading design intent. By manipulating, changing, and altering the location and shape of contours, we create graphically what the resulting landform and ground surfaces will look like as represented in the site-grading plan. The contractor will employ a grid system to transfer the grading plan onto the site, to guide the earth-moving operations. In addition to contours, the grading plan will include spot elevations, which are used where more precisely controlled elevations are necessary, such as the height of walls, built features such as fountains, or paved and landscaped areas.

Design is an activity that involves a back-and-forth conversation between linear and reiterative processing of information. The process is linear in that the activities are done in a sequence, beginning with project definition, site analysis, and programming, then progressing to concept formulation and design development. The process is reiterative in that earlier steps of investigation and analysis might be revisited several times, reworking initial thoughts on the basis of new insights. The design process usually begins with a meeting between the designer and the client. For complex projects, several meetings with the client may be needed to finalize project goals. Next, the designer would make one or more visits to the project site and surrounding neighborhoods, to understand the project site's physical features and contextual considerations that would be important for project programming and later design considerations. Once the project designer or design team have (1) gained sufficient understanding of the project site and its context, (2) completed due-diligence research of governing matters such as zoning, governmental regulations, and design criteria, and (3) established programming requirements, the designer may begin the design process. Working over a base map, the designer develops initial design concepts and their spatial layout. This initial development of a project design is referred to as the schematic design (SD). This is the first phase of a professional service contract between the client or owner and the project design consultant.

At the beginning of the site-grading process, the designer will start with a property map and topographic land survey. The land survey map will include topography (usually in the form of contours and key spot elevations of existing land or built features on the property). It will also contain property lines, existing built structures, vegetation (usually trees), existing driveways, roads adjacent to the property, infrastructure (power and telephone lines), servitudes (drainage channels or electrical rights-of-way), hydrologic features, and other pertinent information that can be mapped. As the designer works to develop site design concepts, he or she will consider the existing site features, and, initially, what was learned walking the site and conducting a site analysis. Initial site design concepts will be informed by the existing physical features of the property, most importantly the landforms and drainage patterns. Guiding the site design are the client's programmed activities, including proposed new structures, circulation (vehicular and nonvehicular), infrastructure, and environmental influences such as sun and wind patterns and climate, to list a few. The experienced designer will have the requirements of grading and existing topography in mind while developing initial design concepts during the site investigation. The details of the grading that will be necessary to support the design will consist of arranging program elements requiring level surfaces on the more level topography of the site, and locating other program elements on steeper portions of the site. There is always a balancing act involved in making these design and location decisions, as it is not always feasible or desirable to utilize the level areas of a site for activities requiring level areas, in which case a more aggressive modification of existing site topography to accommodate design elements will be required.

One of the precepts of grading is to pair design elements requiring level surfaces with level areas of a site, and fit other program elements that can appropriately be accommodated into steeper topography. As a goal, this would make sense in order to reduce the amount of grading (the moving of earth)—an approach that serves to respect site integrity and reduce construction costs at the same time. This approach of matching program to suitable site characteristics is not always feasible, given other considerations. For instance, access to an existing road may be situated on steep, hilly topography that cannot be avoided, assuming there are no alternatives for an entrance onto the property. The result may require significant grading to accommodate the entrance road and entrance feature. Regardless of the circumstances, grading will be required—minimally, when matching program elements with site suitability, or substantially, when the match is less achievable.

The devil, however, is in the details. While an experienced designer may be successful in matching the design elements with site topography, the actual grading requirements will not be fully appreciated until the designer launches the phase of design that comes after the client has approved the schematic design (SD) phase, and the design development (DD) or detailed design phase is begun. A preliminary site-grading plan is usually the first step of the design process after the client approves the schematic design. It is during the detail design phase that a more precise, accurate site design plan is developed. Using the site design plan as a base, a grading plan is developed at a level of detail pretty close to the final grading plan. During the design development phase, a planting plan, early detail sections and construction details, and selection of materials will be developed. A staking or layout plan is created, whereby horizontal control is provided for the contractor, demonstrating how to locate and lay out all construction elements, including buildings and structures, paved and planting areas, roads and walkways, and all the elements to be constructed. Material selection for paving and walls is also a part of what is detailed in the design development phase. Decisions on other material and equipment selections are also made, such as for lighting, site furnishings, and irrigation.

GETTING FROM THE SITE AND THE DESIGN TO GRADING THE SITE

Grading is a creative process informed by an understanding of simple geometric concepts used to manipulate an existing topography to achieve a set of landform design intentions. The grading design intent might be as simple as creating a series of earthen mounds to given another layer of form and interest to a landscape planting. Grading to create a variety of landforms is used to add a layer of physical and visual challenge for a golfer approaching a hole. Manipulation of a project's topography might be necessary to direct surface water off a sports field or paved surface, or might be necessary to reduce the potential of flooding a building. Site grading may include an earthwork strategy for detaining surface water by creating a system of ponds and bioswales. The experienced designer considers grading as a useful tool for achieving both functional and aesthetic objectives. So, where to begin? We shall begin with the landscape itself. The scene in Figure 11.2 is a landscape, a rural agricultural landscape in central China.

If we had the task of designing, say, a cluster of cultural-tourism cottages somewhere on these slopes, we would need at least two items, before we should commence developing some preliminary ideas for the project. First, we would need a scaled map showing property boundaries, and second, a topographic map comparable to the quad maps available from the USGS. The Chinese equivalent to a USGS-type map is useful for an initial site evaluation. In the case of a large tract of land, this topographic map will help us identify the areas most suitable for potential development and could be used as the basis of preparing a preliminary master plan. At the outset of the site design phase, a more precise topographic survey of the portion of the property to be designed would be necessary. The survey would be done through the services of a professional land surveyor.

The topographic survey of a site in the USA might look like the one shown in Figure 11.3. In studying the topography in Figure 11.3, we are able to glean very useful information to inform and inspire our work. The contour lines that are close together tell us the areas on the property that are steep; in some cases they are too steep for locating building clusters, and perhaps too steep for an entry road, but they may be perfect for a walking trail. Where the contours are spread further

Figure 11.2 First start with the landscape

apart, we can see areas more suitable for grouping the buildings, parking, and perhaps sport facilities. The existing central landform winding horizontally across the map delineates upper and lower less steep areas, suggesting perhaps the creation of two separate developments that share the central more mountainous area. This central area could serve valuable watershed management and greenbelt purposes, including recreation.

Figure 11.3 A topographic survey with contours reveals a diversity of landforms and suggests the ideal locations for different program elements and circulation

Figures 11.4 and 11.5 illustrate what contours might look like if they were drawn on actual landscapes. Figure 11.4 represents a more or less uniform slope of 10 to 15 percent. The contours are spaced (horizontal distance) approximately 7 to 10 feet apart. Figure 11.5 is a hillside slope with a constructed pond at the foot of the sloping ground. In both cases the contours are conceptual, drawn as diagrams and not intended as accurate representations.

Figure 11.4 Visualizing a slope with contour lines

Figure 11.5 Contour lines reveal a sculpted landform

CONTOURS USED TO SHOW LANDFORM

There are two major reasons for site grading. The first—and we will discuss this and the other reason more fully in the following sections—is to modify the existing landforms of a site to accommodate the programmed elements, creating level areas for building pads, for instance, or gently sloping ground to accommodate a road or walking trail. The second is to reshape the existing landforms to direct water away from areas where it is not wanted. For example, the designer may direct surface water away from the front of a building, to prevent flooding, or use grading to avoid ponding (standing water) in a programmed use area on the site. To accomplish either goal, the designer prepares a site-grading plan. The creation of this plan involves a combination of contour modifications and spot elevations supplemented with other conventions, including slope direction arrows and sections to graphically represent the grading design intentions.

CREATING LANDFORMS FOR PROGRAMMED USES

Figures 11.6-A through 11.6-D each provide a snapshot of the same scene. Figure 11.6-A is a photograph of the site and serves as a base for the next images. Figure 11.6-B is the same site, but with hypothetical contour lines drawn in. The elevation of each contour is added in Figure 11.6-C. As additional information is added, we gain a greater understanding of the site, and we can use that information to be more precise in determining the degree of slope of its topography. Figure 11.6-D contains the same information in the previous images, but in plan. Working in plan, the designer has the ability to make modifications of the landform to achieve some specific purpose, such as creating a building pad for a structure.

Contours are a convenience created as a means to visualize in two dimensions what a three-dimensional topography might look like as the designer manipulates the contours. Second, contours are a graphic tool that allows a landscape architect to make modifications of an existing landform. This is accomplished as the designer rearranges the contours to achieve some new landform created for a specific purpose. In Figure 11.6-A, one can see the sculptural relief of a landscape. There is an upper area defined by a fairly steep slope that wraps around to frame a lower, flatter area. To help the viewer better visualize the scene, and to add numerical values of elevation contours, lines have been drawn in Figure 11.6-B. The pattern and placement of the contour lines could have been interpolated visually; however, they would normally be derived from a land survey conducted on the property. The contours themselves require elevation values to be useful. The elevation values are shown in Figure 11.6- C. The contours in Figure 11.6-C are labeled starting at the lower end of the slope, beginning at 100, which designates 100 feet above sea level or 100 feet above a known physical bench mark established by the local jurisdiction. The contours gain a foot in elevation as we go higher up the slope to an elevation of 107 feet. Figure 11.6-D was created to show what the contours would look like in plan.

Figure 11.6-A Landscape without contours

Figure 11.6-B Landscape with contours

Figure 11.6–C Landscape with contours and their elevations

Figure 11.6–D The landscape with the contours shown in plan

Figure 11.7 illustrates how manipulating the contour lines can create a level area, identified in the center of the photograph. The arrows represent the creation of a swale to guide the flow of water from the 106 contour around the level area, and direct the water onto the lower

Figure 11.7 A level area created with contours on a rolling landscape. Dashed lines are existing contours and solid lines are proposed.

elevations of 105, 104, and lower. Figure 11.8 is a professional landscape architect's grading plan that shows a level area created with contours for a playing field. The central area of the grading plan is a large open grass field with steep slopes surrounding the playing area, as represented with contour lines drawn closely together. A small crescent-shaped mound appears in the upper left of the grass field, to partially buffer a water tank to be constructed.

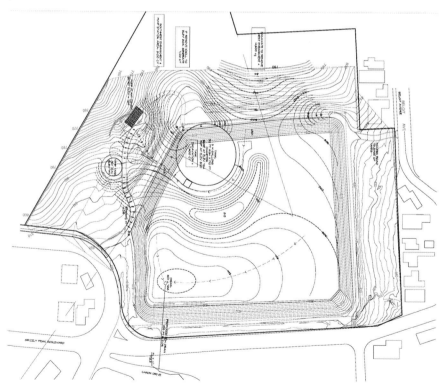

Figure 11.8 Grading plan showing landform created with contour lines
COURTESY OF DILLINGHAM ASSOCIATES

Figures 11.9-A and 11.9-B A portion of sloping farmland with a retention pond at the bottom of the slope

Compare Figure 11.9-A with 11.9-B. Although they are the same scene, 11.9-B includes contour lines. The contours provide additional information about the scene. They emphasize the undulating landform and serve to give the viewer a better understanding of the elevation difference from the lower pond to the upper, planted area. Take an additional step, and a land survey could produce an accurate topographic map of the scene in two dimensions with the contours accurately provided.

From the topographic map one could manipulate the contours to change the landform, for instance to create several small terraced areas on the now sloping ground, to accommodate a meandering walk from the upper area to the pond.

A picture of a culvert inlet is shown in Figure 11.10. You may have often passed by a similar culvert but never stopped to look at it or even noticed its existence—not that you had any reason to do so. Figure 11.10 shows one end of a culvert going under an entrance driveway with a drainage swale that carries water from the upper end of the

Figure 11.10 The drainage swale is directing water toward a culvert

site to the culvert. The culvert is a large-diameter pipe installed under an entrance driveway. The water from the swale is carried downstream through the culvert to the swale that continues on the other side of the access road. The swale is sloping at 2 percent (a 2-foot drop in elevation for every 100 feet of horizontal length). The lines drawn on the image represent contours and where they would fall if they actually existed. Without the photograph, the shape of the contours would be a graphic means to visualize the same landscape in plan, in this case the adjacent slope and swale that carry the water to the culvert entrance.

CONTOURS USED TO SHOW SURFACE DRAINAGE

First, through the activity of site grading, we can transform an existing site's landform to accommodate specific program elements. Another important goal of site grading is to make sure surface water flow across the site landscape avoids flooding and ponding where it is not wanted—for example, the ponding in an entry drive and parking lot shown in Figure 11.11. This ponding could have been avoided by forming the ground surface to direct surface water flow to another location, such as a drainage swale, catch basin system, detention pond, or bioswale. There is a reasonable chance that when the original grading and construction of the area shown in Figure 11.11 were done, they were done correctly. However, the resurfacing of the neighborhood road or some other main-tenance operation may have caused a blockage, allowing water to pond with no way to exit to the adjacent drainage swales. Another possibility is that ground subsidence may have occurred, creating a pond-like sur-face where surface water could collect.

Seemingly paved surfaces such as parking lots and plazas appear level but almost always are sloped, either in one direction as a mono-lithic whole, or, more often, as a series of watersheds with water directed as low as 1 percent to a catch basin, drainage swale, or drain-age system. Catch basins are commonly employed to receive surface water, as in the parking lot shown in Figure 11.12. The photograph was taken several hours after a rain. From the picture you can easily see the pavement is sloping and how the water is directed to the receiving catch basin. The catch basin is connected to an underground, sloping pipe. The water flows through the pipe to a larger storm water system, perhaps located in an adjacent street.

Figure 11.11 Water ponding in a parking lot

Figure 11.12 Area catch basin in a parking lot

In the lawn area of Figures 11.13-A and 11.13-B, you can see how the ground has been sculpted with gently rolling topography and a drainage swale. The swale roughly bisects the lawn area, directing surface water to a catch basin at the top of the image. From the catch basin it is carried by underground pipes to a storm water system, in this case located to an adjacent campus-wide storm drainage system

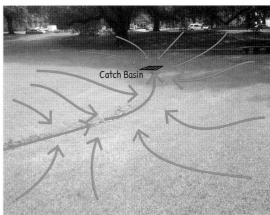

Figures 11.13-A and 11.13-B Lawn area with central drainage swale and catch basin

Stepping back 100 or so feet, we have a broader view of the context, in Figure 11.14, with the same catch basin in the distance. In Figure 11.14 you can see the flow path of surface water shown as arrows directing water to a catch basin located at the lowest elevation of the grass area labelled. The landform created in the space creates a pleasant glade surrounded by massive oak trees. The ground was shaped to direct rainwater to the swale, and from there to the catch basin. The ground, including the paved walkway, has been shaped with gradual slopes of 1 and 2 percent. The slope is adequate to direct excess water, while the actual speed of flow is sufficiently slow to allow time for some of the water to percolate into the soil deep below the surface and provide moisture for the oak trees.

Figure 11.15 shows a drainage swale paralleling a roadway, and Figure 11.16 is a view taken 180 degrees toward a culvert looking along the same swale further downstream. Notice that the slope of the swale was 3 percent in the first photograph and was made less steep as the swale approached the culvert, to slow down the water. The uphill alignment of contours shown in Figure 11.15 is a contour signature (more on contour signatures to be covered in Chapter 12) that represents a drainage swale, valley, ravine, gorge, or gulley on a topographic map.

Figure 11.14 Paths water flows across a landscape

Figure 11.15 A drainage swale collects and carries surface water from the road and adjacent tree-covered slope

The photograph with graphic annotations in Figure 11.17 follows the same contour signature of the swale. This contour signature characterizes a valley or ravine in a mountainous landscape. Note how the contours move up the highway, creating an inverted V shape. This inverted V shape is a contour signature for a valley, swale, or ravine landform. Notice further how the contours bow or follow around the hills on either side of the highway valley. This rounded or bowed-out form of successive contours is the signature of a hill, mound, or embankment.

The pattern of trees—in some instances planted by the farmers—and the country road found in Figure 11.18 follow the terrain much as contours would do. Notice how the lines of trees roughly approximate how contours would follow the terrain in the landscape and bow out to reinforce the hill signature, as opposed to how they turn upslope to form a valley following the contours in Figure 11.17. While the same landscape without the pattern of trees would still be seen as a hilly landscape, the tree pattern accentuates the sculptural quality of the hilly terrain. If you were to look at a topographic map of this same landscape, with the contours, you should be able to distinguish and visualize the valley and the hill-forming patterns.

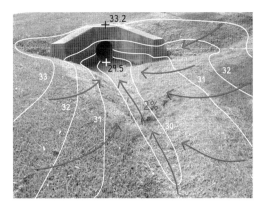

Figure 11.16 The culvert allows water in the swale to pass under an entrance road

Figure 11.17 The path of the I 405 Freeway in Los Angeles follows the base of a mountain and valley landscape, in this case a mountain pass

Figure 11.18 Rural farmland in Northern Spain

PAVED SURFACES WATER FLOW

One does not think of paved surfaces such as plazas, parking lots, and trails and roads as being plastic in the same sense as earthen landforms, which can be shaped like clay. But paved surfaces (made from concrete, asphalt, and even modular precast forms) can be warped to shapes that are undulating to a certain degree of sculptural fluidity. Visualize a skateboard park with its undulating, daredevil-challenging ramps and sunken, bowl-shaped areas. The parking lot shown in Figures 11.19-A and 11.19-B is another, less extreme example of a warped, modestly sculpted paved surface. The asphalt was laid down with a purposefully warped surface so as to direct water drainage (runoff) toward a catch basin located next to the curb on the left of the parking spaces. The diagram in Figure 11.19-B shows what the contours might look like to achieve a warped surface. The contours together with the arrows showing the direction of surface water should give you some idea of the shape of the warped paved surface. The parking lot is set at a higher elevation at either end near the entranceways. The surface is tilted or sloped (perhaps 2 percent) toward the middle of the lot, with a crown along the central drive lane. At the same time, the surface is warped toward either side of the drive lane, with water flowing toward catch basins at the curb located at the front end of the parking spaces.

Figures 11.19-A and 11.19-B Campus parking lot

Figures 11.20 and 11.21 show two different views of the same parking lot. Follow the drainage arrows in the parking lot shown in Figure 11.20. The surface water sheet flows toward the curb and is allowed to drain to the adjacent entry drive though a channel. The view of the same parking lot in Figure 11.21 was taken to help the viewer visualize the drainage pattern. In this case, the parking lot surface was divided into several sections with each section sloped toward the curb and catch basin. The sections of pavement were designed so that water is directed toward the curb; at the same time, the lot has been graded so that water flows along the curb toward either a catch basin or drainage channel outlet. Surface water is directed by elevating the driving lane forming a crown at a higher elevation than the parking spaces, thus directing surface flow to the curbs.

Figures 11.22-A and 11.22-B show two diagrams graphically representing two approaches for contour grading a simple parking lot. The contours in Figure 11.22- B direct the flow of surface water toward the center of the driving lane, while the surface water is directed toward the perimeter of the parking spaces in Figure 11.22-A. Note the location of the catch basin in the figure. The arrows show the direction surface water directed from centerline (dashed line A) of the parking lot toward the catch basin.

Figure 11.20 In this view the water from the parking lot is directed to a channel crossing through a planting area toward an adjacent entrance driveway

Figure 11.21 View of parking lot showing how surface water might be directed across its surface to catch basins

Figures 11.22-A and 11.22-B Two parking lots with different approaches for directing surface water

HOW TO CREATE A LEVEL AREA ON SLOPING GROUND

One of the common tasks in grading is to create a level area on sloping ground to accommodate a building structure. The first step in the process is to establish an elevation for the level area. A good place to start is to set the elevation somewhere close to the elevation of the middle ground of the slope. For instance, if the contours where you intend to create the level area are between 101 and 105, you might set the level area at elevation 102.5. After working to develop a solution using 102.5, you might find that setting the elevation a foot[1] higher or lower may work out better for a variety of reasons that become evident as you work to devise a solution using 102.5.

Once a working elevation is established for the level area, the next steps involve redrawing and modifying the existing contours, first to create the level area and second to direct the surface drainage of water around the level

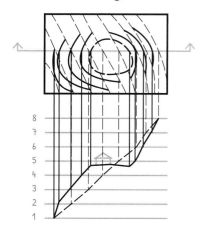

Figure 11.23 Plan and section views representing the use of contours to create level surfaces

. . . .

1 You may raise or lower the elevation less than one foot, or alternatively two or more feet, depending on your design intent and site limitations.

area toward the lower elevations below. Figure 11.23 and Figures 11.24-A and 11.24-B are diagrams showing how these two goals are graphically portrayed. The assumption here is that one of the design intentions is to create a level area that is to remain dry. That is, an area where surface waters are directed away, so as not to allow water to flood the structure, in the case of a residence, school, or other building. Seems a reasonable goal. Think of Figure 11.24 as representing a signature landform a designer can employ in solving many grading and surface drainage situations.

Now let's look a little more closely at the various elements involved in creating a level area on sloping ground. Considering Figure 11.25, let's look at the specific contour grading details commonly used to create a building pad with swales. Notice in this example that the ground is sloping from the bottom of the figure, beginning with contour 35 downward toward contour 27. Area E is the general area in which we want to create a level area. This could be for a building or a site for a group picnic area. Area E could be graded level or slightly sloping, perhaps at 1 or 2 percent toward contour 31. We might also want to set the elevation of the level area. Elevation 31.5 would be a good starting elevation. If we use 31.5, we next need to establish the elevation of point A (the beginning of the swale we will create to direct water runoff away from pad). The elevation should be lower than 31.5, somewhere between, say, 31.4 and the next lowest contour, which is 31. A good average would be 31.25; that way, surface water

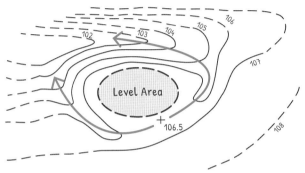

Figures 11.24-A and Figure 11.24-B Oblique plan view depicting the grading plan signature for creating a building pad. The same plan view superimposed over a photograph of the actual site to better visualize the form the grading signature takes for creating a building pad and directing surface runoff away from the area.

coming from the level area and from the 31 contour would flow to the 3.25 elevation (not into the building site), and then the water would flow following the arrows (labeled B on both sides of the area E) around the level area to the lower slopes of contours 31, 30, 29, and so on. Notice that the new contours in the area labeled C have been realigned toward the uphill, which in effect is producing cut or removal of earth material. The contours noted in the D area have been moved downhill, which in effect is filling the lower slope in order to create a level area shown in E. By realigning some contours uphill (cut) and downhill (fill) we are working towards balancing cut and fill.

Also notice that in this example the area where cut will take place, the 32-contour is the last contour to be moved. Contours 33 and higher will not have to be moved, as we have not shifted any lower elevation contours on top or pass the 33. Likewise, contour 27 is the last contour moved in the downhill area as the 27 does not overlay past the 26-contour.

Figure 11.26 is an example of what a grading plan might look like, applying this contour signature with drainage swales. Note that in this figure the finish floor elevation (FFE) is shown as 80.25´ on the building pad. It is customary to assign a finished floor elevation in grading plans. The contours that form the pad are at elevations decreasing as they move away from the building area. This configuration of contours ensures that surface water flows away from the pad and down-slope.

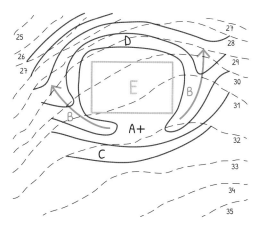

Figure 11.25 Diagram of how contours are used to create a level area

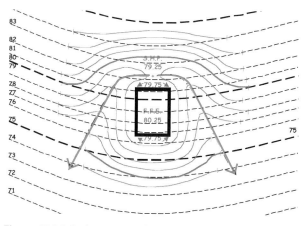

Figure 11.26 Preliminary grading plan showing signature swale solution

COURTESY OF SADIK ARTUNC

Figure 11.27 is of a proposed small parking lot in a park. A grading solution with proposed contours (the solution) is illustrated, with solid lines and existing contours shown as dashed lines. Note how the designer divided the parking lot with the center island made the highest elevation, similar to a crown. The contours are laid out to slope surface water diagonally from the center island toward the back corners of the parking lot. At these corners a catch basin was installed. Another solution would have been to create a curb break and install a channel opening in the curb, allowing the water to sheet flow downhill, perhaps into a rain garden. Either solution would have solved the problem of what to do with the water coming off the parking lot surface. The catch basin may be the preferred solution, depending on the sensitivity of the surrounding undisturbed landscape—for example, if there was a wetland system nearby. Also notice how the designer created a hill-like feature in the back area using the 86 and 87 contour lines.

The last example to demonstrate the use of contour lines with spot elevations and slope arrows is shown in Figure 11.28. In this example a grading design having both a walkway with steps and a ramped walkway (to provide for handicapped access) is presented. From this site-grading plan you are able to see the number and location of spot elevations needed. The solution is a straightforward one requiring minimal

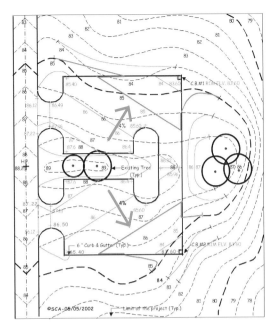

Figure 11.27 Small parking lot preliminary grading plan
COURTESY OF SADIK ARTUNC

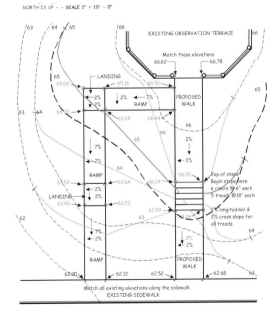

Figure 11.28 Preliminary grading plan for a proposed set of entrance walks
COURTESY OF SADIK ARTUNC

movement of earth. Another design approach to this site-grading solution would be to round or bow out the new contours located between the two walkways in an arrangement that mimics the existing landform. This grading design would tend to blend the walkways with the adjacent landscape forms.

The next step the designer would take would be to estimate quantities of cut and fill. The quantity estimate is needed when putting together an estimate of probable cost for all aspects of the project, including concrete, landscape planting, irrigation, and any other designed elements that make up the project. As long as the estimate of probable cost falls closely within the project budget, there may not be a reason for considering design changes to reduce costs. In the case of site grading, cost reduction may not be feasible, given the minimal amount of grading needed for this particular site-grading plan. The same assessment could apply to the site-grading plan in Figure 11.29. The grading design for this example required minimal grading, since the new contours do not extend very far into the surrounding landscape, but instead remain pretty close to the outline of the parking lot. A method for estimating cut and fill quantities is covered in a later chapter.

Figure 11.29 Retention pond, Hamilton College Theatre and Studio Arts
COURTESY OF REED HILDERBRAND ASSOCIATES

12

SIGNATURE SOLUTIONS

In this chapter you will learn about:

- Eight common signature solutions for solving most site-grading problems
- Applying several of the signature solutions in combination to create a site-grading plan

INTRODUCTION

Each landscape site is unique, complete with its own idiosyncratic physical qualities and complex natural processes. The human component, in the form of constructed improvements or activities, adds further layers of complexity to a project site. In the activity of site grading, the focus is primarily on the topography and the movement of water onto and across the site. Site grading provides the foundation that can integrate landscape and design into an experiential, aesthetic, and functional whole. Although each landscape site is different, the solutions to site grading often follow one of several standard approaches known as signature grading solutions. Even though grading plans may look different—and they are different in detail—there are more similarities than one might realize. In this chapter the basic approaches to solving grading problems will be presented. A step-by-step process that will lead the reader through several grading solutions will be presented. The goal of presenting these step-by-step approaches is not to minimize the complexities involved in arriving at a site-grading plan, but to provide insight on how to think about and work through the grading process for most grading situations that might be encountered.

The common signature grading solutions that a designer might consider in preparing a site grading have been distilled to eight. The eight are shown in Figure 12.1. It is likely that any combination of the eight might be used to solve the grading for any single site design. A brief description of the eight signature grading solutions follows.

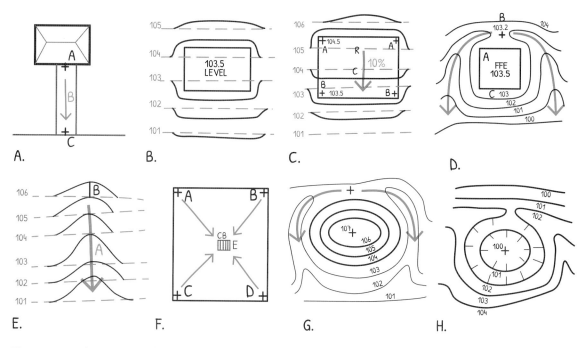

Figure 12.1 **A** Creating a simple slope, **B** Creating a level area on sloping ground, **C** Creating a sloping surface, **D** Creating a swale around a level surface, **E** Creating a swale, **F** Creating a watershed to collect water, **G** Creating sculpted landform, **H** Creating a detention pond or depression

SIGNATURE GRADING SOLUTIONS

Creating a Simple Slope

One of the most common tasks in preparing a grading plan is to create a sloping surface such as a section of walk, paved surface, or sloping landscape area or playing field. To create a sloping surface involves establishing or determining the elevations (spot elevation) of two points, one at the uphill point and one on the downhill point of the sloping feature. To create a 5 percent slope, as shown in Figure 12.2, the designer would need to establish the elevations for spot elevations A and B. The elevation is given for spot elevation A: 34.5´. In order to calculate the ele-

vation of point B, the designer would need to first know and be working with a scaled plan, and then would have to decide the percent of slope of the walkway wanted between points A and B. Once the slope is determined—in this case it is 5 percent—the designer would measure the horizontal distance between the two points, then apply the formula S = V / H to calculate the elevation of point B. Assume the horizontal distance between the two points as measured with a scale on the plan is 35 feet.

Figure 12.2 Sloping walkway leading from a parking lot to an upper building area

$$S = V / H$$

$$.05 = V / 35$$

$$V = -05 \times 35 \qquad = 1.85 \text{ feet}$$

Finally, to calculate the elevation of point B, subtract the answer from the given calculation (1.85) from the elevation of point A. If point A was 35.5´ then the elevation for point B is:

$$35.5 - 1.85 = 33.65'$$

The same procedure for determining the elevation of a spot elevation of the ground could also be used in locating the new position of a contour, assuming a desired percent

Figure 12.3 Locating the contours that help create a 5 percent slope on this walkway. Knowing elevations and the beginning of a slope (A) and the bottom of a slope (B) one can determine location of intermediate contours between the two points.

of slope. In this case, we want to determine the distance of the next contour going downhill from point A. The elevation of point A is 34.5, and the contours we are trying find are 33 and 34.

S = V / H

S = .05

V = (34.5 – 34) = .05′

.05 = .5′ / H H = .5 / .05   H = 10′

Contour 34 is located 10 feet downslope from point A. If this were a site-grading plan, the designer would use an engineer's scale and locate the contour 10 feet on the walkway from point A. Next, locate contour 33:

S = V / H

S = .05

V – (34 – 33) = 1.0′

.05 / 1.0′ / H   H = 1.0 / .05   H = 20′

Contour 33 is located 20 feet downslope from contour 34. Using an engineer's scale, the designer would locate the contour on the site-grading plan 20 feet on the walkway from contour 34.

CREATING A LEVEL AREA ON SLOPING GROUND

Another common requirement is to create a level area (for a building or structure) on sloping ground. In the case of creating an area for a building such as a residence, the designer would need to assign an elevation for the level building pad, as shown in Figures 12.4-A and 12.4-B. This elevation is referred to as the finish floor elevation (FFE or FF are interchangeable). The simplest approach for assigning this elevation is to find the average elevation between the highest and lowest contour where the pad is located. In the example the upper end of the pad is located between contours 104 and 105, and the lower end of the pad is located close to the 102 contour between the 102 and 103 contours. To determine

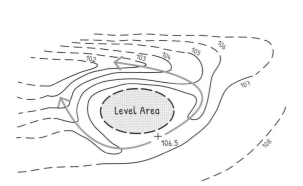 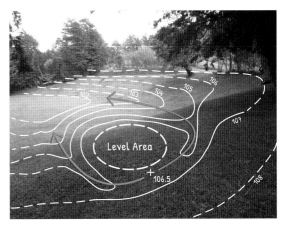

Figures 12.4-A and 12.4-B Figure 12.4-A is a plan view of the contours shown in Figure 12.4-B

the finish floor elevation in this example, the average slope is calculated as follows:

104.5 − 102. 5 = 2.0′

2.0′ / 2 = 1.0′ then

Add the result of 1.0´ to 102.5 = 103.5. This is your initial elevation for the proposed building.

Once the finish floor elevation is determined, the other existing contours would be manipulated following the example in Figure 12.1-D.

SIGNATURE SOLUTION: CREATING A SLOPING SURFACE

Grading an existing site to accommodate a building, a paved surface for a parking lot, or a sports field considers two basic grading operations: (1) creating a level or moderate sloping surface, and (2) collecting and directing surface drainage to direct excess water away from the level surface being prepared for a structure, paved surface, or sports field. Figure 12.1-D is a diagram that combines the two grading procedures: creating a level or sloping surface and creating a swale to carry surface water away from the level area. Figure 12.4-A represents what this grading operation would look like in plan, and Figure 12.4-B overlays the grading plan with its contours onto the landscape to help the viewer visualize the three-dimensional aspect of the grading solution.

Figures 12.5-A through 12.5-E provide a closer look at this signature grading solution. In this example, the building pad is a rectangular shape with a uniform slope of 2% beginning at corner B and sloping toward corner C. The designer would need to begin by establishing an elevation for corner A. Once an elevation is established for corner A, the designer would next calculate the elevations for the other corners, then reposition the contour lines that will create the sloping plane and surrounding drainage swales. The process for creating this grading solution is shown in Figure 12.6.

Where the designer has placed a sloping paved surface such as a tennis court, patio, or parking lot on sloping terrain, spot elevations as well as contours will need to be calculated and located, representing the desired modifications of the existing terrain. The signature solution shown in Figure 12.1-C can be thought of as the application of two signature solutions, 12.1-A and 12.1-B, to solve the grading situation. Also consider that in this example it is not necessary to inhibit the flow of surface water onto the pad surface, as we will do in the signature solution shown in Figure 12.1-D.

In the example shown in Figure 12.5 -A, the spot elevation (B) for the uphill corner of the pad surface is 104.5. Notice that this spot elevation falls between two existing contours: 104 and 105, so the designer decided to set the elevation of the corner at 104.5´. Next, the designer would begin at the 104.5 spot elevation and use the slope designation of 2 percent to determine the elevation of spot elevation (C), using the formula $S = V / H$. The elevation for spot elevation (C) was calculated as 102.5´ (Figure 12.5-B).

Considering Figure 12.5-B, the designer would notice that two contours could be located between the two spot elevations 104.5 and 102.5. These contours are 103 and 104. To find their location the designer would use the formula $S = V / H$. For instance, to find the location of contour 104, take the vertical elevation difference of 104.5 and 104, which is 0.5´:

$$S = V / H$$

$$.02 = .5 / H$$

$$H = .5 / .02 \qquad = 25 \text{ feet}$$

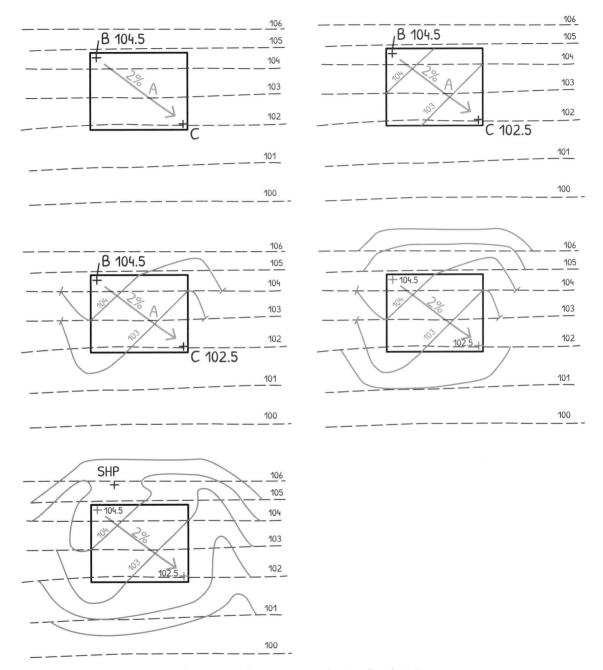

Figures 12.5-A through 12.5-E Plan view with beginning spot elevation B and existing contours

The designer would then locate the 104 contour by measuring 25 feet downslope from point B. To find the location of contour 103, take the vertical elevation difference between 104 and 103, 1.0´. See Figure 12.5-C.

S = V / H

.02 = 1 / H

H = 1 / .02 = 50 feet

The designer would then locate the 103 contour by measuring 50 feet downslope from contour 104. See Figure 12.5-C.

In Figure 12.5-D the designer has connected the 103 and 104 contours that cross over the pad surface to meet their respective existing contours outside of the pad surface. The contractor would grade the slope following the grading plan directions depicted with the new position of the two contours. The contractor would complete the grading following the contours shown in Figure 12.5-E.

CREATING A SWALE AROUND A LEVEL SURFACE TO DIRECT SURFACE WATER FLOW AWAY FROM A BUILDING OR ACTIVITY AREA

Now let's look at the process of applying the signature grading solution, beginning with Figure 12.6-A. The figure shows a level area delineated with black lines where a proposed building structure is to be located. In order to establish a working elevation for the level area, an elevation midway between the two extreme elevations of the proposed building location must be determined. The two points A and B on the uphill and downhill outlined pad area represent the elevation range on the existing topography.

Establish an elevation for the pad. Assume the designer wishes to balance cut and fill so the elevation can be midway between point B on the uphill side and point A at the lowest downhill point from point B. The existing elevation of point A is 103´, and the elevation of point B is approximately 105.2´.

- Pad elevation is: 105.2 – 103 = 2.2´.

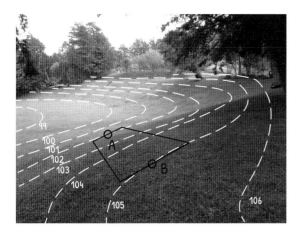

Figure 12.6-A Step One: Location of proposed building pad with elevation showing points A and B to be used in determining the elevation of the pad (FFE)

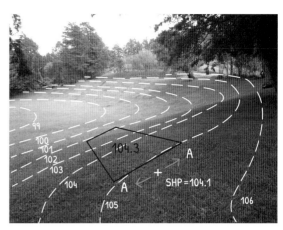

Figure 12.6-B Step Two

- Half of 2.2′ = 1.1′.

- Adding 1.1′ to 103′ gives the midway elevation of the pad at 104.1′. See Figure 12.6-B.

Establish the swale high point (SHP) elevation. Establishing this elevation requires us to consider many variables, such as the distance to locate this elevation from the building pad and the planned uses for areas adjacent with the pad. As a rule of thumb, position the SHP upslope from the pad area and midway, so that surface water is divided to flow down-hill equally to either side and away from the pad. The SHP elevation should be lower than the pad elevation so that surface water coming from the back side of the pad follows a 1% slope.

Notice the shape of contour 104 in Figure 12.6-C. This shape characterizes the signature of this solution. The 104 contour wraps around the proposed building pad and forms a swale to direct water from the

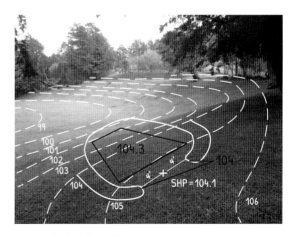

Figure 12.6-C Step Three

upper 105 contour and surrounding in the direction of the 103 contour and below. Notice the arrows marked B in Figure 12.6-D; they show the slope of the swale that should be a minimum of 2%, steeper if the natural ground is steeper, but no more than 5 percent to minimize erosion of the swale.

After establishing the 104 contour signature, the next steps are to continue extending the swale, locating the subsequent swale contours to create the desired bottom of swale slope (see Figure 12.6-E). If the slope were 2%, then the contours would be 50 feet apart.

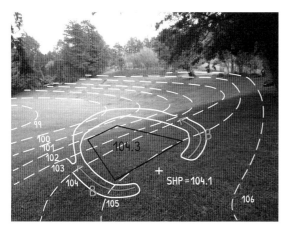

Figure 12.6-D Step Four

Figure 12.6-E Step Five

The remaining swale slope contours are put in place. Notice two things: First, the swale ends at approximately the 100-contour. When the next contours after the last one modified are located so as to achieve the desired swale slope (in this case 2%), then this is where the swale stops.

Notice items A and B in Figure 12.6-E. Item A indicates the horizontal distance from the edge of the pad to contour 104. This distance is calculated considering the desired slope of the ground. If the area is not paved, then the slope could be 1% to 3%, depending on the treatment and use. Generally, the swale would probably be positioned at a greater distance away from the building pad to allow some other use associated with the function of the pad area. If the pad was for a residence there might be space provided for landscape improvement, a patio and walkway, and maybe a pool with deck. If this is the case, the swale could be 20 to 30 feet away from the pad so that the ground slope away from the pad might be set at 1% or 2%.

Item B represents the width of the swale. The width could vary along the length of the swale and should be sized so that the side slope is no greater than 2% to 5% (as a rule of thumb, it could be greater on less erosive soils).

The final steps (see Figure 12.6-F) are to reposition the contours 105 and higher. Notice that in this example contour 105 is

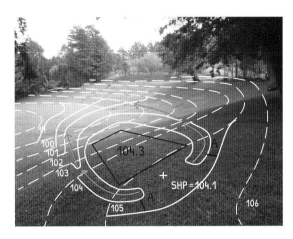

Figure 12.6-F Step Six

modified, as the 104 contour was repositioned to cross over the 105 contour. If other contours were affected they would need to be modified as well. The area where the 105 contour is modified is called the back slope and—in this case—is creating cut. In modifying the 105 the designer should create a back slope that will not cause erosion if too steep.

CREATING A DRAINAGE SWALE

A drainage swale can be created and placed in the landscape with the purpose of collecting surface water and directing it to another location on a project site. The water could be directed to an on-site pond, a neighborhood drainage canal, or a catch basin that is connected by an underground pipe to a storm water collection system. A constructed drainage swale could also be adapted into a system of bioswales that in turn might be components of an on-site detention or retention pond system. While a simple swale is created solely for collecting and directing water, a bioswale is designed for the added purpose of slowing down water flow to allow the water to percolate into the soil, eventually recharging a subsurface aquifer, or into the water table. A bioswale is also designed to incorporate plantings of species that are selected to uptake a variety of pollutants dissolved in or carried by the water entering into the swale, such as oil or various chemicals found in a parking lot, or chemicals such as pesticides or fertilizer carried from nearby planting areas by the surface water flow.

Figures 12.7-A and 12.7-B Photograph diagram of drainage swale along the side of a road and a plan view of same location of drainage swale along the side of the same road

Figures 12.7-A and 12.7-B give an example of a drainage swale running along a road. The process of creating a drainage swale is shown in Figures 12.8-A through 12.8-D. In this example, the designer is to create a drainage swale that also functions as a bioswale.

Decide where you want a swale and the desired slope. Establish a slope for the swale that is a minimum of 2% and no steeper than 12% to 15%. On terrain that has less erosive soils, steeper slopes are possible. Generally, swales with steeper slopes carrying high volumes of water tend to cause erosion.

In this case a slope of 5% is being considered. In order to achieve a 5% slope, contours will be positioned 20 feet apart.

$$S = V / H$$

$$.05 + 1 / H$$

$$H = 20 \text{ feet}$$

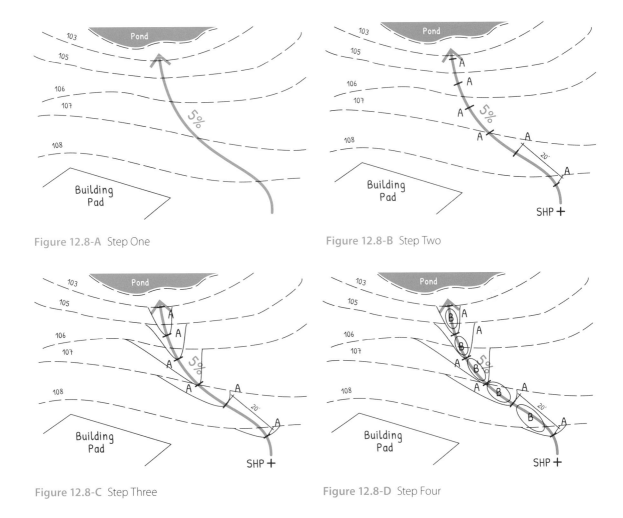

Figure 12.8-A Step One

Figure 12.8-B Step Two

Figure 12.8-C Step Three

Figure 12.8-D Step Four

Tick marks (A) have been placed along the swale alignment with 20-foot spacing.

The next step is to alter each contour along the route of the swale, beginning with the 108, to meet the 20-foot interval A.

Where the designer wishes to retain surface water, to support a wider diversity of plant species along the swale, a bioswale with intermediate small retention ponds or depressions (B) may be created. The depth and area of these depressions may vary, depending on the designer's intent: aesthetics or type of plant species desired.

CREATING A WATERSHED TO COLLECT SURFACE WATER

Often, the desire to grade a project so that water is directed toward other locations on-site—or to create a sheet flow from one area to another—is not entirely feasible. A reasonable alternative is to simply sheet flow or direct surface water to be collected either in a detention pond or a system of catch basins that are connected by underground piping and carried to a city storm water collection system.

One way to visualize a catchment system is to think of such a system as a watershed, a small one perhaps, serving an area of several hundred square feet or less—or a larger area, but less than one acre. The photograph in Figure 12.9-A was taken of a portion of a mountain range in Southern California. The mountains in the photograph make up three adjacent sub-watersheds, and each of the three is further subdivided into drainage courses or natural swales. A watershed is an area bounded by higher landform—for example, a series of ridges with a swale or V-shaped valley or stream—that carries the rainwater that falls within the bounded area ultimately to a single watercourse or body of water, such as a river, lake, wetlands, or ocean. The photograph in

Figure 12.9-A Watershed in Southern California mountains and small watershed-like area within a larger paved walkway

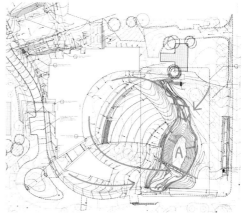

Figure 12.9-B Portion of a professional grading plan designed to gather surface water from amphitheater and behind building to retention pond below
COURTESY OF REED HILDERBRAND

Figure 12.9-B was taken of an expanse of pavement within a larger central campus quadrangle. The area outlined with a dashed line is in effect a small watershed where any water that falls within the dashed area flows toward a central point where a catch basin has been constructed. The purpose of the catch basin is to carry the water underground in pipes to a nearby storm water system (part of a city's storm water infrastructure).

CATCH BASIN DESIGN IN PAVED AREA

Once the designer has created a paved area, consideration will be given to subdividing the area into smaller quadrants or watersheds to handle surface drainage. By doing this, the designer creates the feeling of a level, rather than sloping, paved area. The number and area dimensions of quadrants can vary. See Figure 12.10-A.

The arrows in Figure 12.10-B indicate the desired surface flow of storm water. The arrows within the dashed area show that water is intended to flow toward a catch basin located in the center of the quadrant. The designer would establish an elevation for the perimeter that would most likely be the same throughout the entire perimeter.

Figure 12.10-A Step One

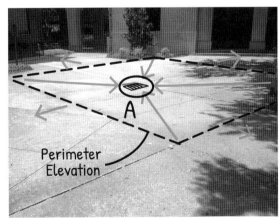

Figure 12.10-B Step Two

The designer would then select the arrows going from the quadrant corners (A) to the catch basin, indicating direction and percentage of slope (see Figure 12.10-C). Starting with a slope of 1 percent, the elevation of the catch basin would be established. To check to see if 1 percent is too steep, calculate the percent of slope from the midway points of the watershed outline to the catch basin. The calculated slope should be less than 2 percent. If it is more, then reduce the slope from the corners to the catch basin as low as .5 percent slope (paved areas in a plaza-like situation can work with .5 or 1 percent slopes).

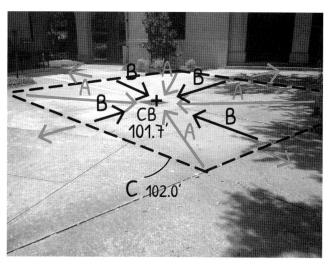

Figure 12.10-C Step Three

The consideration for setting the catch basin elevation is to start by creating a .5 or 1 percent slope along the longest diagonal from the corners to the catch basin. If the slope along the longest diagonal is 1 percent, the shorter distances from the watershed outline to the catch basin will be slightly steeper. In order for the surface to appear "flat" or level—which would be an appropriate design intent in a plaza situation—the pavement where surface water travels the least distance should not be greater than 1 or 1.5 percent. If the slopes for the shorter distances are steeper than 1.5 percent, then revise the longest diagonal to less than 1 percent, say, to .5 percent of slope. In this example, the perimeter elevation is 102.0′, and the catch basin rim elevation is 101.7′.

CREATING A SCULPTED LANDFORM

Site grading can be guided by practical considerations as well as the aesthetic goals of the designer. Successful site-grading solutions pay attention to both the practical and aesthetic potential of a project site. During the process, the designer will work to accommodate programmed design features while seeking to manipulate the existing topography to add three-dimensional interest, as depicted in the example shown in Figure 12.11. In this example, the designer not only modified the landscape to accommodate an entrance road but also created a sculpted landform to enhance the dramatic interest of the landscape and the experience of the motorist. The resulting sculpted landform creates a varied visual experience for the entrance road as well as dramatic views to the surrounding buildings.

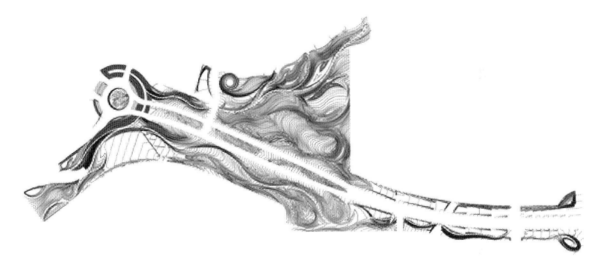

Figure 12.11 Computer-generated grading plan
BY PERMISSION OF DESIGN WORKSHOP, DENVER CO

The park located in a high-rise residential area in Lower Manhattan shown in Figure 12.12 makes use of highly sculpted landforms. The resulting composition creates visual interest and spatial variety reinforced by the designer's intention of creating a diversity of interconnected spaces. The park contains a variety of use areas, made visually cohesive with calculated plantings complemented by a skilled site-grading plan. Figures 12.13 and 12.14 provide a snapshot of the different spaces set within sculpted landforms.

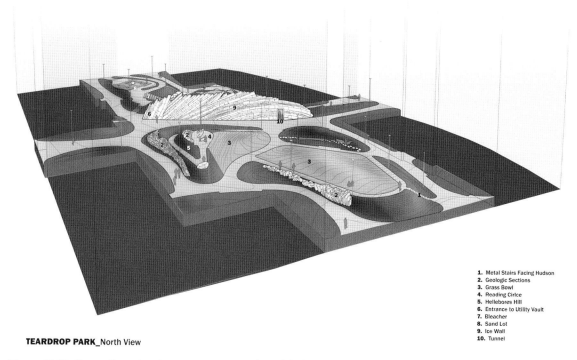

1. Metal Stairs Facing Hudson
2. Geologic Sections
3. Grass Bowl
4. Reading Cirlce
5. Hellebores Hill
6. Entrance to Utility Vault
7. Bleacher
8. Sand Lot
9. Ice Wall
10. Tunnel

TEARDROP PARK_North View

Figure 12.12 Three-dimensional computer generated model of Teardrop Park, New York
BY PERMISSION OF MICHAEL VAN VALKENBURG ASSOCIATES

Figure 12.13 Children's slide and playground in Teardrop Park, New York

Figure 12.14 Carefully sculpted lawn area provides visual and experiential interest at Teardrop Park, New York

CREATING A DETENTION POND OR DEPRESSION

The design of a site-grading plan must include an integrated response to the issue of water that flows across the surface of a project site, whether as the result of natural occurrences such as rain, or of human causes, including changes of topography in the course of construction.in The designer can create a swale, or a system of swales can be used to gather water and direct it to another location on-site. Often there is the requirement to retain or detain surface water on-site rather than direct it to a municipal storm water system. Increasingly, government entities require that best management practices[1] be incorporated into a site-grading plan. The grading plan would then include a water detention or retention basin for storing water runoff, and in some cases cleaning it of pollutants and debris through a designed system of bioswales and bioretention ponds. Figure 12.15 shows an on-site pond created to retain surface water runoff carrying dairy farm related pollutants before it reaches a stream located further downhill. Figure 12.16 is an example of an on-site retention pond created to allow storm water time to infiltrate into the ground as well as to capture water-borne silt.

Figure 12.15 Retention pond constructed on a dairy farm in Costa Rica to prevent pollutants from reaching a lower stream on the property

Figure 12.16 Retention pond in a newly created landscape on the University of Georgia campus

. . . .

1 Best management practices (BMP) simply refers to federal, state, and local government mandated storm water and water pollution control requirements, primarily requiring storm water and runoff to be contained within a site, rather than carried off-site to adjacent natural water bodies (rivers and lakes) or a municipal storm water system.

SITE-GRADING CONCEPTS FOR A SIMPLE RESIDENTIAL LOT

This chapter has presented a way to think about site grading as the application of a variety of signature solutions. The signature solutions approach is a way to visualize site grading; these solutions are not meant to be applied as simply as one applies colors selected from a palette to a canvass. The designer might first consider one or more of these solutions as a means to solving a site-grading problem. In actual application, designers may not think in terms of signatures, but for the beginning student it might be helpful to consider them as a way to get started. The way site grading has been presented in this chapter should not minimize the complexities challenging the designer in arriving at a practical and aesthetically pleasing site-grading solution.

In the following examples, different signature solutions are presented to show how one might approach a site-grading problem. To decide which is the most practical or desirable solution, the designer would consider a number of factors. Cost is always a consideration for selecting what is best, as well as site conditions such as topographic constraints, and the project program and attendant landform.

THREE INITIAL SITE-GRADING STRATEGIES

Figures 12.17-A through 12.17-C provide a diagrammatic overview of three signature solutions for solving the site grading of a simplified residential site. Signature A is an approach that sets the house at the highest elevation on the site and creates four planes to sheet-drain storm water away from the building to the edges of the property. Signature B sets the house at a high elevation then creates two swales to direct storm water around the building toward the street. This solution assumes that the property generally slopes from the back to the front. The signature solution used to solve the grading problem of site C positions a catch basin at the back of the property to collect storm water that cannot be directed toward the front of the property. The solution for the remainder of the property is to direct surface water to the front and street side of the property.

Keep in mind that, for more complex site conditions and site plans, a combination of the signature solutions presented in this chapter might be used. There are also many variations of each signature solution. Again, presenting grading as an approach that utilizes these solutions is a simplification of what may be required in solving projects with more complex physical conditions and governmental requirements. With practice, the designer develops an approach to each site-grading project based on a sound understanding of the site and the best practices to employ to arrive at a practical and aesthetic solution.

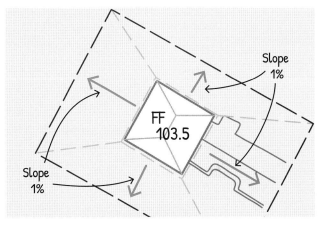

Figure 12.17-A Site grading strategy that sets the building at a higher elevation from surrounding property so that water sheet flows away from building

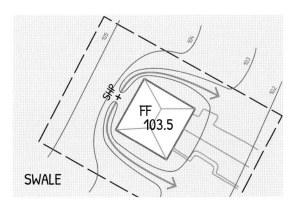

Figure 12.17-B Site grading strategy that sets the building at a higher elevation than surrounding property then creates drainage swale to direct water from back garden toward the front and street

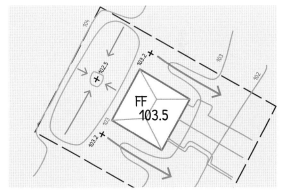

Figure 12.17-C Site grading strategy where a catch basin receives surface water in combination with swales that direct water around building toward the front and street

USE OF SPOT ELEVATIONS AND CONTOUR GRADING FOR A TENNIS COURT OR OTHER LARGE COURT-GAME SURFACE

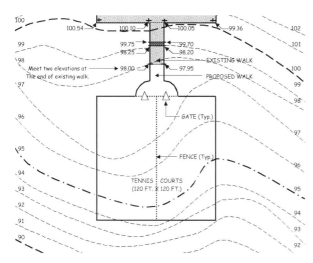

Figures 12.18-A through 12.18-H Plan of double tennis court with existing contours

FIGURES ADAPTED USING IMAGE COURTESY OF SADIK ARTUNC

The next example is for preparing a contour-grading plan for a double tennis court on a sloping site, as shown in Figure 12.18-A. Figure 12.18-B represents the base plan, with existing contours and spot elevations for an existing walk. The process for solving this grading plan would begin with the two spot elevations A and B: 98.0´ and 97.95´. Both spot elevations are at the terminus of the existing walk and are fixed elevations the designer should meet with the new section of walk leading to the tennis court entrance.

STEPS FOR SOLVING THE TENNIS COURT EXAMPLE

- Tennis court to slope as a single plane at 1%

- The centerline of swales to have minimum 2.5% slope starting at SHPs

- Minimum swale width 10′

- Maximum slope in nonpaved areas 20% to 25%

To begin, note that the left side of the existing walk is slightly higher (point A = 98.0´) than the right side (point B = 97.95´). The existing walk was designed with a cross slope of 0.5 or ½ percent. Assume the main slope of the walk is 1 percent and will continue at that slope until it reaches the edge of the tennis court. The spot elevations where the walk meets the tennis court at 1 percent are: point C = 97.86´ and point D = 97.83´.

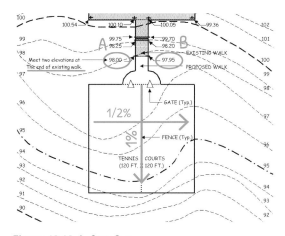

Figure 12.18-A Step One

FIGURE ADAPTED USING IMAGE COURTESY OF SADIK ARTUNC

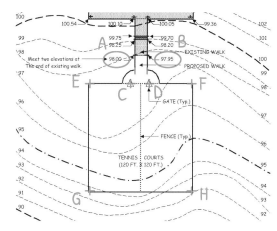

Figure 12.18-B Step Two

FIGURE ADAPTED USING IMAGE COURTESY OF SADIK ARTUNC

Assuming that the .5 percent cross slope continues for the tennis court (along a line drawn between points F and G), we can find the proposed elevations for the two upper corners of the tennis court. Using the formula S = V / H, plug in the .5 percent slope for S, measure the distance H from spot elevations to the respective corners, then solve for V. Point F = 97.86′, and point G = 97.55′. Next calculate points G and H considering the slope from point E to G is 1 percent and the distance H is 120 feet.

S = V / H

.01 − V / 120

V = 120 × .01 = 1.2′

Point E elevation is 97.86′

Point G elevation is 97.86′ − 1.2′ = 96.66′ and

Point H elevation is 97.55′ − 1.2′ = 96.35′

Now that we know the elevations of the two lower corners of the tennis court (points G and H), we might then see that elevation or contour 97′ falls somewhere between the two upper and lower corners. To find the location of contour 97′, let's first find its location between E and G, then between F and H: We need to calculate the horizontal distance H in both cases.

The vertical distance between point E and 97´ is 97.86´ minus 97´ = 0.86´.

$$S = V / H$$

$$.01 = 0.86 / H$$

$$H = 0.86 / 0.01$$

The horizontal distance I from point E = 86´.

Then measure the distance 86´ from point E, and you have the location of where 97 is on the tennis court.

The vertical distance between point F and point H is 97.55´ minus 97´ = 0.55´.

$$S = V / H$$

$$.01 = 0.55 / H$$

$$H = 0.55 / 0.01$$

The horizontal distance H from point F to the 97´ contour is 55´.

Then measure the distance 55 from point F to where the 97´ is on the tennis court. Connect the two points of 97´ as in Figure 12.8-C.

Now that we have located the 97´ contour on the tennis court, we need to connect it to the existing 97´ contours and use them as the signature swale to carry surface runoff water at a 2.5 percent swale slope, as shown in Figure 12.18-D.

See Figure 12.18-E to see how the 97´ contour would be drawn to create the signature drainage swale. Notice the distance of what is shown as the SHP or points A and B to the beginning of the 97´ contour swale. The distance is calculated using the formula S = V / H:

Point A was calculated earlier as 97.5. The start of contour 97 is the distance H at 2.5 percent slope.

$$S = V / H$$

$$0.025 = 1 / H$$

$$H = 0.5 / .025$$

The distance between point A and the 97 contour is 20 feet.

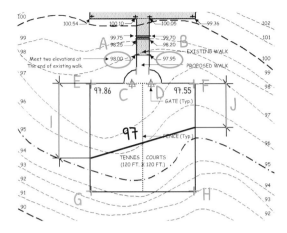

Figure 12.18-C Step Three

FIGURE ADAPTED USING IMAGE COURTESY OF SADIK ARTUNC

Figure 12.18-D Step Four

FIGURE ADAPTED USING IMAGE COURTESY OF SADIK ARTUNC

Point B was calculated earlier as 97.45. The start of contour 97 is the distance H at 2.5 percent slope:

S = V / H

0.025 = 0.45 / H

H = 0.45 / 0.025

The distance between point B and the 97 contour is 18 feet.

In Figure 12.18-F contour 98 is located. The distance along the swale centerline from contour 97 to contour 98 is:

S = V / H

0.025 = 1 / H

H = 1 / .025 = 40 feet

So each next lower contour is located a distance of 40 feet from the next contour.

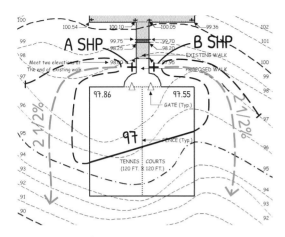

Figure 12.18-E Step Five

FIGURE ADAPTED USING IMAGE COURTESY OF SADIK ARTUNC

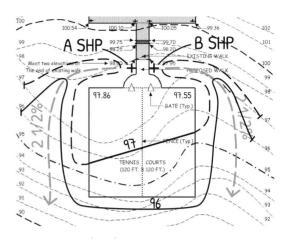

Figure 12.18-F Step Six

FIGURE ADAPTED USING IMAGE COURTESY OF SADIK ARTUNC

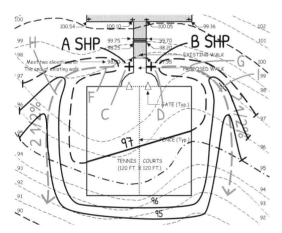

Figure 12.18-G Step Seven shows the location of contours 96 and 95

FIGURE ADAPTED USING IMAGE COURTESY OF SADIK ARTUNC

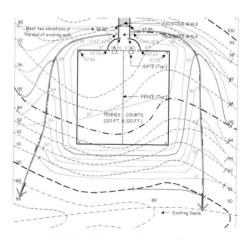

Figure 12.18-H Final grading plan for the tennis court with all the contours drawn

FIGURE ADAPTED USING IMAGE COURTESY OF SADIK ARTUNC

In Chapter 13 we will combine what we have learned about grading using contours and spot elevations in this chapter and others prior to develop more detailed grading solutions for a variety of site grading situations.

13

DETAILED GRADING WITH SLOPES, CONTOURS, AND SPOT ELEVATIONS

In this chapter you will learn about:

- How to employ site-grading tools in solving a variety of common landscape-grading problems
- The sequence of steps for solving common landscape-grading situations.

INTRODUCTION

Now that you have been introduced to the fundamental concepts of grading, we will turn our attention to applying what you have learned to a variety of site-grading situations that you will encounter in the field. To recap, grading is required when the design plans call for the existing topography of a project site to be altered in order to accommodate intended designed elements and activities. For instance, one of the reasons for site grading might be to create a gently sloping broad area for a proposed building pad, parking lot, or set of athletic fields on what may be steep or undulating existing topography. Items A and B in Figure 13.1 are diagrams that graphically portray the grading that may be required to create a level area. Item C in the same figure illustrates a swale needed to carry water from one part of a site to another. Where detailed and subtle grading is required for a proposed plaza or entry and gathering place, more detailed spot elevations are required to regrade the site, as depicted in item D in Figure 13.1.

Then, of course, grading is required for roads, trails, and walkways. Each has its unique design metrics, including considerations for safety, mode of transport (such as motorized or nonmotorized vehicle or bicycle), handicap access, and design speed. In this chapter we will look at a variety of grading design situations. Keep in mind that the formula S = V / H will be universally handy in solving most grading matters. The formula will be useful in creating slopes for paved areas or drainage elements such as swales; establishing critical spot elevations for paved and unpaved surfaces, as well as wall heights (elevations); and for the spacing of contours for creating desired landforms and pavement slopes.

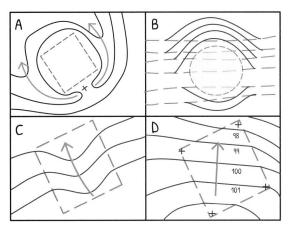

Figure 13.1 Four common-site grading operations that can be used singly or in combination, depending on the site design features

GRADING OF PAVED SURFACES: WALKS AND RAMPS

Paved surfaces such as the one shown in Figure 13.2 can be thought of as monolithic slabs of concrete, asphalt, or modular elements that might be generally level or designed with a slight to moderate pitch or slope to direct surface water to either side and away from the paved areas. In the case of a walkway, plaza, or parking lot, the paved surface often has a main slope, and in the case of a walkway or driveway it may have a secondary slope called a cross slope to modify the main direction of water flow to one side, generally into a landscaped area or storm water structure. You can see in Figure 13.2 that the main slope is 4 percent and generally directs the flow of surface water downslope along the direction of the paved walkway. At the same time, the walkway was given a 1 percent cross slope so as to direct the water flow off to one side of the walkway into an adjacent planting area. You learned in an earlier chapter that water flows perpendicular to the contours, but, when there is a cross slope, the water migrates in a direction somewhere between the direction of the main slope and the cross slope, as depicted by the dotted line in Figure 13.2. The dotted line represents water flow diverging to one side of the walkway.

The 4 percent slope of the walk shown in Figure 13.2 is somewhat steeper than is generally found in a high-use public area such as a large urban space. In this situation, the public space lies on an existing sloping site connecting several anchor public buildings; a 4 percent slope made sense because the overall park space slopes close to this percentage already. A 1 or 2 percent slope may be more common in a large urban plaza. What may also be common is to create a slight crown down the center of the walk pitched at a .5 to 1 percent slope to either side of the walk. However, it is often the practice in an urban space to pitch paved surfaces with one cross slope.

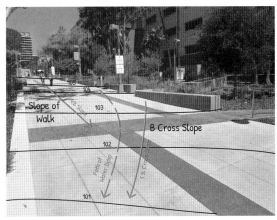

Figure 13.2 Diagram of a sloping walkway at Grand Park in Los Angeles, CA. The walk has a primary 4 percent slope and was designed with a cross slope (B) to ease surface water to the planting area at the left of the walkway. The contours are diagrammatic to help viewers visualize the slope conditions.

DESIGN PROCESS FOR GRADING A PEDESTRIAN RAMP

The process for setting slopes described in this section is to some extent simplistic, but it should serve as a starting point on how to establish the slope and needed spot elevations for paved or other surfaces. In Figures 13.3-A through 13.3-D, the process for establishing the slope and spot elevations for a pedestrian ramp is broken down into a series of steps.

Step One: Arrows A, B, and C represent the direction of slope for three portions of a pedestrian ramp. Slopes A and C can be as steep as 8 percent, while slope B is for a landing and should not be greater than 1 percent to meet wheelchair accessibility standards. In this example the slopes for A and C are in the range of 2 to 4 percent.

Figure 13.3-A Step One showing direction of three sloping sections along the ramp

Figure 13.3-B Step Two

Step Two: Assuming ramp slope A is 2 percent and that the designer using the percent of slope calculated the spot elevation S1 located in the center of the ramp and landing, the dashed line that crosses the width of the landing would be the same elevation. Spot elevation S2 would also be the same elevation as S2.

Step Three: The landing would be given a 1 percent slope. Working up-slope from S2 the designer could calculate the spot elevation of S3 using the formula S=V / H. Likewise, the designer could calculate spot elevation S4 with the same formula. Once the elevation of S4 is established, calculations for the next ramp can be made.

Step Four: Assuming ramp slope C is 4 percent, the designer can calculate spot elevation S5 at the end of the ramp. To complete the grading plan for this portion of the ramp, the designer would need to calculate spot elevations at all the corners of the landings. In many instances, the ramp sections and landings would have a cross slope. This would allow the ramps and landings to meet where they join, thus allowing the paved surface for the landing and ramp planes to meet smoothly where they join together. To achieve the smooth transition of the two planes (ramp and landing) would necessitate a certain amount of warping at the time of the construction process and during the pour of the concrete).

Figure 13.3-C Step Three

Figure 13.3-D Step Four

DESIGN PROCESS FOR GRADING A BICYCLE TRAIL AND PARK WALKWAY

The design of ramps and walks is approached in a similar manner. Figure 13.4-A shows a 10-foot-wide concrete bike trail/walkway in a neighborhood city park. The walkway was designed with a varied slope to conform to the existing terrain. In Figure 13.4-B, the main slope is approximately 1 percent (item A) with a 1 percent cross slope (items B1 and B2). Notice the position of the contours relative to the general direction of the walkway in Figure 13.4-C. They cross the width of the walkway at an angle. This angle is called the cross slope. The left side of the walk is higher than the right side so that the walk surface is tilted downhill toward the right (thereby creating the cross slope).

Step One: The arrow positioned down the center of a 10-foot-wide pedestrian walkway represents the main slope. Sections of the line may have varied slopes,

Figure 13.4-A Step One showing the direction the walkway slopes

with shallower slopes to conform to less steep terrain and steeper slopes for steep terrain. The designer varies the slope to minimize earthwork, and in this case so that the walk fits with the existing terrain.

Step Two: A is the main slope of the walkway, B1 represents the cross slope, and C is spot elevation 103.5, slightly higher by 1 percent than spot elevation F.

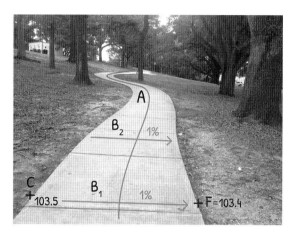

Figure 13.4-B Step Two providing information to make slope and spot elevation calculations

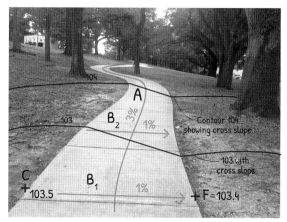

Figure 13.4-C Step Three showing the grading solution with contours and spot elevations

Figure 13.5 A switchback wheelchair access ramp, Grand Park, City of Los Angeles, CA

Step Three: The locations of contours 103 and 104 are shown to help the viewer visualize how they might appear in the landscape. The spacing of the contours would be 33.3 feet apart to achieve a 3 percent slope.

The slopes of the switchback ramp system shown in Figure 13.5 were designed to accommodate wheelchair access and meet ADA design criteria for the recently completed Grand Park, located in downtown Los Angeles. Eight percent is the maximum slope allowed for walkways designed for wheelchair access. The length of the ramp cannot exceed 20 feet. In the case of a ramp that, by necessity, is greater than 20 feet, the ramp should be divided into segments not greater than 20 feet, with a 5-foot landing between ramp segments. The landing should be sloped at 1 percent so as to direct water off the walkway into the adjacent landscape.

INTEGRATION OF WALKWAY, STEPS, AND SEATING AREA

The photograph of a stairway and paved surface feature shown in Figure 13.6-A consists of an upper seating area and informal stage with steps leading down to a walkway, at the Los Angeles County Museum of Art. Figure 13.6-B shows that the upper paved seating area was designed to slope in one direction toward the stairs at 1 percent. Each tread or step has a .5 percent slope toward the next step. The steps end at a lower paved walkway, and this surface was designed with a 2 or 3 percent slope, directing water diagonally toward a walkway leading beyond the wall to a lawn area and street beyond. Note that both full 1-foot contours are shown supplemented with .5-foot contours to help viewers visualize the 1 percent sloping surface of the lower gathering area. Arrows point in the direction in which surface water is to flow—in this case, surface water flows perpendicular to the contours.

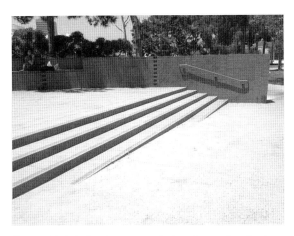

Figure 13.6-A Seating area and place for small gatherings at the Los Angeles County Museum of Art, Hancock Park

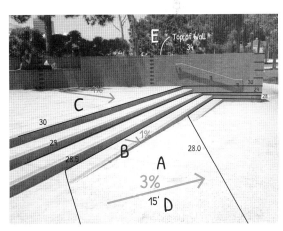

Figure 13.6-B Seating area with contours and spot elevations superimposed over photograph

GRADING DESIGN WHERE PAVED AREA MEETS BUILDING ENTRANCE ACCESSIBLE BY STAIRS

Another example of how contours, spot elevations, and slope indications are used to communicate the design intent of a grading plan is shown in Figure 13.7. A few items worth pointing out in the photograph: Note the spot elevation of 105.5′ at the top of the flight of stairs. Most likely the building finish floor elevation (FFE) was set first. The designer used stairs as a device to get from the building to the paved area below. Since the project involved public buildings, a ramp would be required but is not shown here. At the bottom of the stairs is the 100′ contour. The walk that passes in front of the stairs was given a 1 percent slope and is a continuation of the larger paved area. The paved area is also sloped at 1 percent, and the hypothetical contours are shown. Normally, the designer would use primarily spot elevations without contours in paved areas. Contractors expect to see and work with spot elevations in paved areas to construct the forms before pouring concrete or setting pavers.

Figure 13.7 Paved forecourt and access to public building at Grand Park in downtown Los Angeles, CA

PARKING LOT GRADING DESIGN

The diagrams in Figure 13.8 depict the three basic approaches for directing surface water across a paved area—in this case a parking lot. The central drive in Diagram A is situated higher, in the form of a crown with water directed to the curbs at the parking spaces. The water flows to the lower corners of the parking lot, necessitating the installation of a catch basin at either corner or a channel installed to allow the water to flow out of the parking lot. Diagram B shows the driveway as a valley with surface water flowing from the parking space curbs to the center of the driveway. A catch basin could be placed at the parking lot outlet or the water could be allowed to flow to some point outside the parking lot to a street storm water inlet, drainage swale, or detention area. The parking lot grading solution shown in Diagram C simply tilts the parking lot in one direction toward a catch basin or exit channel to be installed in the lower corner of the lot. All three solutions are commonly used to drain surface water in parking lots, large expanses of pavement, and grass fields. Generally a selection is made based on the designer's preference or in response to site design considerations or governmental regulatory requirements.

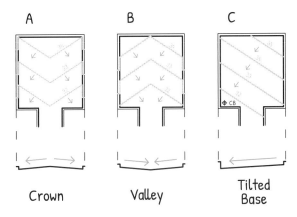

Figure 13.8 Three approaches for grading a parking lot or large paved surface

A parking lot with a crown down the center is shown in Figure 13.9. Notice that the contours are curved, with the top of the curve at the center of the lot, labeled as B. Point B is located at the top of the crown in the center of the parking lot (high-points) so that surface water is directed by a cross slope formed by the curvature of the contours toward the curbs running along either side of the parking lot. The water then runs along the curb to a catch basin or drainage channel constructed at the lower end of the parking lot. Tree islands may protrude from the curb with catch basins installed at the higher side of the island, or a channel might be used to allow the surface water to continue flowing down-slope along the curb.

Figure 13.9 Parking lot with crown

In the next chapter the topic of storm water management will be presented. While the use of catch basins has traditionally been the "go to it" solution for disposing of surface water runoff, current trends in site grading seek grading solutions that keep surface water within a property site. This is achieved through the use of detention/retention ponds, creation of bioswales, and selection of pervious paving materials. The use of these site-grading approaches complements larger site design strategies of creating sustainable and responsible surface water management. Recharging groundwater, reducing the need for irrigation, and minimizing the use of costly municipal storm water infrastructure are goals achieved when site-grading solutions find innovative ways of keeping storm water on-site.

The grading design for a soccer or football field is similar to that of the parking lot shown in Figure 13.10-A. However, the contours would have an elliptical crown surface, not an angular, V-shaped contour. A crown is formed down the center of the playing field in Figure 13.10-B, directing water to the sidelines where it is carried away by a swale or a series of catch basins. The slope of the crown could range from 1 percent to 2 percent, depending on applicable sports field design standards.

Figures 13.10- A and 13.10-B Soccer field, Kincaid Park, Anchorage, AK

Figure 13.11 shows a detail of a parking lot designed with a crown so that the surface water flows toward a 6˝-high curb around the perimeter of the lot. Items marked C indicate the elevations at the top of the curb and coincide where contours 104, 105, and 106 meet the top of the curb. The contours then continue across the adjacent lawn area. Notice that spot elevations C are located half the distance between two

contours (for instance, halfway between 103 and 104). The spot elevations at the top and bottom of the curbs for the four contours shown in
the figure are summarized as follows:

Table 13.1 Relation of Spot Elevations along a Curb to Contours

	TOP OF CURB ELEVATION	BOTTOM OF CURB ELEVATION
D 103	103.5'	103.0'
C 104	104.0'	103.5'
C 105	105.0'	104.5'
C 106	106.0'	105.5'

Curb, slope, spot elevation, and contour line mark-ups have been
added to the photograph in Figure 13.11 to facilitate visualizing a parking lot as it would be drawn in a site-grading plan. A 2 percent cross
slope was created with the contours (Item A).

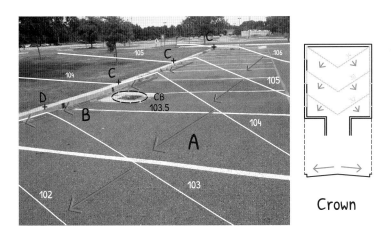

Figure 13.11 Parking lot with crown shown in photograph with diagram to right

The photographs in Figure 13.11 show how water flow is directed in
a parking lot using contours and spot elevations. The contours shown in
Figure 13.12 have been drawn to create a valley down the center of the
drive with surface water sheet flowing at a 1 percent slope. The valley
solution concentrates water down the center of the drive lane, reducing
water in the parking spaces so that people stepping out of their vehicles

are not stepping into a puddle, as they would if the lot were graded with a crown along the drive lane.

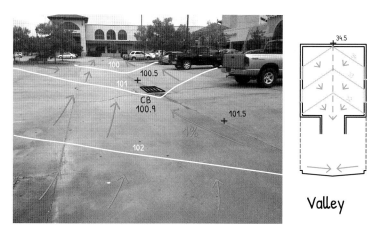

Valley

Figure 13.12 Parking lot with valley down center shown in photograph with plan to right

SITE-GRADING DESIGN IN LAWN AREA

The lawn shown in Figures 13.13-A through 13.13-C is a new addition to what was previously an undeveloped, poorly draining area. To solve the drainage problem, and as a means to carry water away from the wood-lot in the background, a drainage swale was created and a catch basin installed in the lawn. The earth removed in creating the swale was used to create gentle earth mounds to either side of the swale.

Figure 13.13-A Step One

Step One: A catch basin is located in the center of the lawn area, with a swale directing surface water to the catch basin.

Step Two: Contours represent the landform consisting of a central swale with mounding to either side of the swale. Arrows show the direction surface water flows to the swale and catch basin. The rim elevation of the catch basin was established as the lowest elevation within the grassy area.

 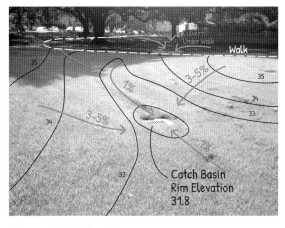

Figure 13.13-B Step Two   Figure 13.13-C Step Three

Step Three: Note the percent of slope indicated for the mounding landforms. Note the culvert in the background to allow surface water coming from the woodlot walk to flow under the walk (through a culvert) to the lawn area.

SCULPTURAL LANDFORM SOLUTIONS IN LAWN OR LANDSCAPED AREAS

Figures 13.14-A and 13.14-B provide an example of a sculptural grading solution in a campus landscape. The photograph in Figure 13.14-A was taken of a lawn area fronting a street that borders the campus. The design intent was to provide visual interest and greater visual impact for what could otherwise have been a simple level lawn area. The goals of increasing visual impact and interest are achieved by the creation of rolling mounds with gentle swales depicted as an oblique plan view in Figure 13.14-B. In Figures 13.15-A and 13.15-B, the pedestrian walkway system, with its gentle 1 and 2 percent slopes, traverses an adjoining landscape that has been sculpted with grass-covered mounds. The mounds add visual interest and serve to define the various spaces connected by the walk. The mounding landforms provide partial screening of views into adjoining outdoor study spaces and along the corridor of the walk. As the pedestrian approaches these spaces, the view into them opens up to reveal the full space. Sunlight accents the sculpted landscape, casting shadows and providing bright openings that together articulate the space and add another layer of visual interest, particularly as the alternating shade and sunlight move across the landscape during the day.

Figure 13.14-A Lawn area along the street fronting the California Institute of Technology, Pasadena, CA

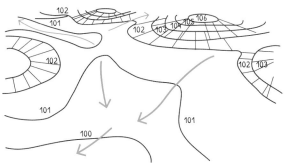

Figure 13.14-B Plan view of lawn area along the street fronting the California Institute of Technology, Pasadena, CA

Figure 13.15-A Internal pedestrian walkway connecting buildings at the California Institute of Technology, Pasadena, CA

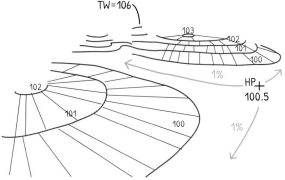

Figure 13.15-B Plan of internal pedestrian walkway connecting buildings at the California Institute of Technology, Pasadena, CA

SOME FINAL EXAMPLES OF USING SPOT ELEVATIONS AND CONTOURS IN SITE-GRADING DESIGN

Figures 13.16-A through 13.16-C show a series of photographs of a sunken, terraced gathering area at the California Institute of Technology, Pasadena, CA. Essentially, the design of this terraced gathering area is composed of a watershed-like low point at the lowest elevation of the space. A series of steps and terraces was designed to define and articulate the seating and gathering spaces on higher ground. Some of the steps, identified in Step Two as item E, continue to wrap around the space, morphing into broad terraces while maintaining a 6-inch step or rise with varying tread widths.

Step One: The area outlined with a dashed line in Figure 13.16-A represents the lowest elevation of the gathering area and serves as a watershed to collect surface water that drains from the upper terraces to the catch basin (item I).

Step Two: Item A in Figure 13.16-B is the spot elevation at the entrance to the gathering area. Item B is a spot elevation at the bottom of the sloping ramp (item C). Item D is the elevation at the top of the highest seat wall. Item E circles four steps with the highest step serving as a seat wall. Each dashed line that runs along each paved terrace would have an elevation.

Step Three: The arrows with G1 and G2 in Figure 13.16-C represent the direction each terrace would slope; in this case, they slope at 1 percent. Items G1a and G2b are the elevation set for each terraced step.

Figure 13.16-A Step One shows arrows indicating direction of surface water flow to catch basin

Figure 13.16-B Step Two

Figure 13.16-C Step Three

Detailed grading plans will place a greater emphasis on spot elevations in cases where paving and hardscape features are to be constructed, such as the business campus entry plaza shown in Figure 13.17. Spot elevations would be found at all corners, tops, and bottoms of stairs and walls, and where slope changes occur throughout the paving and hardscape areas. For a project with many complex changes of grade and constructed fountain and wall features, the designer would also prepare a series of technical cross sections to communicate the grading design intent to the contractor. Contours have greater use in areas where landscape, turf, and earth forms are to be constructed, as in the grounds

Figure 13.17 Williams Square, Dallas, Texas
SWA GROUP

Figure 13.18 Getty Museum, Los Angeles
ROBERT IRWIN AND THE OLIN PARTNERSHIP

of the museum shown in Figure 13.18. Slope indications would also be shown along swales and where steep cut and fill slopes occur. Technical sections would also be provided where the designer wishes to ensure that the contractor understands the grading design intent for subtle or critical earth forms and slope changes.

CONSTRUCTION SEQUENCE FOR A BUS SHELTER

The contractor lays out the construction area using the staking or layout plan included in the construction document packaged prepared by the landscape architect. The staking plan is the basis for the contractor to establish the locations of all the design elements. The contractor may hire a land surveyor to locate the design elements following the staking plan or may do the work with in-house employees. After staking is completed, the contractor does rough grading then constructs the wood forms following the staking plan and grading plan. The forms contain the poured concrete and are positioned on the ground conforming to the elevations shown on the plan. The contractor sets the top of the forms following the spot elevations shown on the site-grading plan. Stakes are installed to secure the wood forms so they do not move or bow out when wet concrete is poured.

The sequence followed in erecting the forms and setting the elevations can be seen in Figures 13.19-A through Figure 3.19-J. Figures 13.19-A and 13.19-B show the overall layout for a bus shelter next to a street. The center area of Figure 13.19-A is the location

Figure 13.19-A Wood forms to contain concrete in the construction of a bus shelter area

Figure 13.19-B Wood forms for ADA access ramp and walk to lead to bus shelter

of the bus shelter, with the wood forms for the paving work around the periphery. Figure 13.19-B is a detail of the access ramp and curb from the street leading to the sidewalk. The forms for the curb are set in place at the proper elevation by a system of stakes. The use of surveyor's string is shown Figure 13.19-C. The elevation of the string line is fastened to a nail on a stake. The position of the nail represents a spot elevation taken from the grading plan. The surveyor's string line shown in Figure 13.19-D guides the location of the proposed curb and pavement taken from the staking plan,

Figure 13.19-C Method of establishing correction elevation of wood form. The nail represents the spot elevation shown in grading plan and the string guides the construction of the wood concrete form to correct height.

Figure 13.19-D String level used to guide the location of wood concrete forms at their correct elevation before pouring concrete

Figure 13.19-E Concrete truck in position before concrete pour

Figure 13.19-F Concrete is distributed to meet height of wood forms and fill in low spots

with the elevation of the string corresponding to the spot elevations from the grading plan. Figures 13.19-E and 3.19-F show the stage of construction after the staking is complete and the forms have been positioned to the proper elevations for the concrete to be poured. The contractor has ordered delivery of the concrete, and the crew can be seen spreading it in Figure 13.19-F. Figure 13.19-G shows the concrete finishing working in progress, and Figure 13.19-H is the bus shelter project after the concrete has dried and the forms have been removed. The work remaining is the finish work for the bus shelter, installation of the landscape materials, and cleanup. Figures 13.19 -I and J show the completed bus shelter and waiting area.

Figure 13.19-G Concrete finishing work in progress

Figure 13.19-H Completed concrete paving after wood forms removed

Figure 13.19-I Completed ADA access ramp and walk to bus shelter

Figure 13.19-J Completed bus shelter area

Figure 13.20 is a portion of a professional site-grading plan. Notice the use of contours in the landscaped areas and spot elevations for the hardscape. Exiting contours are shown as dashed lines, and proposed contours are solid lines. The plan guides the work of the grading contractor. The grading plan package would also include multiple section drawings. To guide the actual earth-moving activities of the grading contractor, a series of cross sections following a grid system would be established by a team of land surveyors. Wood stakes are placed in the ground along the grid lines with elevations marked on the stakes corresponding to grade elevations found in the grading plan. Wood surveyor's stakes are typically placed at the intersections of the grid lines and at key locations such as at building corners or critical elevations where the designer wants to control the elevation of landscape or paved surfaces, and needs to indicate heights of walls or other design elements. The elevation is written directly on each stake, with the proposed elevations interpolated by the land surveyor or taken directly from the grading plan.

In the next chapter various approaches to handling storm water will be presented.

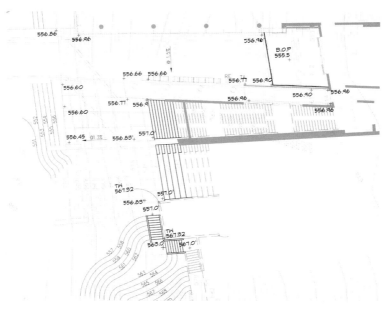

Figure 13.20 Grading plan detail: Tarrant County College District, East Trinity Campus, Fort Worth, Texas

COURTESY OF STUDIO OUTSIDE AND BING THOM ARCHITECTS

14

STORM AND SURFACE WATER DRAINAGE MANAGEMENT

In this chapter you will learn about:

- The wide variety of options for a designer to manage storm water

- How storm water management can serve multiple uses

INTRODUCTION

Approximately 70 percent of the earth's surface is covered by water, and over 96 percent of this water is saline, found in the oceans. The remaining 4 percent of this water, found on the land, is in the form of lakes, rivers, glaciers and ice fields, and wetlands. Water also exists in the earth's atmosphere in the form of water vapor. The water vapor is one part of a cyclic system called the water cycle, whereby water vapor condenses in the form of rain or snow to fall to the ground, then disperses across the Earth's surface to either infiltrate into the ground or travel across the ground as water run-off. Water that infiltrates into the ground saturates the soil, is taken

Figure 14.1 Neighborhood street scene reflection in one of the urban canals in Delft, the Netherlands

up by plants, or migrates beyond the surface to recharge the underground aquifer. As runoff, surface water feeds streams, lakes, and other water bodies. Water on the surface that permeates into the soil later will transpire or evaporate from the soil and water bodies as water vapor. The water vapor returns to the atmosphere later to resume the natural water cycle.

Water is vital to life, offering a multitude of positive attributes that sustain life and natural processes. Without water, life on this planet would not exist. However, there are situations when life with less water is necessary, particularly when water enters our lives as heavy storms and surface runoff. Storm water that moves across the ground can cause damage and havoc where human beings live, play, and work. Unwanted surface water can cause flooding and damage within the built environment. Moving surface water can cause erosion and undermine walls and structures, causing structural damage. One of the goals of landscape grading is to manage and direct rain and surface flowing water to eliminate or minimize the damage and calamities caused by uncontrolled water. In other cases, it may be desirable to collect and store storm water, as opposed to disposing of it. Stored water can be used for irrigation and other desirable and sustainable water management practices.

Figure 14.2 Leaves as a watermark or witness to the level of storm water that filled the grassy swale after a late afternoon rain

If you look carefully in the right of the middle ground in Figure 14.2, you will see a pattern of leaves that echoes the swale almost precisely. The position of the leaves serves as a reminder of the amount of water that filled the swale during evening rains that fell several hours earlier. The swale was filled at the height of the storm to the level where the leaves were deposited. The area is not a great expanse of lawn, but it managed to receive a significant amount of water that moved at a sufficient speed and force to cast the leaves uphill from the swale.

Managing storm water is one of the important purposes of landscape grading. In addition to modifying existing topography to accommodate the various program elements, further modification of the topography has the purpose of redirecting surface water flow from places water is not wanted to other locations on the project site. Storm water management can take many forms and includes a variety of systems.

Figures 14.3-A and 14.3-B Drainage problems: Handicap parking space (A), Apartment parking lot (B)

Scenes such as the ones shown in Figures 14.3-A and 14.3-B illustrate storm water drainage problems. Unwanted storm water has been left standing in the handicap parking space in Figure 14.3-A, making the space temporarily unusable. This situation could have, and should have, been avoided. In this case, one grading solution would have been to change the slope of the parking lot so that surface water is directed away from the curbs, to either a planting area or driveway. Another solution, if the topography would not allow surface water to be directed to another location, would have been to install a catch basin where the water is now collecting. The standing water in Figure 14.3-B is the result of several possible causes:

1. An inadequate grading plan created a depression where storm water could collect.

In nearly every site-grading design problem, there are several alternative solutions for handling storm water. Which is the best solution depends on project budget, governmental requirements, design considerations, and functional activities and uses.

Soil erosion is caused by water moving across the ground surface as a concentrated, fast-moving flow, or by a surface water sheet flowing over a steep slope. Figure 14.4 shows the result of storm water that has backed up along a parking lot curb, spilling over the side then moving down a steep, poorly maintained slope. Over time the erosion became worse as the slope became increasingly exposed with the loss of grass to protect and hold the soil.

Examples of different approaches to handling surface storm water are described in the following sections. The examples represent a broad range of approaches to collecting, storing, and transporting storm water. In some cases the water is stored on-site, and in other examples the water is collected then carried off-site by an underground pipe or canal to a municipal storm water disposal system. In today's world, where sustainable design and best water management practices are steadily becoming the norm, site-grading designs incorporate a range of strategies for maintaining water on-site, in retention ponds or water gardens, or stored for later uses such as for irrigation. Other grading design approaches direct and slow down surface water to allow absorption into the soil and to recharge underground aquifers.

Figure 14.4 Slope erosion adjacent to a parking lot

TRADITIONAL HANDLING OF SURFACE STORM WATER

Site grading can be approached in a number of ways, ranging from an art form to a means of solving practical physical problems. The ultimate grading plan is one that integrates art and practical requirements. The landscape grounds at Parc de Sceaux, Paris, accomplish both. In Figure 14.5, the artful carving and shaping of an existing landscape into an expansive, terraced parkland make this garden a visual pleasure. Underlying the creative approach that went into manipulating the landscape to create such a grand view, André Le Nôtre, the designer of Versailles, manipulated the ground form in subtle ways to disperse surface water to either side of terraced lawns. The designer not only accomplished the creation of a beautiful scene, but also solved the dispersal of surface water without compromising the smooth transition of the terraced panels of lawn to the tree-lined frame. The subtleness of the rolling topography and the efficient dispersal of storm water were achieved through contour grading.

One of the more common grading strategies for placing a building or structure in the landscape is to set its finish floor elevation on high

Figure 14.5 Parc de Sceaux, André Le Nôtre, Paris, France

Figure 14.6 Building set on high ground so surrounding pavement slopes away to direct water away from the building on the J. Paul Getty Museum campus in Westwood, CA

ground, then slope the landscape, walks, plazas, and driveways so that surface water drains down and away from the building. Figure 14.6 shows this approach very well. The ground and paved areas around the building are set at elevations below the first-floor elevation and sloped to direct water away from the building entrances and the structure itself. The paved areas and ground adjacent to the building are more gently sloping, with slopes farther away from the building becoming relatively steeper.

CONTOUR GRADING

One of the simplest and most direct ways of directing water away from a building is to elevate the structure and surrounding area, then create a slope that will direct surface water to drain away to an area designed to receive the excess water. The grass slope in the photograph in Figure 14.7 was created to do just that. In this example, the surface water is directed downhill to an extensive planting bed that receives the water, allowing it to soak into the soil. Any excess water moves farther downhill into the dense tree cover and landscape understory.

Figure 14.7 Simple slope to drain water away from building

Surface water is directed to either side of the lawn area shown in Figure 14.8-A. An underground storm water collection system has been installed along either side of the lawn in the form of catch basins. Look carefully at the picture in Figure 14.8-B, and you will be able to see a crease in the walk that represents the top of the crown that runs along the center of the space.

The slopes shown in Figure 14.9 conform to a series of terraces created to absorb runoff from the walkways before it reaches the soccer field below. The

Figures 14.8-A and 14.8-B Expanse of lawn graded with a crown to direct water to either side of the central space

slope will be planted with soil-holding shrub and tree plantings. These plantings will slow down the water moving down the slope, facilitating absorption of much of the water into the soil before it reaches the playing field. The undulating slopes in the right part of the photograph were created to divide surface water, directing portions of the water to be carried by swales in different directions so as to minimize the concentration of storm water flowing across the lawn area. The undulating landform provides visual interest in what would otherwise be an expansive lawn facing the adjacent street.

In both cases the two sections of the same sidewalks shown in Figures 14.10-A and 14.10-B were designed to bring people from an upper sidewalk to a parking lot down-slope. The designer had to grade the area to ensure that storm water was directed away from the adjoining building, and at the same time grade the sidewalk so that surface water was directed with a cross slope to one side of the sidewalk.

Figure 14.9 Landform created to direct surface water to other locations on-site

Figure 14.10-A Sloping sidewalk made with modular, concrete pavers that allow some absorption of water to enter the ground underneath. Figure 14.10-B The same sidewalk located further uphill with a poured in place concrete surface. Both sections of the same walkway were graded to conform to the existing sloping landform.

Figure 14.11-A and 14.11-B Two design options for linking an upper area to a lower area using steps (A) and terracing or steps (B)

Figures 14.11-A and 14.11-B show two examples in which the grading strategies of steps and terraces are used to provide transitions from an upper to a lower area, in addition to the use of contour grading to make transitions from one elevation to another. While steps and terraces may allow movement from an upper area to a lower area, each step and terrace is graded or sloped to allow water to drain off, to prevent it from collecting and puddling, and causing a potential slipping or other hazard. Typically, individual steps are designed with a .05 or 1 percent slope, while the slope of a terraced landscape can vary depending on the program conditions and the surface of the material (paved or planted). Paved terracing with rough and irregular stone, such as shown in Figure 14.11-B, would be designed with a 1 percent slope in regions with low rainfall such as Southern California and the U.S. Southwest (to facilitate water percolation to recharge the aquifer). A slightly steeper slope of 1.5 percent might be preferable in wetter climates or those with heavy snowfall such as the U.S. Pacific Northwest or Northeast.

DESIGN OPTIONS FOR HANDLING STORM WATER

Catch Basins

Catch basins are often used to collect surface water in grading situations where swales and simple topographic modifications are not feasible. Catch basins are set at the lowest elevation of an area that is shaped to direct surface water to the catch basin. Catch basins can be installed in narrow spaces (such as planting areas next to a building) or can be positioned within a large expanse of paving (such as a plaza or parking lot) or in planted and lawn areas. Site-grading plans that use catch basins for extensive areas will position them in a grid pattern rather than installing a single catch basin, whenever possible. A single catch basin has the initial high cost of making a connection to a storm water system. The cost can be spread out when multiple catch basins are used.

Figure 14.12 Note the catch basin next to the curb in the middle of the photograph. Its purpose is to collect surface water from the parking lot

The parking lot shown in Figure 14.12 may appear flat at first glance, when in fact the pavement is divided into sloping planes. The sloping pavement is formed to create a ridge-like crown in the center of the parking lot, directing storm water toward the edges, where it is intercepted by catch basins positioned at the curb.

Figure 14.13-A In this photograph one can see how the creation of a warped, paved surface can effectively collect and direct water to a catch basin

Figure 14.13-B The arrows in this photograph show the direction that surface water is made to flow across paved parking lot surfaces

Figure 14.13-C The catch basin noted as item A in the photograph receives surface water flow from multiple directions

Figure 14.13-D The pavement in a campus quadrangle has been subdivided into multiple mini-watersheds. A catch basin has been positioned at the lowest elevation and the center of each watershed.

Four examples of the use of catch basins are shown in Figures 14.13-A through 14.13-D. The area in each example is graded to act as a watershed, as shown in Figure 14.3-D, or graded in a series of warped paved surfaces sloped to carry surface water to a system of catch basins. Water flows across the surface of a paved area such as those shown in Figures 14.13-A and 14.13-C, where the water drops into the basin to be carried in pipes by gravity to some other area on the site or to a municipal storm water system. The catch basin in Figure 14.13-B was positioned to gather water flowing from several directions in the parking lot. The parking lot paving was shaped to direct surface water toward the curb, then along the curb to the catch basin.

Figure 14.14 Storm water street inlet

More common, and perhaps the norm 25 or more years ago, was the ubiquitous use of area catch basins to collect storm water on a site. The water was then carried underground in pipes to the municipal storm water system. Storm water inlets were part of municipal storm water infrastructure and were installed in the streets to collect runoff from the street or from adjacent properties, as seen in Figure 14.14. In rural areas or in less dense residential neighborhoods, swales are installed along streets and roads to receive and carry away surface runoff water, as shown in Figure 14.15. Notice in Figure 14.15 that curbs and gutters are absent, so the storm water inlet structure is not necessary. The use of swales along streets is an alternative to a piping storm water system, and generally is less costly than an underground municipal system. Sometimes the swale is preferred for aesthetic reasons, providing what some designers and their clients consider a soft, less visually obtrusive solution.

Figure 14.15 Essentially a brick-lined swale to direct surface water to the catch basin

Other solutions for collecting and disposing of surface water are shown in the examples in Figures 14.16-A and 14.16-B. The standard approach for collecting storm water in paved areas such as concrete surfaces, roadway, or parking lots is to warp the surfaces so as to direct water to a central low point such as a catch basin. Where large expanses of pavement are involved, a gently sloping surface is formed to direct the water to a series of evenly spaced catch basins. This system of water collection is a good solution where there is not a lot of elevation change within the paved area. The designer is able to maintain the visual effect of a level brick area while creating gradual slope sufficient to direct the water to the central catch basins. The drainage system shown in Figure 14.16-A is a variation where a strip catch basin called a French drain was installed down the center of a campus walkway. The walk was graded to sheet-drain surface water to the central drain. The drain itself has a sloping bottom where water is collected and distributed by an underground pipe to the campus storm water infrastructure. Figure 14.16-B shows a variant application of a French drain system with a central catch basin to collect surface water.

The ponding that occurred shortly after a hard morning rain (Figure 14.17-A) may not have been anticipated at the time the campus space was constructed. Quite possibly, in this case, the original grading plan provided for adequate sheet drainage to a nearby catch basin; however, over the years since the original construction, the ground may have settled, forming a low area to collect storm water in a temporary pond.

Figure 14.16-A and 14.16-B Alternative designs to catch basin: French drain (14.16-A) and combination French drain with catch basin (14.16-B)

Figure 14.17-A Rainwater ponding in low area where ground subsidence occurred

Figure 14.17-B Area catch basin positioned in low point (elevation) between buildings and pedestrian walk

The ponding probably does not pose any problem, because the water does dry out after a few days, making the lawn area usable, but several solutions are available to correct the periodic ponding. Installation of a catch basin, as shown in Figure 14.17-B, is one solution, probably a costly one. Bringing in topsoil to raise the area so that water can flow to a more desirable location is another possibility. Most likely, nothing will be done because of the costs involved in correcting a situation that is a temporary nuisance, one that students and the university groundskeepers can live with, at least for the time being.

In many cases it is not possible to manipulate the topography to sheet-drain water to another location. In those instances, installation of one or more catch basins would ensure that storm water is dispersed to another location to reduce flooding or unwanted detention of surface water around the building. Figure 14.18 shows a catch basin in a lawn area. The cross section shows the basic components of a catch basin with underground pipes to

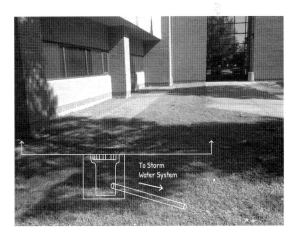

Figure 14.18 Catch basin in lawn area

carry collected water to another location on-site or to a storm water collection system.

Figure 14.19-A and 14.19-B Use of catch basins to receive surface water in two adjacent sculpted lawn areas

Figures 14.19-A and 14.19-B are examples of how catch basins can be used to gather surface water within a sculpted lawn area where the designer chose to use the swale to articulate the sculptured landform. In Figure 14.19-A the catch basin receives the water from the swale before allowing it to cross the walk. In Figure 14.19-B swales bring water from either side of a great lawn area to a central low point where a catch basin collects the water. The collected surface water could then be transferred to a storm water collection system or to another adjacent area, perhaps to a detention pond or water garden.

Canals and Swales

The constructed drainage channel shown in Figures 14.20-A and 14.20-B was installed in a new parking lot adjacent to an existing campus road. The designer may have had the option of installing a drop inlet catch basin at the curb in the road to handle the storm water but chose to divert the water from the road to a catch basin located in the adjacent. A channel, similar to the one in Figures 14.20-A and B, is often used to direct water from one paved surface, such as a parking lot, to another.

Ultimately, the surface water is collected in a catch basin or directed to a rain garden or planting area, where the water may be absorbed into the ground or held in a landscaped retention area.

Figures 14.20-A and 14.20-B Concrete drainage channels to carry surface water from a parking lot to an adjacent road

Roadside Drainage Swale

The swale shown in Figure 14.21 was created to carry surface water from the adjacent roadway and the surrounding sloping landscape area. Note the culvert at the end of the swale, which allows surface water to continue under an entrance drive to a continuation of the swale along the road.

Surface water is carried by gravity in a grassy swale toward the culvert that allows the water to flow under the access driveway. The grass serves to slow down the water, allowing some percolation into the soil. The grass also protects the swale from erosion, particularly when water run-off is high and large quantities of moving water could cause soil erosion. Grass or other vegetative ground cover also serve to

Figure 14.21 This drainage swale was created along a campus road, instead of using a curb and gutter design

collect much of the debris that could clog the culvert and cause water to back up and potentially flood the street.

Aquifer Recharge

With the current emphasis on creating sustainable landscapes, the application of and reliance on traditional storm water removal infrastructure—such as municipal storm water systems—are being subsumed by on-site water reuse and water conservation strategies. Grading solutions that allow water to be absorbed in the soil to recharge the underground aquifer or stored in a retention pond for later uses, such as for onsite irrigation, are becoming increasingly common. Methods for conserving surface water on-site include the creation of water gardens and detention ponds, the creation of minimal slopes to allow surface water to percolate into the soil, and use of porous paving surfaces such as crushed rock, modular units, or even porous concrete and asphalt. The photograph in Figure 14.22 provides an example of surfacing an expansive level or slightly sloping area with compacted crushed rock, a design approach with definite aesthetic appeal which at the same time contributes to water recharge of the area's aquifer.

Figure 14.22 Surfacing an expansive area with compacted crushed rock, The Hague, the Netherlands

Figures 14.23-A and 14.23-B show examples of the use of modular paving set in sand to provide a smooth surface comfortable for walkers, bikers, or parents pushing strollers. Rainwater can penetrate to the subsoil below the paving or be directed to the adjacent landscape areas. Puddles, which commonly occur with nonporous paving, are minimal where porous or modular paving surfaces are used. Figure 14.23-A shows a walkway and street surfaced with modular concrete pavers, and the surface in 14.23-B is a walkway surfaced with modular granite rock. Figure 14.23-C shows a dense, highly urbanized shopping setting where the designer selected a combination of concrete pavers and compacted crushed rock for the paving surfaces. Water can penetrate into the soil below both paving surfaces to provide moisture for the trees.

Figure 14.23-A Use of modular concrete units set in sand for a Delft, the Netherlands, neighborhood walkway and road

Figure 14.23-B Use of modular granite units set in sand for a Delft, the Netherlands urban walkway

Porous concrete is seeing increased use as a means to return surface runoff to the ground, rather than directing it for disposal via a municipal storm water system. In the example of porous concrete use shown in Figure 14.24, a new walk that crossed near the base of an older Live Oak resulted in minimal impact on the surface root system and, at the same time, provided moisture where encroachment of paved surfaces were threatening the health of the tree.

Figure 14.23-C Mixed use of modular concrete paving units and compacted gravel surface in the new central shopping district in Almere, the Netherlands

Figure 14.24 Porous concrete walk (A) and conventional concrete pavement (B) on the Louisiana State University

Retention Ponds

Retention ponds have become increasingly common in jurisdictions requiring that storm water be contained and made use of on-site, as opposed to being directed off-site via a storm water system. The ponds are designed to maintain a certain level of water, as shown in Figures 14.25-A and 14.25-B. Additional water-holding capacity is provided based on assumed storm water events. The canal-like basin shown in Figures 14.25-A was designed to allow the upper area of the basin to serve some purpose such as passive, or in some cases active, recreation uses. The upper slopes (14.25-B) are planted to hold the soil and to serve as a surface for passive uses such as picnicking or field sports. In the case of Figures 14.25-A, the upper slopes provide wildlife habitat and serve nature study purposes, while the area in Figures 14.25-B provides for valuable park and recreation uses, serving adjacent residential neighborhoods.

Figure 14.25-A Retention pond with upper slopes supporting native plants in a residential neighborhood in Voorhof, the Netherlands

Figure 14.25-B Retention canal located in a more dense residential neighborhood in Voorhof, the Netherlands

The example in Figure 14.26 of a retention basin and surrounding grassy slopes was designed to serve a diverse range of active and passive park uses for surrounding neighborhoods. A sandy beach was created for sunbathing and access for wading. The steep slopes forming a basin were designed as a visual amenity while providing excess-water-holding capacity in the event of heavy rains.

The slopes of the retention basin at Sud Park in Rotterdam, shown in Figure 14.26, were planted in grass, most likely to reinforce the park-like nature of the area in what is a dense, highly populated mixed cultural residential area. In the examples in Figures 14.27-A and 14.27-B, the edges are treated to provide biodiversity, to support wildlife as well as to improve water quality. In both examples the narrow greenways serve as a visual buffer between two adjoining residential areas that line the waterways. Even though both situations are located in dense residential areas, one can enjoy walking along the greenways surrounded by vegetation, with minor visual intrusion of the adjacent townhouses or office complex.

Figure 14.26 Retention lake in Sud Park, Rotterdam, the Netherlands

Figure 14.27-A Greenway with retention canal in Voorhof, the Netherlands

Figure 14.27-B Narrow retention canal with diverse planting to filter water and stabilize steep side slopes adjacent to road and parking lot in Voorhof, the Netherlands

The examples shown in Figures 14.28-A and 14.28-B present the range of landscape and slope design treatment of two drainage canal and water retention systems. The canal example 14.28-A is concrete lined, primarily treated with a hard, smooth surface to allow a swift flushing of the canal and reduce maintenance (area A). The upper slopes are planted with grass, allowing for informal recreation use (area B). The grass is easy to maintain but provides little in the way of visual variety or biodiversity. The canal example in Figure 14.28-B serves similar storm water conveyance and park functions but is more of an amenity, given the lush and diverse plantings. The canal in 14.28-B was designed to retain water at a prescribed level year-round, whereas the canal in 14.28-A is allowed to dry out during low-rainfall months.

Figure 14.28-A Drainage canal also provides valuable park and greenway functions in Shreveport, Louisiana

Figure 14.28-B Retention canal and greenway in Voorhof, the Netherlands

Water Detention Swale

Water detention ponds or swales can serve to slow down storm water and store it for later use, or function as a site design feature. In the examples shown in Figures 14.29-A, 14.29-B, and 14.30, a wide drainage swale was created in two parks, allowing for the detention of extreme storm water during heavy rains. Both were designed to accommodate a large quantity of water with a minimum slope that would slow the water, to let it penetrate into the soil, and would eventually become dry, allowing for informal park uses. A rock trail, seen in Figures 14.29-A and B, provides passage across the swale during low-water events and connects to a paved walking trail on the higher ground. A narrower and deeper swale could have been constructed, providing for a similar flood capacity, but that would limit the use of the area for recreation, at the same time creating a physical and visual barrier that would unnecessarily divide the park. A bridge would be required for passage across the deeper and narrower swale, potentially a more

Figure 14.29-A Stepping stone trail traversing drainage retention swale, Rotterdam's Sud Park

Figure 14.29-B Stepping stone trail traversing drainage retention swale connecting to upper asphalt paved walkway, Rotterdam's Sud Park

costly solution. In cases where open space is limited, the narrower swale would be an appropriate solution. An example of the bridge and swale solution is shown in Figure 14.30. Figure 14.31 provides an example where a bridge (A) solution was designed over a narrow and deep canal (B) to accommodate a tight space. The bridge in this example is a less visually integrated approach, but with straightforward functional advantages.

Figure 14.30 Manzanaras Park, Madrid, designed by West 8 landscape architects

WEST 8 LANDSCAPE ARCHITECTS, MADRID, SPAIN

Figure 14.31 Pedestrian bridge over canal solution, Delft, the Netherlands

Figures 14.32-A and 14.32-B An example of water retention and storage for later use to irrigate urban gardens. Item A is for water retention, and B is a flower and vegetable garden. Amersfoort, the Netherlands.

The extensive urban garden shown in photographs in Figures 14.32-A and 14.32-B serves a second and important purpose as a water retention strategy. The gardens are primarily planted with seasonal flowers, herbs, and vegetables. The canal in the same picture adds interest as only a water feature can in a dense urban setting. The area, which is essentially a large basin or vessel, has been designed with a capacity for detaining water during heavy storms. Eventually the water is absorbed in the soil or evaporates. Some of the water stored in the concrete canal is used to supplement irrigation of adjacent planting. Item A in figure 14.32-B is the same canal as in Figure 14.32-A. The area marked B shows the variety of plants including perennials and herbs to add visual interest at the same time can detain water overflow from the canal during heavy rains.

A dry stream was created in the dense urban commercial area shown in Figure 14.33. When not containing water, the dry streambed can serve a variety of creative functions such as a skateboarding park or a site for programmed uses and events hosted by the city or merchants.

Figure 14.33 A dry stream channel in Almere, the Netherlands

Rain Garden and Related Water Storage or Absorption Strategies

A rain garden is a design strategy to collect and detain surface water runoff on-site. In the example in Figure 14.34-A, the neighborhood street and walkway are graded to slope and direct surface water toward the central planting area. In some cases the rain garden itself is designed to slope—in the way that a swale slopes—farther downstream to a larger-capacity retention area. Figure 14.34-B shows a French drain (item B in the photograph) that was installed to carry excess water from a rain garden on the upper side of the street to a lower garden downstream (item A). Figure 14.35 is a detail section of a bioretention swale or rain garden similar to the ones in Figures 14.34-A and B.

Figures 14.34-A and 14.34-B Creation of rain gardens to manage storm water along a neighborhood street in the Netherlands

While not designed as a rain garden, the planting areas in the two examples in Figures 14.36-A and B are located between the sidewalk and an adjacent neighborhood street to collect surface water and facilitate its absorption to the soil. Additional shrub and tree planting could be installed later and the areas now planted with grass could be graded to form a basin to increase water detention capacity. Items A, B, and C in Figure 14.36-A demonstrated three approaches for providing a driveway and roadway a porous surface. The materials used in items A and C are modular concrete units set in a sand base. Item B is a modular concrete unit with voids so that grass could be planted. Items A and B in Figure 14.36-B are the same modular paving units for the roadway and entry walk. Item C is a grass area that can detain runoff water from the street and allow it to percolate into the soil.

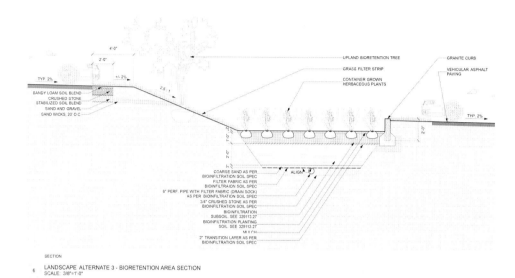

Figure 14.35 Bioretention section detail
COURTESY OF REED HILDERBRAND ASSOCIATES

Figures 14.36-A and 14.36-B Modular concrete pavers on sand (A) for road drive surface (C) and grass with pavers (B) for driveway, which allow for water percolation to subsurface soils in a residential neighborhood outside of Delft, the Netherlands

The photograph in Figure 14.37 is an example of either a clever design or the unfortunate result of poor site grading or delayed maintenance. Sometimes a designer considers subtle grading solutions to handle rainwater. The designer of this solution chose to create a gravel path with a crown so as to direct surface water to either side of the walkway into the adjoining grass or planting beds. The standing water could have been the result of ground subsidence or long-term erosion exacerbated by heavy foot or vehicle traffic. In either case, the crown makes much of the walk accessible during rain events.

Town Planning That Incorporates Sustainable Storm Water Management

The photograph in Figure 14.38 was taken of a model of a new town plan constructed in the central Netherlands. The plan for this new town development incorporated a variety of storm water management strategies. At the heart of the plan is a greenway that winds through the development. It was designed to hold maximum detention capacity during heavy

Figure 14.37 The Hague, the Netherlands   **Figure 14.38** Model of new town plan, the Netherlands

rains as well as to accept excess surface water from the internal storm water management systems integrated throughout the development. The models represent a comprehensive approach to managing storm water, integrating diverse systems of canals, water retention basins and swales, rain gardens, and other systems to reduce flooding of structures and to accommodate multiple uses.

15

ESTIMATING VOLUME OF CUT
AND FILL USING CONTOUR METHOD

In this chapter you will learn about:

- How to determine areas in a site-grading plan that will result in cut and those that will result in fill
- How to calculate the quantity of cut and fill based on the site-grading plan by determining area of cut and fill, using square inches based on a scaled site-grading plan
- The difference between a square foot and cubic yard, and how both are used to determine cut and fill quantities

CUT AND FILL IS THE PROCESS OF EARTH MOVING

The topography of a site is not always opportune for the purposes of project. In most cases portions of a site's topography will need to be modified so as to accommodate the uses and activities envisioned in the site design. What this means is that the designer will need to shift soil around from some parts of the site to others in order to create topography suitable for the designed elements. To achieve the topographic modifications detailed in the site grading plan, earth—and in some cases, rock—may need to be removed (cut) from areas of the site then used to build up other places requiring additional material (fill). In other situations, it may be necessary to transport excess earth material from the project site and dispose of it at an off-site location. In other instances,

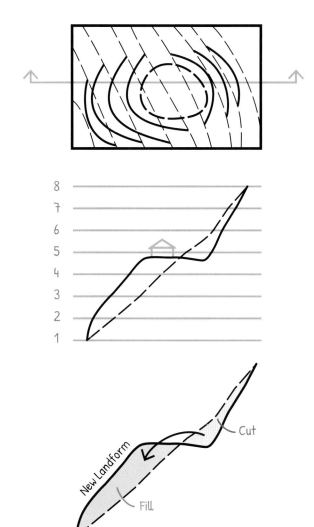

Figure 15.1 Section of a slope showing area of cut and area of fill. The dashed line represents existing slope and the solid line the proposed newly created shape or section of the modified slope.

soil may need to be transported from an off-site location to supplement areas where additional fill is needed. Both disposing of and purchasing material will add to the project budget. The process of moving and shifting earth around a site involves cutting and filling. Cutting away a portion of a hill slope to create a gently sloping area and placing the cut material at another area on the site is common. However, the goal is to balance cut and fill whenever feasible to minimize costs of taking away or importing material.

Figure 15.1 should help viewers visualize the concept of cutting a slope in one area then moving the earth to another area. Cutting and filling creates a level area to build a structure such as a house, picnic shelter, or playing field.

The Figures 15.2-A and 15.2-B visually represent the concept of cut and fill by modifying or changing contours on a site. Notice that when contours are adjusted in an uphill direction, as in Figure 15.2-A, one is creating cut. The dashed lines are existing contours, and the solid lines are the same contours in their new position as shown in the site plan prepared by the designer. Notice the lower contours moved uphill with—for instance—the 104 contour was repositioned to cover the 105 and 106 contours. Conversely, by adjusting the contours downhill, as in Figure 15.2-B, one is filling. In Figure 15.2-B, the higher-elevation contours are moved to cover over the lower-elevation contours. For instance, the 106 contour was repositioned to fill over (or raise the elevation of) the old 105 and 104 contours.

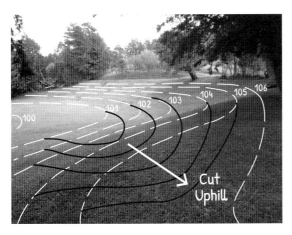

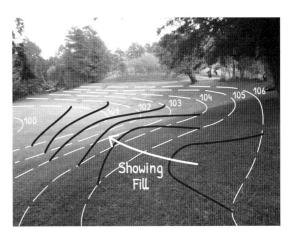

Figure 15.2-A Contours 101 through 107 have been repositioned uphill, thereby creating a cut slope

Figure 15.2-B Contours 101 through 107 have been repositioned downhill, thereby creating a fill slope

INTRODUCTION TO ESTIMATING EARTH-MOVING QUANTITIES

The work done by a contractor for site grading—referred to as earthwork in technical specifications and contract documents—can represent a substantial proportion of a construction budget. For example, earthwork would represent the major expense of a construction budget for constructing a set of soccer fields or other sport facilities, including a golf course. In order to estimate the cost for earthwork, several calculations are required to determine the amount of cut and fill required to implement the grading plan. There are several commonly used methods for calculating the volume of cut and fill, representing varying degrees of accuracy and amounts of time required to make the calculations. Many offices use AutoCAD, Land CAD, and other computer software to prepare their grading plans. Most software applications have an earthwork calculation function that makes determining the amount of earthwork fairly easy as one becomes proficient with the software. In this chapter we will consider a graphic means for estimating cut and fill. With practice accuracy will increase, as will speed.

When going through the process of calculating earthwork quantities, keep in mind that there is a factor that often contributes to over- or underestimating these quantities. The factor has to do with shrink-swell. The undisturbed soils on a project site are generally dense, having been in place for hundreds, thousands, and more years, going through daily and seasonal cycles of rain and sun, giving the soils ample time to consolidate and become dense. One only has to take a shovel and begin digging a hole to understand how the existing soils can be somewhat difficult to penetrate. Some soils are more dense and thus more difficult than other soil types. Next, after digging a hole, shovel the removed soil back into the hole, and you will find there is an excess of soil after the hole has been filled. By compacting the soil as you shovel it in, you can replace most of the removed soil, but often an amount on the order of 10 percent is left, with no more room in the hole for any more soil. This same concept is experienced when doing earthwork on a site. Even after making careful cut and fill calculations, the landscape architect may find an excess amount of soil remaining after the contractor has completed most of the earthwork. As one goes about the process of calculating the quantities of cut and fill of a site grading plan, an excess of 10–25 percent may occur during the actual earthwork operations. Consider 10 percent for sand and sandy soils, and as much as 25 percent for common earth. Rock removed may result in as much as 65 to 70 percent overage—that is, rock that is removed can produce a quantity 165 percent of the quantity calculated from the site-grading plan unless it is crushed into finer material.

To start, consider the grading diagrams in Figures 15.2-A and 15.2-B. Dashed contour lines represent the existing topography, and the solid lines represent the proposed contours. The solid proposed contours that move downhill from the original contour location represent fill. Note that an upper

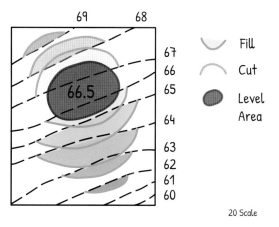

Figure 15.3 Grading plan diagram for creating a level shelf area

contour is pulled down and is drawn over existing contours, creating fill. Where the proposed contours are moved to higher elevations, these contours represent cut that is being proposed. The area created between the existing and proposed contour is what will be measured, followed by a calculation of the volume of earth moved either as fill or cut. The grading proposed in Figure 15.3 is meant to create a level shelf at 65.5 elevation. Contours 67, 68, and 69 have been moved uphill, creating cut, or the removal of material. Some of this material can then be used to fill downhill over contours 66, 65, 64, 63, and 62.

CONTOUR METHOD FOR ESTIMATING CUT AND FILL

The simulation in Figure 15.4 shows how fill is created when moving contours downhill from their original location. The material to create this fill could come from another location on-site that requires cut, or

Figure 15.4 Dashed contour lines are existing contours, and solid lines are proposed contours. The shaded areas (A, B, and C) represent fill.

taking away material. This material could then be placed as shown in the shaded areas in the figure. Contours 55, 60, and 65 have been repositioned downslope, creating three shaded areas: areas requiring fill from some source on-site or trucked in from an off-site source. The areas of fill required can be measured to determine the volume required. Considering the contour interval is 5 feet (five feet between each pair of contours), you would multiply each contour area by 5 feet to determine the volume of fill material. The steps for calculating the volume of fill are outlined as follows:

1. Measure the shaded area created by each contour. Since grading plans are done at a specified scale, the shaded area measured would be in square inches. If the scale of the grading plan is 20 scale, then each square inch is equal to 400 square feet. A one-inch square is the equivalent of 20 feet to each side. If the scale is 1 inch = 50 feet, then each measured inch covers an area of 50' × 50' or 2500 square feet.

2. To calculate the volume on a grading plan at 20 scale, measure the number of square inches represented by the shaded area created by each contour. Referring to Figure 15.4, assume we measure the number of square inches for contour 55 (the measurement would be made directly off the grading plan, not the photograph). Let's say the number of inches of shaded area for contour 55 is 12 square inches:

    12 square inches at 20 scale: 20' × 20' × 12 = 4800 square feet

3. To calculate the cubic volume in cubic feet, first multiply the number of square feet by the contour interval, in this case 5 feet:

    4,800 square feet × 5 = 24,000 cubic feet.

    The standard unit of measurement for earthwork and soil is cubic yards. Earth material and soil are bought and sold in cubic yards.

4. To calculate the volume in cubic yards, first consider the following:

The diagram in Figure 15.5 shows a cubic yard, the standard unit of measurement used for calculating earth volumes. A cubic yard consists of three, 1-foot rows. To convert to cubic yards, multiply $A \times B \times C$ or $3 \times 3 \times 3 = 27$, or 27 cubic feet. Divide 27 into the number of cubic feet calculated in Step 2, and the result is the number of cubic yards.

5. To calculate the volume in cubic yards:

   Divide 24,000 cubic feet by 27 to get the volume of fill in cubic yards.

   24,000 CY / 27 = 889 cubic yards

6. The next steps are to continue calculating the volume of fill for contours 60 and 65 in Figure 15.4, then add up the grand total to give the total cubic yards of fill required to follow the grading plan. Then apply the same process to calculate the volume of cut for each contour.

To put in perspective the amount of fill material required for contour 55, divide 889 cubic yards by 15 CY (the amount of material a fully loaded dump truck can hold).

   889 CY / 15 = 59.2 fully loaded dump trucks.

In the example of a grading in Figure 15.6, note that the higher contours will overlap the contours below them. Contour 55 extends beyond the existing 54 contour. We could have an example where contours are extended to cover three, four, and many more contours in cases where a greater modification of the existing terrain is necessary to provide the appropriate landform to accommodate particular site design elements. If a tennis court were to be constructed on a steep hill slope, considerable modification or grading of that slope would be necessary.

The steps necessary to calculate the volume of fill for contour 55 in Figure 15.6 are as follows:

1. Note the scale of the grading plan drawing: 20 scale.

2. Measure the number of square inches:

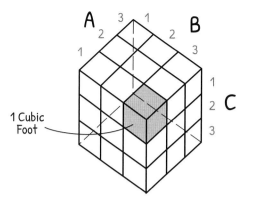

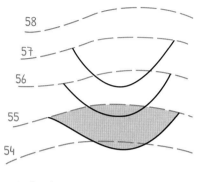

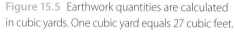

Scale: 1" = 20'

Figure 15.5 Earthwork quantities are calculated in cubic yards. One cubic yard equals 27 cubic feet.

Figure 15.6 Overlapping contours showing fill. Contours that are moved downhill are fill, those moved uphill are indicating cut.

Using a 20-scale ruler, measure the number of square inches of the shaded area created by the 55 contour overlapping the 54 contour: 1.5 square inches.

3. Calculate number of square feet:

Multiply the number of square inches (let's estimate 1.5 square inches) by the square of 20 or $20' \times 20' = 400' \times 1.5 = 600$ square feet

4. Calculate number of cubic feet:

First note the contour interval of the grading plan. In this case it is 1 foot.

600 square feet $\times 1 = 600$ cubic feet

5. Calculate number of cubic yards:

600 cubic feet $/ 27 = 22.2$ cubic yards

6. Calculate cubic yards for remaining contours.

It is desirable to organize your earthwork volume calculations. One way to organize oneself is to set up a spreadsheet such as shown in Table 15.1.

Table 15.1 Cut and Fill Spreadsheet Example

CONTOUR	CUT SQ. INCHES	CUT SQ. FEET	CUT CUBIC FEET	CUT CUBIC YARDS		FILL SQ. INCHES	FILL SQ. FEET	FILL CUBIC FEET	FILL CUBIC YARDS
54									
55									
56									
57									
58									
59									
60									
Totals									

OTHER METHODS OF ESTIMATING EARTHWORK VOLUMES

There are other methods for estimating cut and fill quantities. They include the grid method and the average end-area method. The grid method is useful for estimating pool, pond, and building excavation. The average end-area method is commonly used for estimating earthwork volumes for roads and linear features. In this method a series of cross sections are made at set intervals of 10, 25, and 50 or 100 feet, depending on the complexity of the terrain. The curious student could investigate the various methods of calculating cut and fill and compare their results. In actual practice, most professional offices use computer software to make the calculations. The use of the contour method for calculating cut and fill quantities is a quick and easy method for checking accuracy or when computing is not available.

16

PROFESSIONAL EXAMPLE OF SITE GRADING BY DESIGN

INTRODUCTION

Up to this point, the emphasis has been placed on concepts, theory, and application of site-grading principles. Now, it will be useful for students to see selected works of professional landscape architects, to both inspire them and further their understanding of the design potential of landscape grading. Figures 16.1 through 16.4 show a range of site-grading projects where site grading was an integral component of the landscape designs. Obviously these built works did not drop out of the sky, but were the result of a lengthy process involving the collaboration of many professional disciplines. The works followed the process or steps described in Chapter 3, including the preparation of several reiterations of site-grading plans, technical details, and technical specifications.

This chapter presents a selection of award-winning landscape design projects. The intent of this chapter is to provide students with a range of technical site-grading drawings representing the level of quality and detail required to guide the execution of the landscape-grading design in the field.

Figure 16.1 Stern Grove amphitheater, San Francisco, CA

Figure 16.2 Common open space, Phoenix, AZ

Figure 16.3 Pixar Campus, San Francisco, CA

Figure 16.4 Levi Plaza, San Francisco, CA

All images for the following projects were provided with permission by the firms, unless otherwise noted.

RHAA (Royston Hanamoto Alley & Abey)

MILL VALLEY AND SAN FRANCISCO, CA

PROJECT: El Dorado Beach, South Lake Tahoe, CA

The El Dorado Beach project is the first phase of a new civic and recreational center for the City of South Lake Tahoe. Prominently located on Lake Tahoe, the intent of the project is to reconnect the city to the lakefront. As the prime consultant, RHAA led a multidisciplinary and multiagency team to engage the community in a collaborative, one-year-long process to design a special place that weaves together an array of design objectives and reinterprets local design vernacular to create a recreational and community gathering space. The resulting design consists of stone terraces, a plaza, beach access, and a multiuse boathouse. The project is certified LEED Gold and received the 2013 ASLA Award of Excellence.

Figure 16.5 Project location map
COURTESY OF RHHA

Figure 16.6 View of stepped seating at lake edge
COURTESY OF RHHA

Figure 16.7 Ramp passing through stepped seating to lake

COURTESY OF RHHA

Figure 16.8 Stepped seating

COURTESY OF RHHA

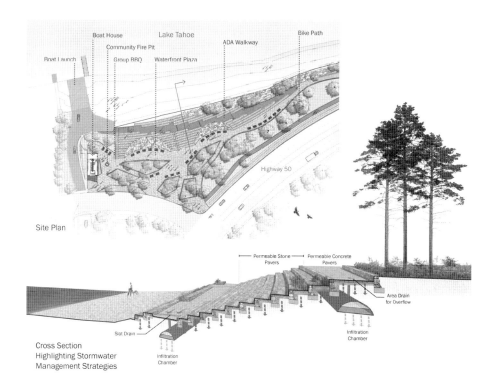

Boat House

Community Fire Pit

Boat Launch

Group BBQ

Waterfront Plaza

Lake Tahoe

ADA Walkway

Bike Path

Highway 50

Site Plan

Permeable Stone Pavers

Permeable Concrete Pavers

Area Drain for Overflow

Slot Drain

Infiltration Chamber

Infiltration Chamber

Cross Section
Highlighting Stormwater
Management Strategies

Figure 16.9 Design plan and section view

COURTESY OF RHHA

Reed Hilderbrand Associates

CAMBRIDGE, MA

PROJECT: Stone Hill Center, The Sterling and Francine Clark Art Institute, Williamstown, MA

Working with architect Tadao Ando, Reed Hilderbrand Associates developed a museum campus master plan that enhances the institute's woodland setting, expands the facilities for its public and academic programs, and reconfigures its galleries to broaden the ways in which visitors experience art. Key elements of the landscape design include:

- New entrance drive reorienting visitors' arrival on campus, highlighting the lily pond and surrounding vistas

- Two miles of new walking trails providing greater access to Stone Hill's meadows, woodlands, and seasonal streams

- Interpretive trail markers highlighting geological features and conservation initiatives

- Plant installations of native species, including more than 350 trees

- A reflecting pool adjacent to the new Visitor, Exhibition, and Conference Center

- Landscaped parking area for 340 vehicles

- An integrated water management system that reduces potable water usage by 50 percent, including: reflecting pool that also acts as a self-sustaining reservoir to harvest storm water for reuse in plumbing and irrigation, and a rooftop rainwater collection system that will capture approximately 120,000 gallons per year for reuse. The project included the design of constructed wetlands, rain gardens, and infiltration meadows to detain, infiltrate, and benignly treat water before it flows into existing water bodies.

Figure 16.10 View from the air of the project site
COURTESY OF REED HILDERBRAND ASSOCIATES

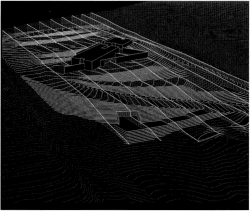

Figure 16.11 Computer generated site grading study
COURTESY OF REED HILDERBRAND ASSOCIATES

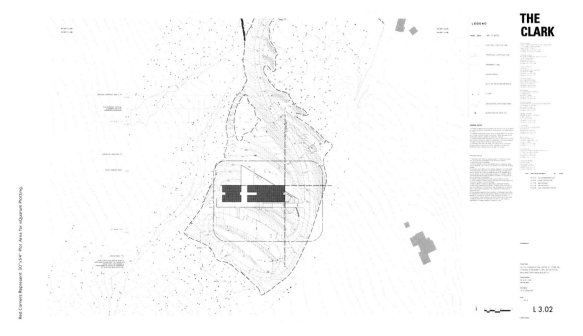

Figure 16.12 Site grading plan
COURTESY OF REED HILDERBRAND ASSOCIATES

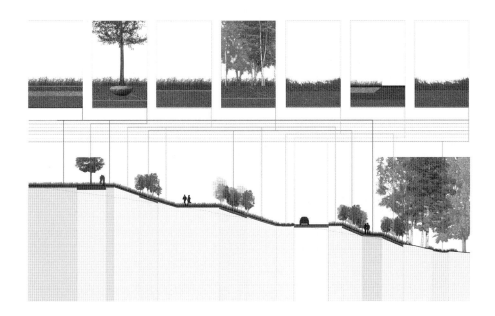

Figure 16.13 Illustrative sections of site grading
COURTESY OF REED HILDERBRAND ASSOCIATES

Figure 16.14 Illustrative site grading section
COURTESY OF REED HILDERBRAND ASSOCIATES

Reed Hilderbrand Associates

CAMBRIDGE, MA

PROJECT: Hamilton College Theater and Studio Arts, Hamilton College, Clinton, NY

This college was physically divided for a long time into two campuses separated by a busy road. This project bridges that gap with a new arts area consisting of three buildings, a network of pathways, and an extended watercourse. A series of lawn-covered ramps weaves through a sloping site and serves to physically connect the buildings to outdoor terraces and extensive landscape. Three ponds were constructed to manage storm water and, at the same time, give new life to a woodland stream corridor.

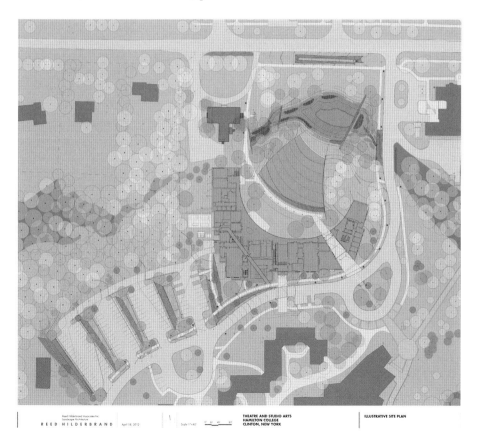

Figure 16.15 Illustrative master plan

COURTESY OF REED HILDERBRAND ASSOCIATES

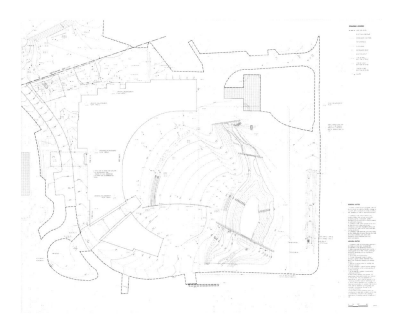

Figure 16.16 Site grading plan for building area
COURTESY OF REED HILDERBRAND ASSOCIATES

Figure 16.17 Site grading plan of parking lot area
COURTESY OF REED HILDERBRAND ASSOCIATES

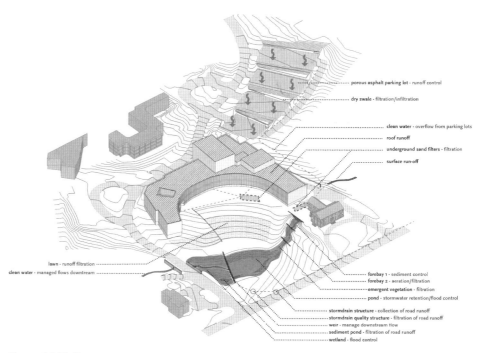

Figure 16.18 Storm water management system

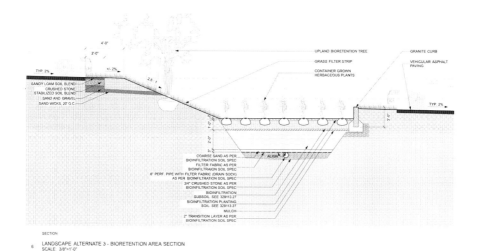

Figure 16.19 Bioretention section detail

Figure 16.20-A Panoramic view of theater site
COURTESY OF REED HILDERBRAND ASSOCIATES

Figure 16.20-B Panoramic view of theater site in winter
COURTESY OF REED HILDERBRAND ASSOCIATES

MVVA (Michael Van Valkenburgh Associates)

NEW YORK, NY

PROJECT: Teardrop Park, New York, NY

Teardrop Park is a 1.8-acre public park in lower Manhattan that transcends its small size, shady environment, and midblock location through a bold topographic design strategy consisting of complex irregular spaces and dense plantings. Teardrop's design and construction were coordinated with the development of four surrounding apartment buildings, each ranging from 210 feet to 235 feet in height.

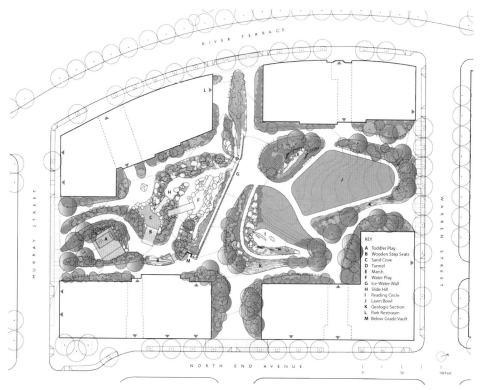

Figure 16.21 Plan

COURTESY OF MICHAEL VAN VALKENBURGH ASSOCIATES

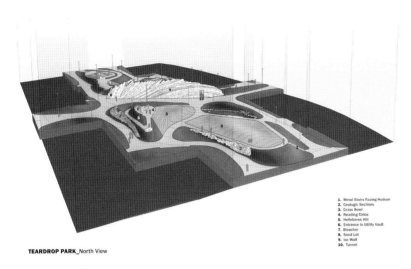

TEARDROP PARK_North View

1. Metal Stairs Facing Hudson
2. Geologic Sections
3. Grass Bowl
4. Reading Cirlce
5. Hellebores Hill
6. Entrance to Utility Vault
7. Bleacher
8. Sand Lot
9. Ice Wall
10. Tunnel

Figure 16.22 Plan
COURTESY OF MICHAEL VAN VALKENBURGH ASSOCIATES

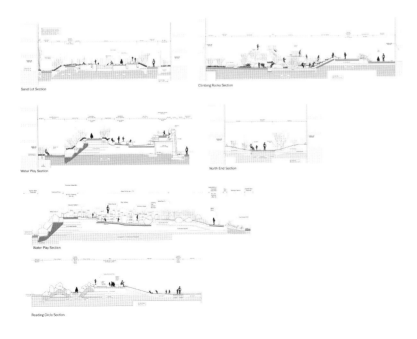

Figure 16.23 Technical sections
COURTESY OF MICHAEL VAN VALKENBURGH ASSOCIATES

Professional Example of Site Grading by Design   279

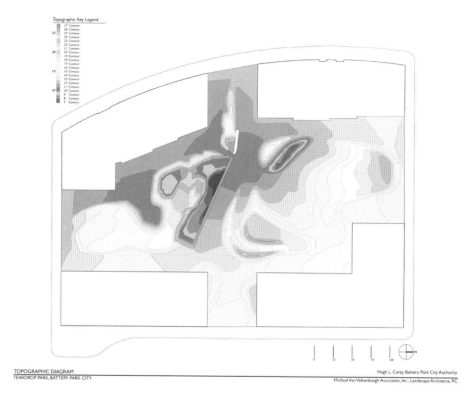

Topographic Key Legend

TOPOGRAPHIC DIAGRAM
TEARDROP PARK, BATTERY PARK CITY

Hugh L. Carey Battery Park City Authority
Michael Van Valkenburgh Associates, Inc., Landscape Architects, PC

Figure 16.24 Elevation diagram
COURTESY OF MICHAEL VAN VALKENBURGH ASSOCIATES

Figure 16.25 Photograph of central lawn

Figure 16.26 Children's play environment

PROJECT: Connecticut Water Treatment Facility, New Haven, CT

Located on the outskirts of suburban New Haven, the facility is a reserve water source for the South Central Connecticut Regional Water Authority. It draws water from nearby Lake Whitney, at the base of the Mill River Watershed. On a limited budget, this project raised the bar for municipal infrastructure design. Using techniques adapted from restoration ecology and bioengineering, the landscape architect created a microcosm of the surrounding regional watershed, from mountain source to reservoir. The result is a visually rich, humanely scaled terrain that invites neighbors to engage with the land from the perspective of the water that flows through it.

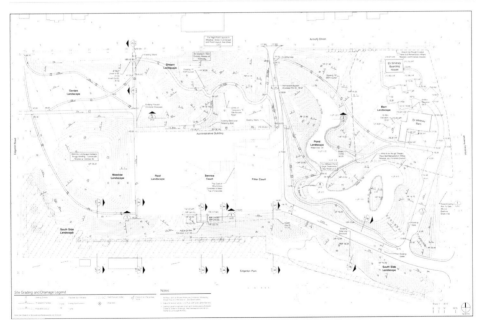

Figure 16.27 Grading plan

COURTESY OF MICHAEL VAN VALKENBURG ASSOCIATES

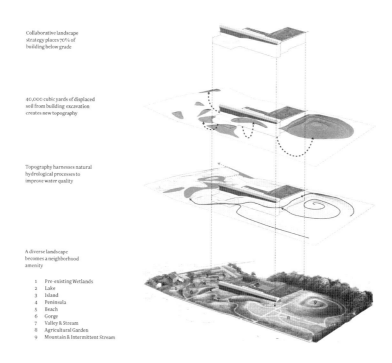

Collaborative landscape
strategy places 70% of
building below grade

40,000 cubic yards of displaced
soil from building excavation
creates new topography

Topography harnesses natural
hydrological processes to
improve water quality

A diverse landscape
becomes a neighborhood
amenity

1   Pre-existing Wetlands
2   Lake
3   Island
4   Peninsula
5   Beach
6   Gorge
7   Valley & Stream
8   Agricultural Garden
9   Mountain & Intermittent Stream

Figure 16.28 Water management system diagram
COURTESY OF MICHAEL VAN VALKENBURG ASSOCIATES

Figure 16.29 A pedestrian path meanders through constructed
landforms to create a sense of anticipation to the arrival of the building entry
COURTESY OF MICHAEL VAN VALKENBURG ASSOCIATES

Studio Outside, and Bing Thom Architects

DALLAS, TX, AND WASHINGTON, DC

PROJECT: East Trinity Campus, Tarrant County College District, Dallas, TX

This detailed design study for this proposed urban campus includes a plaza and park entrance offering site accessibility while creating opportunities for visitors to access the lower-level main pedestrian axis of the campus via stairs, ramps, or elevator. The landscape architects developed a detailed integration of hardscape and landscape within the small but complex group of buildings that offer virtually no right angles, while also incorporating an elegantly detailed fountain and two-story waterfall along the main pedestrian axis. The public spaces and landscape serve as the primary organizational device for the campus, while providing a welcoming image for the surrounding neighborhood and region.

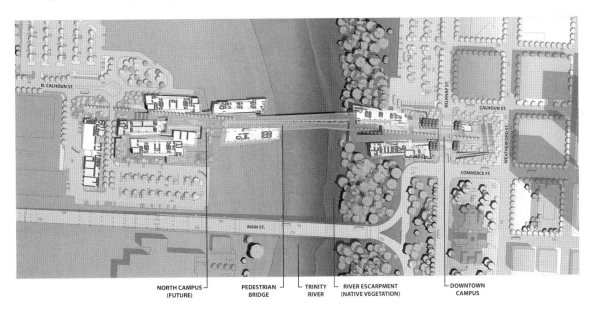

Figure 16.30
COURTESY OF STUDIO OUTSIDE

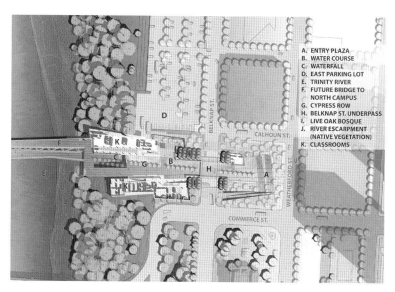

A. ENTRY PLAZA
B. WATER COURSE
C. WATERFALL
D. EAST PARKING LOT
E. TRINITY RIVER
F. FUTURE BRIDGE TO
   NORTH CAMPUS
G. CYPRESS ROW
H. BELKNAP ST. UNDERPASS
I. LIVE OAK BOSQUE
J. RIVER ESCARPMENT
   (NATIVE VEGETATION)
K. CLASSROOMS

Figure 16.31 Illustrative plan
COURTESY OF STUDIO OUTSIDE

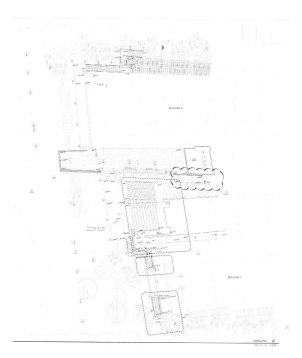

Figure 16.32 Site-grading plan
COURTESY OF STUDIO OUTSIDE

Figure 16.33 Artist's rendering
COURTESY OF STUDIO OUTSIDE

Studio Outside

DALLAS, TEXAS

PROJECT: Red Butte Garden, University of Utah, Salt Lake City

The Red Butte Conservation Garden master plan provides a road map for expanding the visitor experience onto a steep hillside and former quarry. The site affords a spectacular view of the surrounding native mountain landscape. The intent of the program and plan was to feature conservation gardening in arid climates. Major goals include expanding educational programming spaces, adding visitor destinations, communicating a water and resource conservation message, and celebrating the beauty of the native Utah flora. Site grading will serve as the physical framework integrating planned conservation gardening improvements on steep terrain with paths that will engage visitors with the landscape through an ADA-accessible trails system weaving through and binding together the various display gardens.

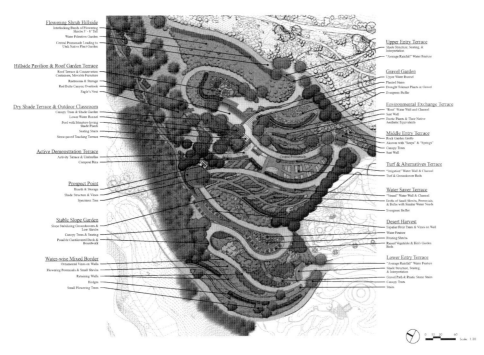

Figure 16.34 Illustrative plan
COURTESY OF STUDIO OUTSIDE

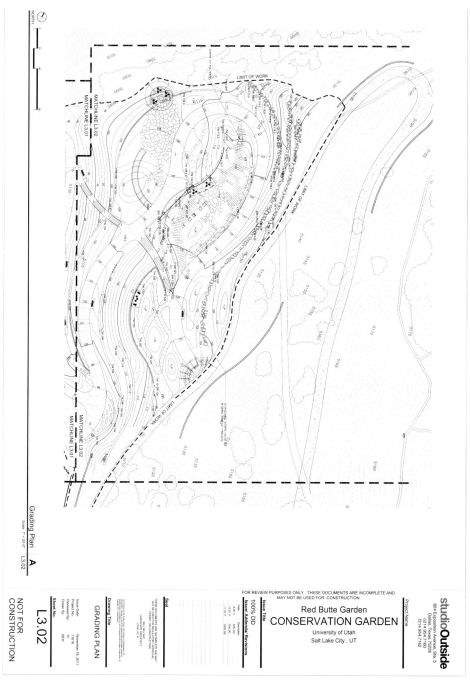

Figure 16.35 Grading plan
COURTESY OF STUDIO OUTSIDE

SWA Group

HOUSTON, TX

PROJECT: Buffalo Bend Park, Houston, TX

Buffalo Bend Park is a conversion of a waterfront industrial landscape into an urban wetlands demonstration project. The plan will divert urban runoff into a series of connected wetlands before returning the flow to the bayou, removing bacteria, nutrients, and toxic materials from the flow on the way. The plan includes parking, trails, wetlands, a small hill, boardwalks, interpretive signage, and reforestation. The underlying goal of the project is to create a working wetland system that will improve the local water quality and be used as a teaching tool for residents. All cut and fill for the project was balanced on-site.

Figure 16.36 Illustrative grading plan
COURTESY OF SWA GROUP, HOUSTON, TX

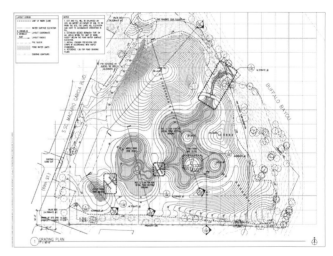

Figure 16.37 Preliminary grading plan
COURTESY OF SWA GROUP, HOUSTON, TX

Olin Studio

PHILADELPHIA, PA

PROJECT: Washington Monument, Washington, DC

The Washington Monument is an iconic American open space located in Washington, DC. The 72-acre grounds provide a public space for demonstrations, celebrations, entertainment, and recreation for millions of people each year. A need to upgrade exterior security provisions came to the forefront after 9/11, leading to an invited design competition for the Monument grounds. The Olin Studio won the competition with an elegant security solution, and in the process, successfully proposed much-needed landscape improvements. The revitalized Washington Monument open space enhances the site's character and identity within the context of the National Mall. It is an outstanding example demonstrating the art and craft of landscape architecture in a very prominent place. The design is bold and clear: a minimalist solution that turned a project originally funded to prevent terrorism into a handsome civic amenity.

Figure 16.38 Illustrative site design
COURTESY OF OLIN STUDIO, PHILADELPHIA, PA

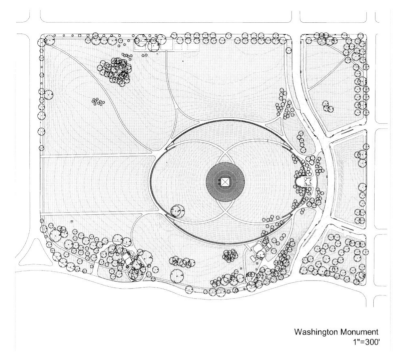

Washington Monument
1"=300'

Figure 16.39 Preliminary grading plan
COURTESY OF OLIN STUDIO, PHILADELPHIA, PA

Figure 16.40 Washington Monument
IMAGE BY PERMISSION OF PHOTOGRAPHER: SAHAR COSTON-HARDY AT THE OLIN STUDIO

Morrow Reardon Wilkinson Miller, Ltd.

ALBUQUERQUE, NM

PROJECT: Alamosa Skate Park, Albuquerque, NM

This project was commissioned in 2004 to be the city's second in-ground large-scale skate park. In order to provide alternative skating opportunities in the city, the West Side facility was designed as a park with the focus on skating. It draws inspiration from Albuquerque's world-renowned arroyo system as well as site-specific elements in the city that are now off-limits to skating. The park is designed for skateboarders, in-line skaters, and BMX bikers of all skill levels.

The skate park is composed of two distinct main areas, the Trenches and the Skylit Bowl. The Trenches is a linear flow area with a mix of banks, ledges, walls, stairs, gaps, and rails in various combinations and arrangements. The majority of the Trenches is poured-in-place concrete with a brick central plaza. The linear arrangement of this area is inspired by Albuquerque's drainage arroyos, and it allows users to ride lines or session-specific elements. The arrangement also disperses users throughout the park instead of congregating them in the middle.

Westside Skatepark: Site Plan

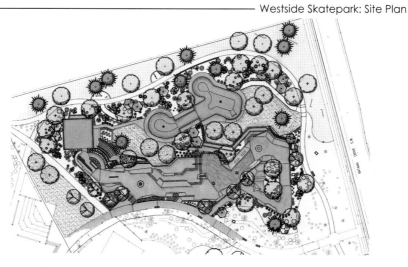

Figure 16.41 Illustrative site design

COURTESY OF MORROW REARDON WILKINSON MILLER, LTD., ALBUQUERQUE, NM

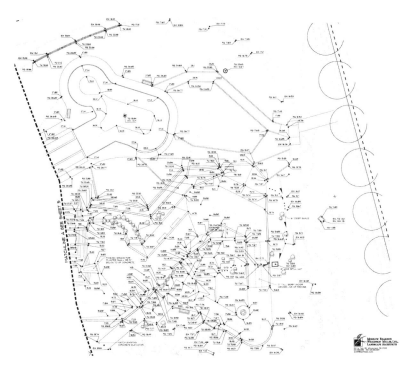

Figure 16.42 Site-grading plan

COURTESY OF MORROW REARDON WILKINSON MILLER, LTD., ALBUQUERQUE, NM

Figure 16.43 View of skateboard park showing sculptural forms created to challenge skateboarders

COURTESY OF MORROW REARDON WILKINSON MILLER, LTD., ALBUQUERQUE, NM

Design Workshop

ASPEN, CO

PROJECT: Daybreak, South Jordan, Utah

Daybreak is a model community plan applying innovative and sustainable design principles. Design Workshop worked as an integral consultant team member from master planning through design and construction. Design Workshop developed design guidelines for the project, which creates a mixed-use walkable community with a full range of services and amenities. The place types include various scales of civic, commercial, residential, and recreational uses. The guidelines address rights-of-way, setbacks, architecture, streetscapes, landscaping, and parking. All project phases will meet the requirements for LEED certification.

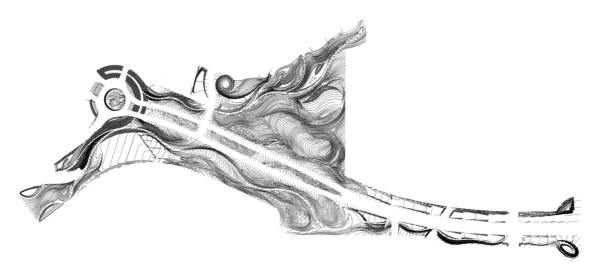

Figure 16.44 Schematic grading diagram

COURTESY OF DESIGN WORKSHOP, ASPEN, CO

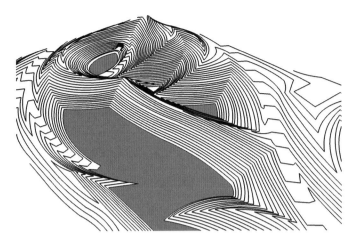

Figure 16.45 SketchUp file
COURTESY OF DESIGN WORKSHOP, ASPEN, CO

Figure 16.46 Panoramic view of site showing sculptured landforms
COURTESY OF DESIGN WORKSHOP, ASPEN, CO

Figure 16.47 Walking trail and overpass with sculpted landforms
COURTESY OF DESIGN WORKSHOP, ASPEN, CO

PROJECT: Pima Community College, Northwest Campus, Tucson, Arizona

Situated on 60 acres, the Northwest Campus is designed to be implemented in a phased strategy. Once completed, the campus will contain memorable spaces, appropriately characterized architecture, and a landscape designed specifically for the Sonoran Desert region.

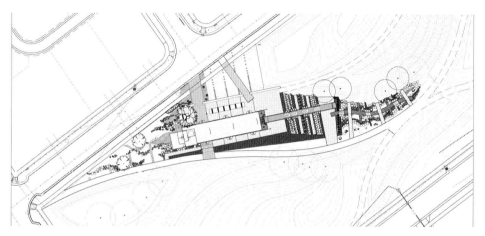

Figure 16.48 Illustrative site design
COURTESY OF DESIGN WORKSHOP, ASPEN, CO

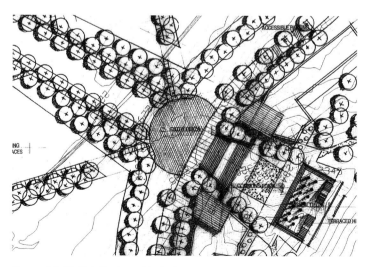

Figure 16.49 Detail schematic design
COURTESY OF DESIGN WORKSHOP, ASPEN, CO

Figure 16.50 View of interior access space
COURTESY OF DESIGN WORKSHOP, ASPEN, CO

Figure 16.51 View of interior access space showing integration of landforms with flights of stairs
COURTESY OF DESIGN WORKSHOP, ASPEN, CO

REFERENCES

Aymer, Valerie. Landscape Grading: A Study Guide for the LARE Grading Examination. Lulu.com, 2011.

Greenwood, David. Mapping. Chicago: The University of Chicago Press, 1946.

Hopper, Leonard. Landscape Architectural Graphic Standards. Hoboken, NJ: John Wiley & Sons, 2007.

Parker, Harry S. and John W. McGuire. Simplified Site Engineering. Hoboken, NJ: John Wiley & Sons, 1954.

Petschek, Peter. Grading for Landscape Architects and Architects. Basel: Birkhauser Verlag AG, 2009.

Strom, Steven, Kurt Nathan, and Jake Woland. Site Engineering for Landscape Architects, 6th edition. Hoboken, NJ: John Wiley & Sons, 2013.

Untermann, Richard. Grade Easy: An Introductory Course in the Principles and Practices of Grading and Drainage. Washington, DC: American Society of Landscape Architects, 1967.

INDEX

The letter t following a page number indicates a table.

definition of, 120, 122

equation, 121–122, 124–125

failure, 18

grading guidelines, 36, 37t

and horizontal distance, 121–122, 124

intentional, 10

of landscape surface, 120, 122

negative, 123

of paved surface, 120, 122

positive, 122–123

prescribed, 10

requirements of, 10, 122

and spot elevations, 120–121, 122, 130–134, 186–187

uniform, 111, 136, 143

and vertical elevation difference, 121–122, 124–125

in water management, 236–238

Smith, Kyle, 42

Spot elevations:

 calculation of, 151–153, 154

 communicating with, 140, 141, 150–151, 156

 and contour lines, 91, 92, 100, 120–121, 139, 141, 151

 contractor use of, 151, 156–157, 159

 conventions of, 140, 150, 157–159

 definition of, 139, 140

 drains, 146

 on grading plans, 140–150, 156–159, 226

 hardscape elements, 147–149

 need for, 10, 139–141, 142–150, 164

 ramps, 143–144

and slope calculation, 121, 122, 125, 130–134

on sloping surface, 154–156

special landscape features, 149

stairs, 142–143

swales, 146–147

trees to save, 149

walls and fences, 144–146

Stakes, wood (surveyor's), 230

Stamping, 12

Standing water. *See* Ponding

Stein, Gertrude, 78–79

Sterling and Francine Clark Art Institute, 271

Stern Grove Amphitheater, 3, 268

Stern Grove Concert Meadow Amphitheater, 18

Stone Hill Center, 271–273

Storm and surface water, management of:

 aquifer recharge, 246–247

 canals and swales, 244–245

 catch basins, 239–244

 and contour grading, 236–239

 design options for, 219–220, 239–255

 detention swale, 250–252

 French drain system in, 242, 253

 importance of, 232–233

 and modular paving, 246, 247, 253–254

 nature of, 231–232, 233

 in paved areas, 241–242

 and porous concrete, 247

 rain garden, 253

 retention ponds, 248–250